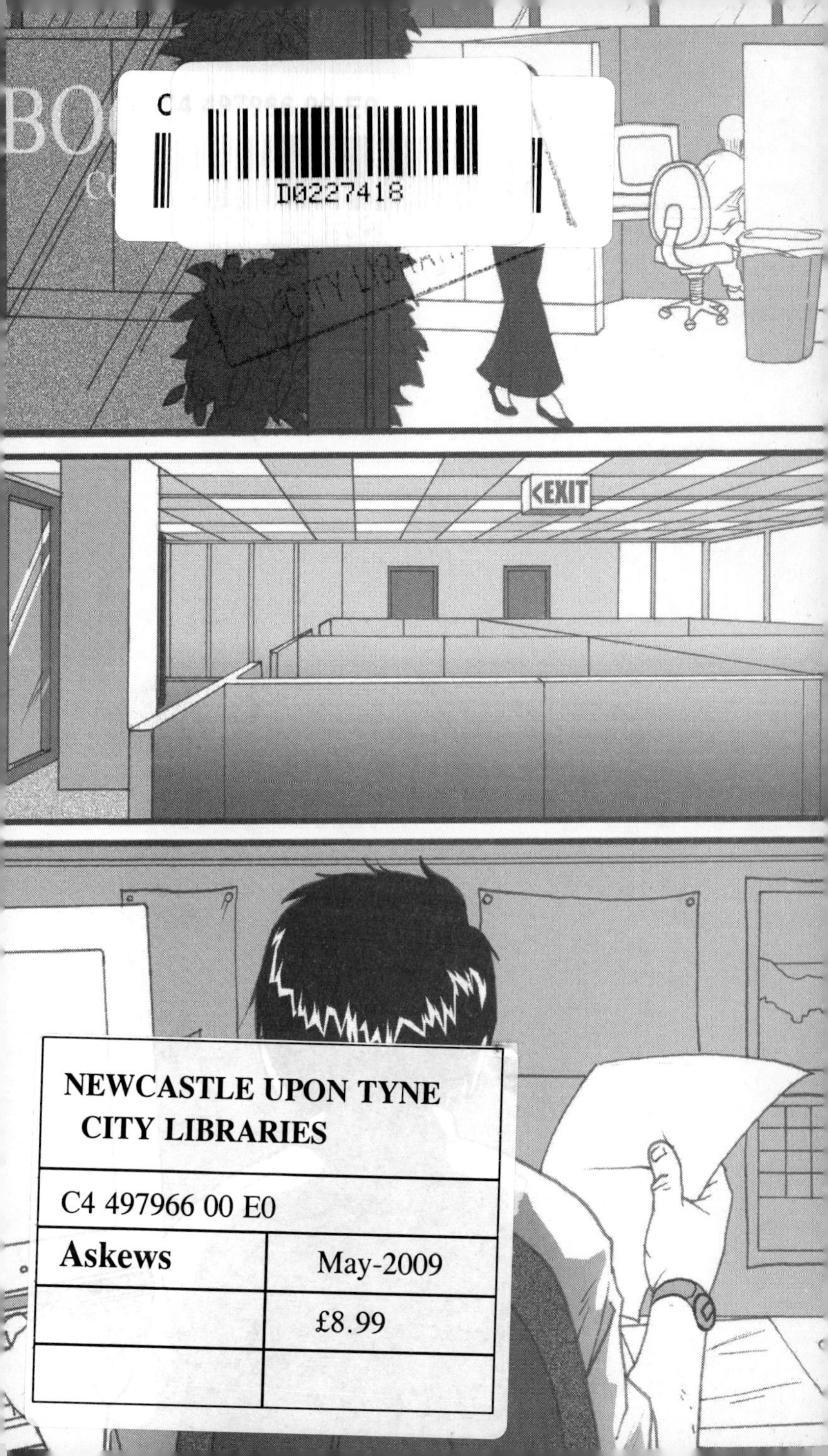
EXIT

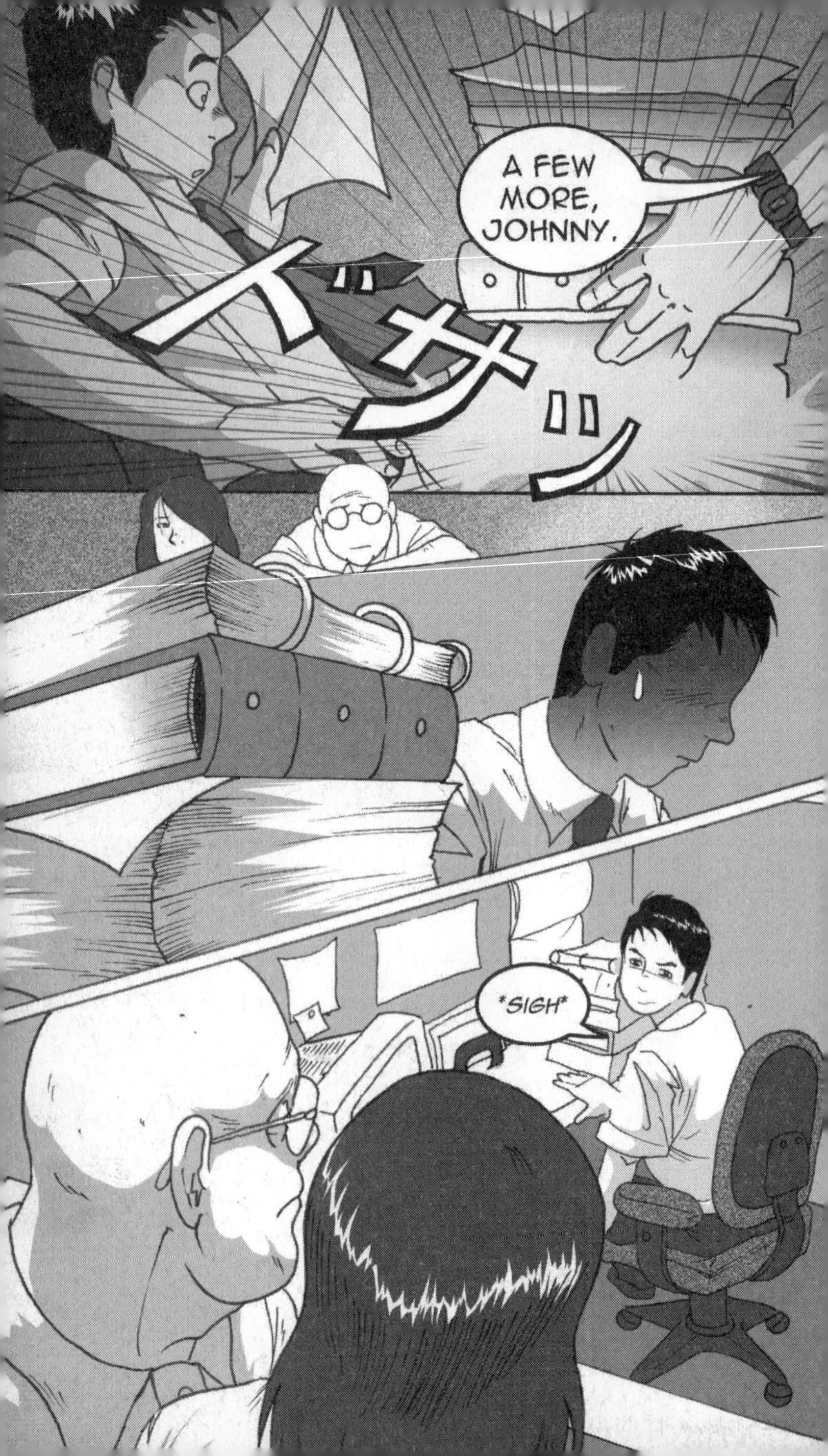
A FEW MORE, JOHNNY.
ドザッ
SIGH

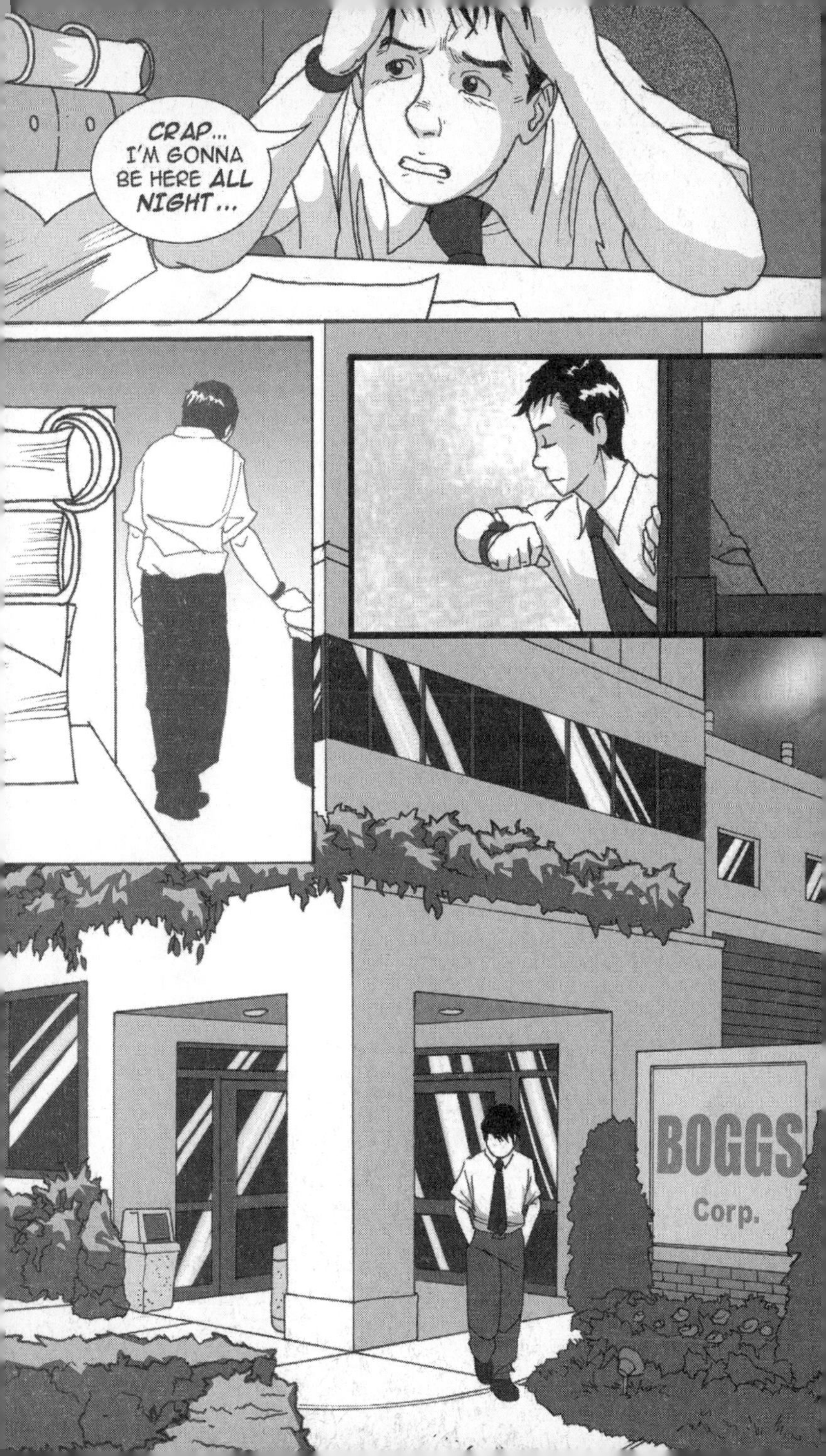
CRAP... I'M GONNA BE HERE ALL NIGHT...
BOGGS Corp.

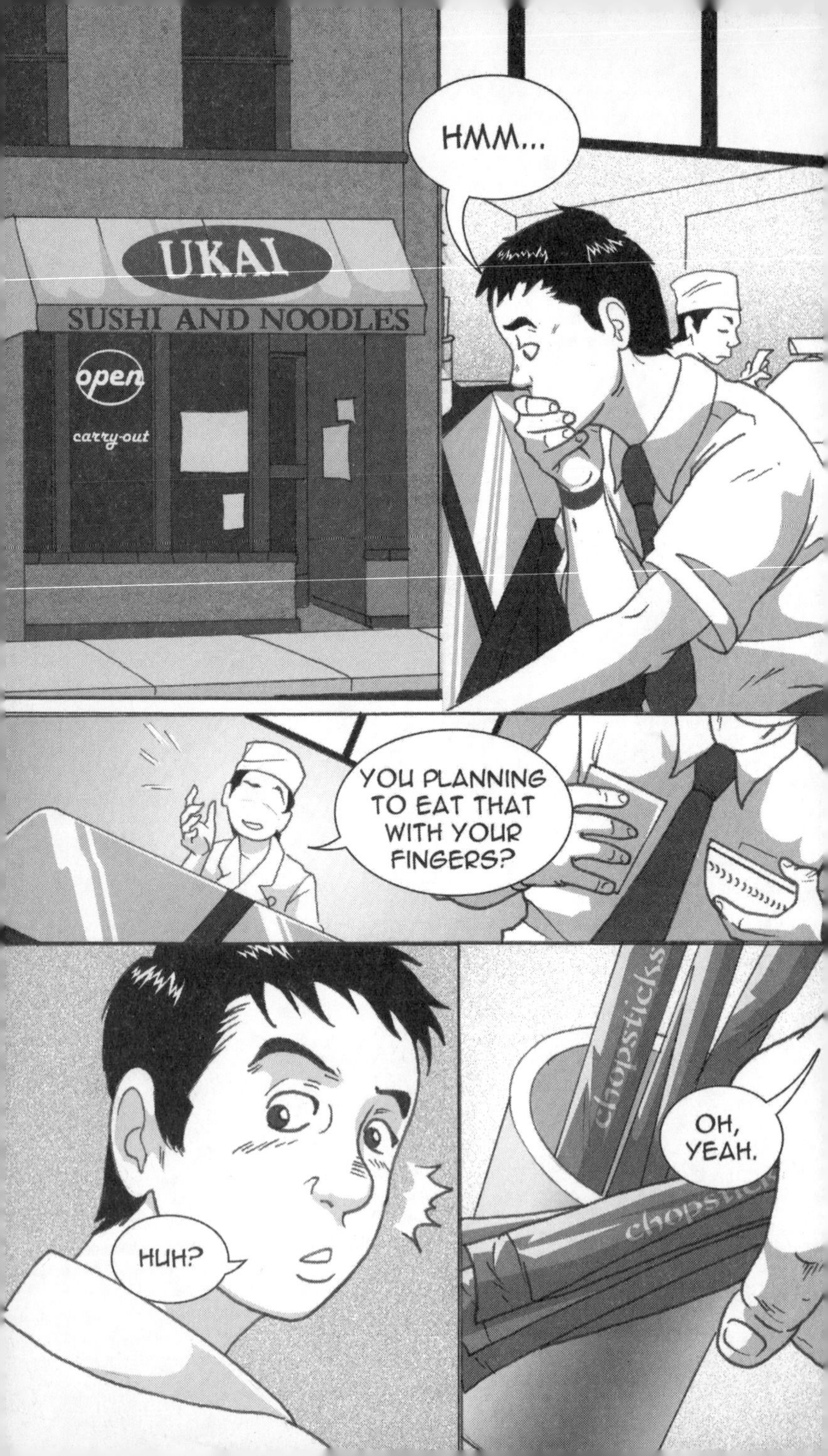
UKAI
SUSHI AND NOODLES
open
carry-out
HMM...
YOU PLANNING TO EAT THAT WITH YOUR FINGERS?
HUH?
chopsticks
chopsticks
OH, YEAH.

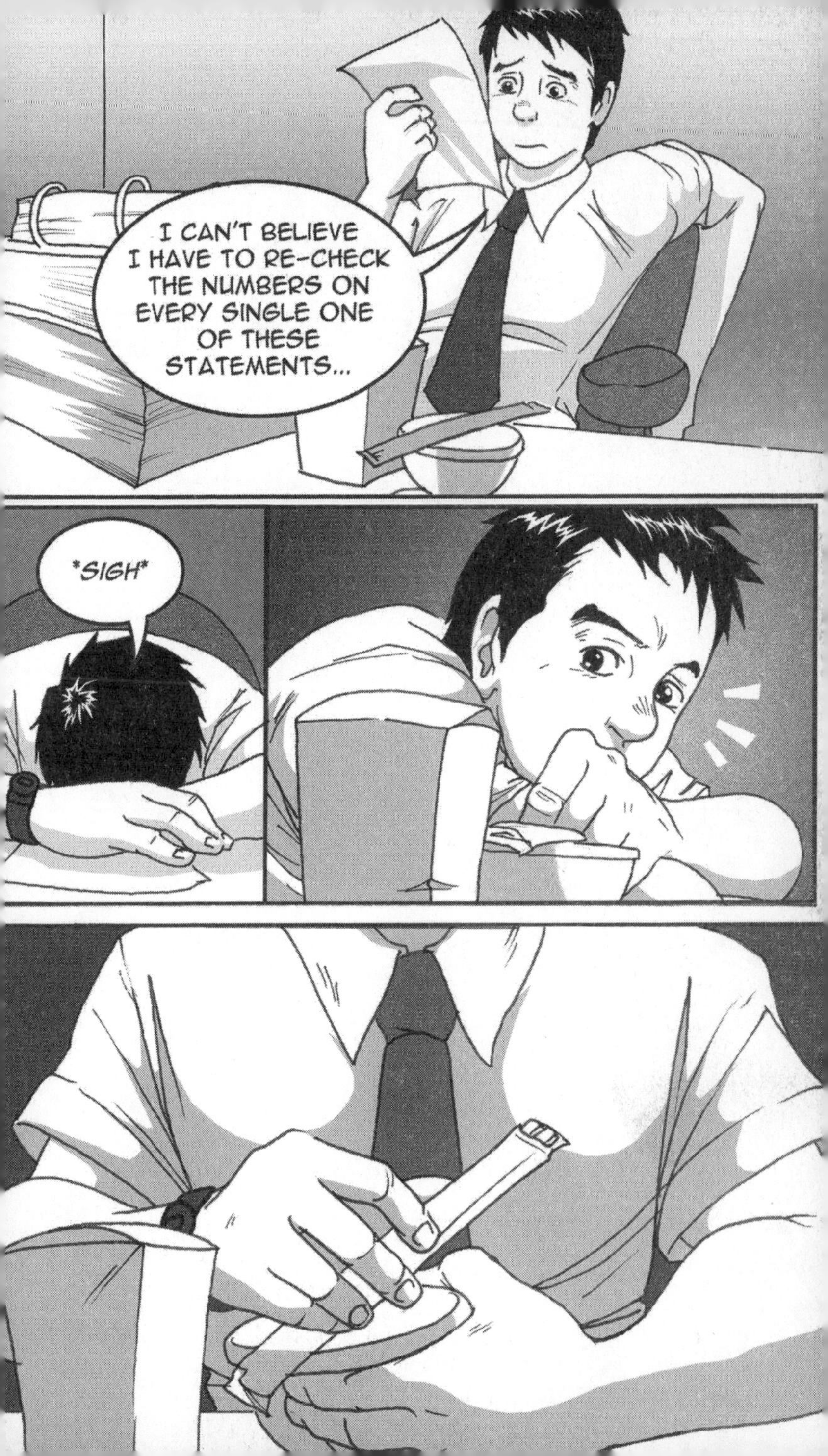
I CAN'T BELIEVE I HAVE TO RE-CHECK THE NUMBERS ON EVERY SINGLE ONE OF THESE STATEMENTS...
SIGH

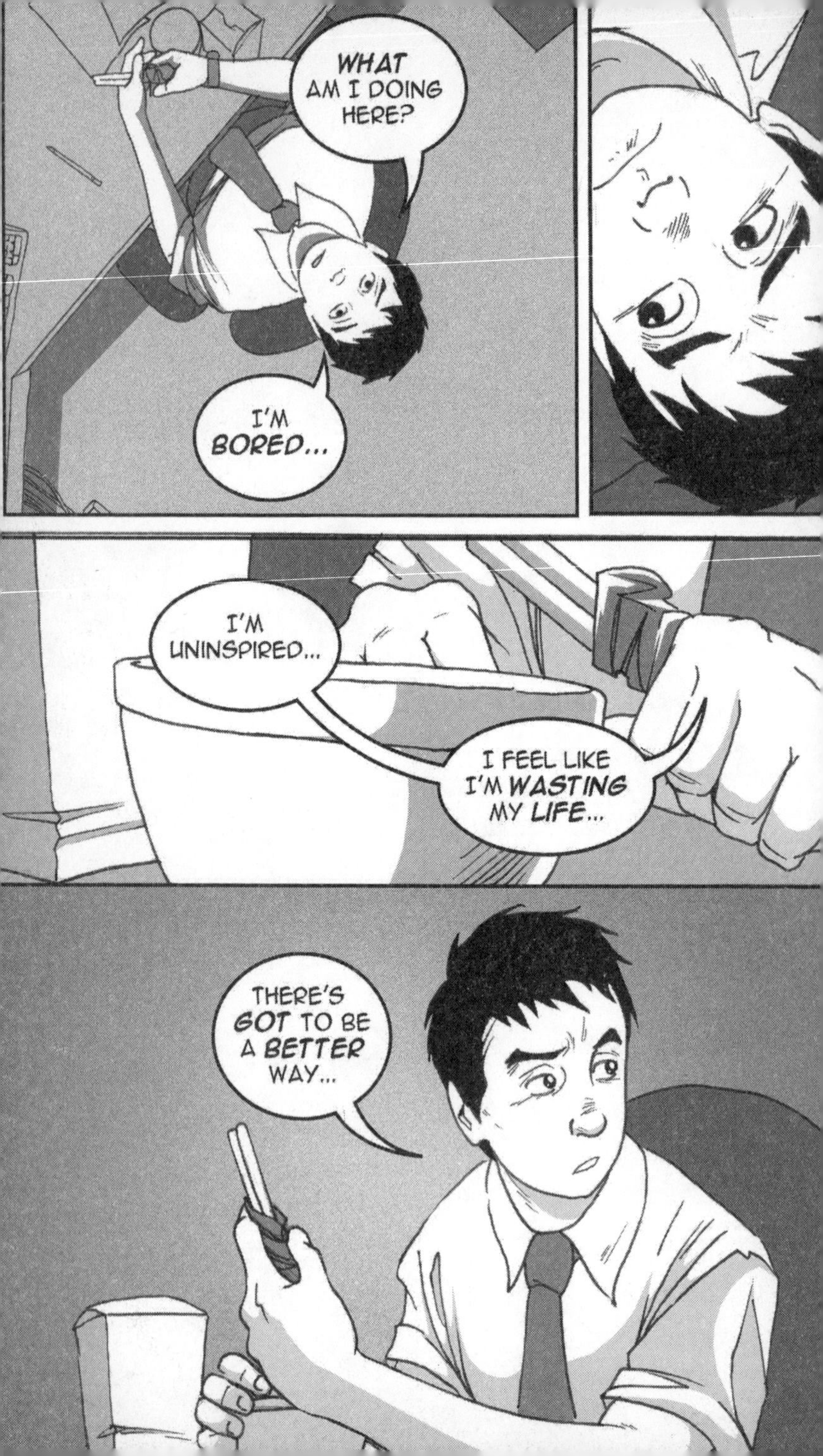
WHAT AM I DOING HERE?
I'M BORED...
I'M UNINSPIRED...
I FEEL LIKE I'M WASTING MY LIFE...
THERE'S GOT TO BE A BETTER WAY...

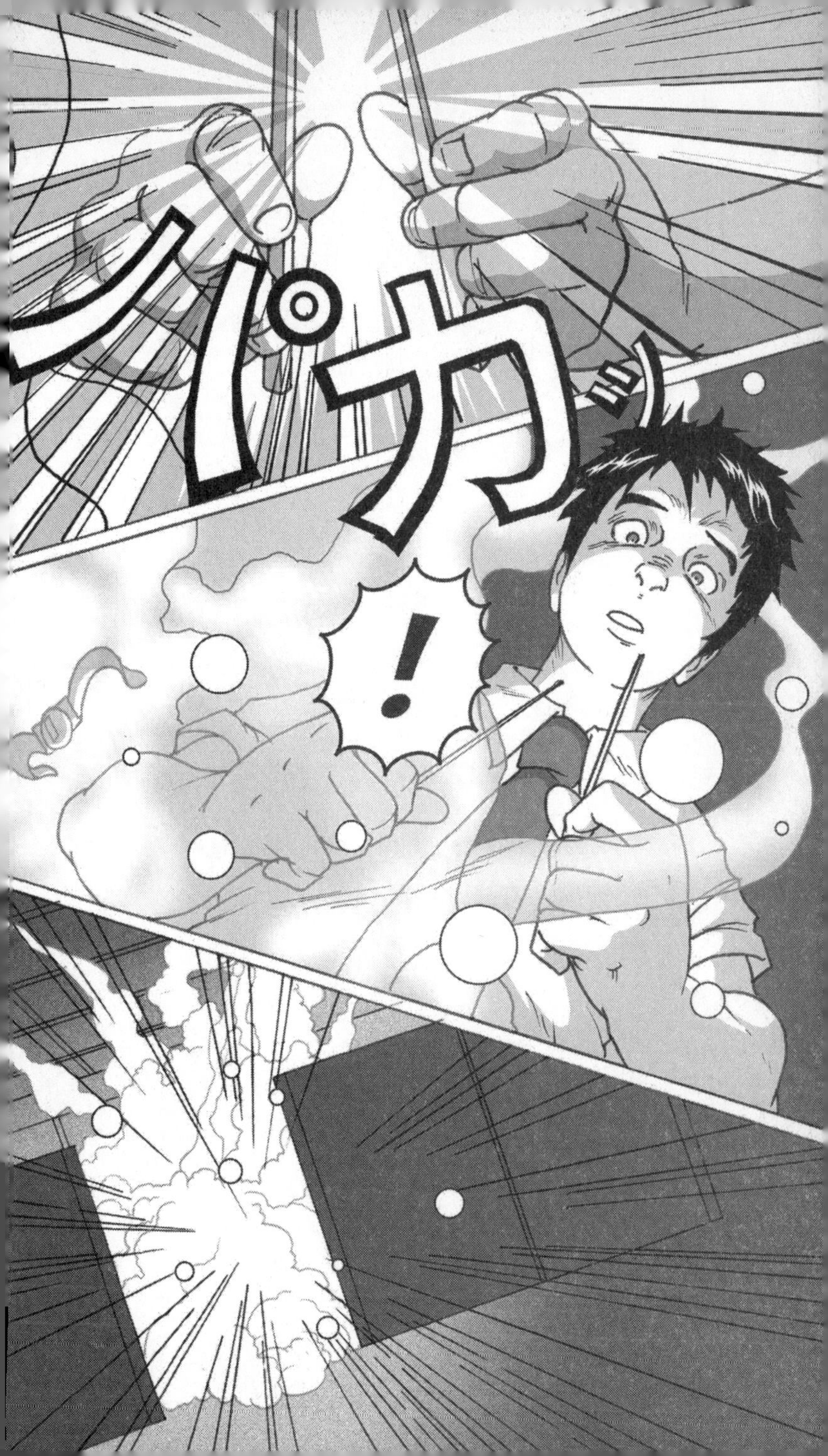
パカッ
!

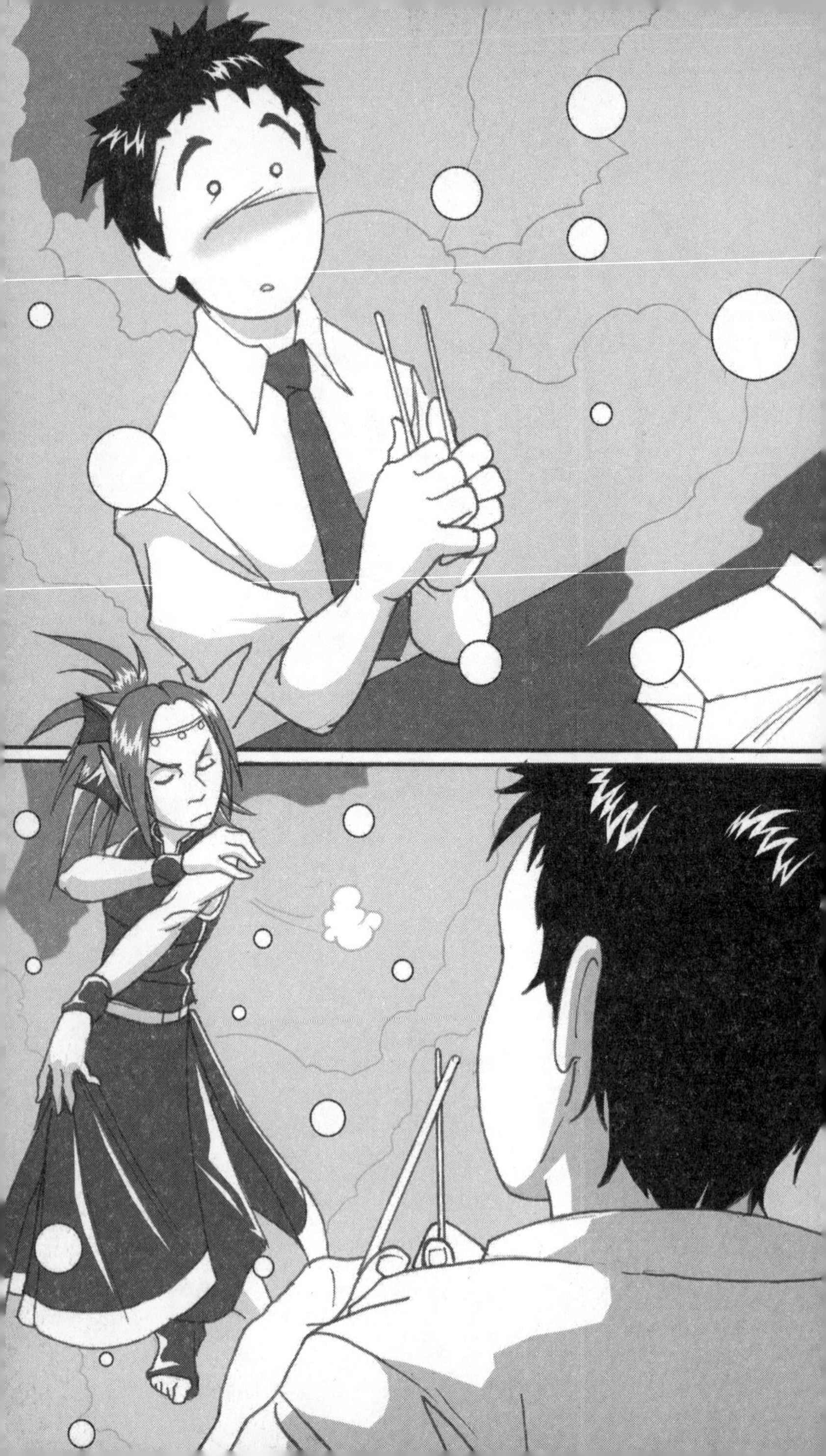

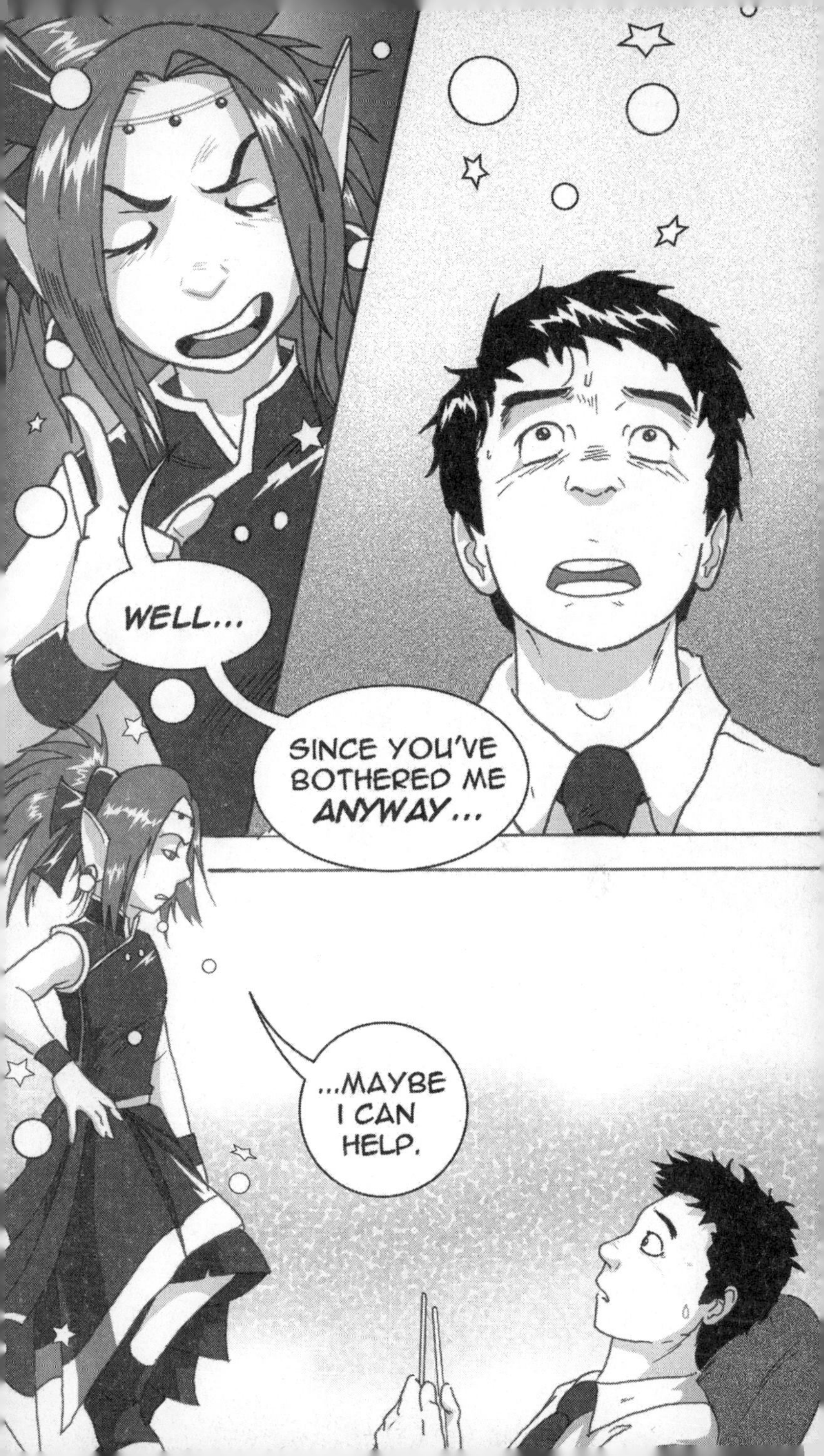
WELL...
SINCE YOU'VE BOTHERED ME ANYWAY...
...MAYBE I CAN HELP.

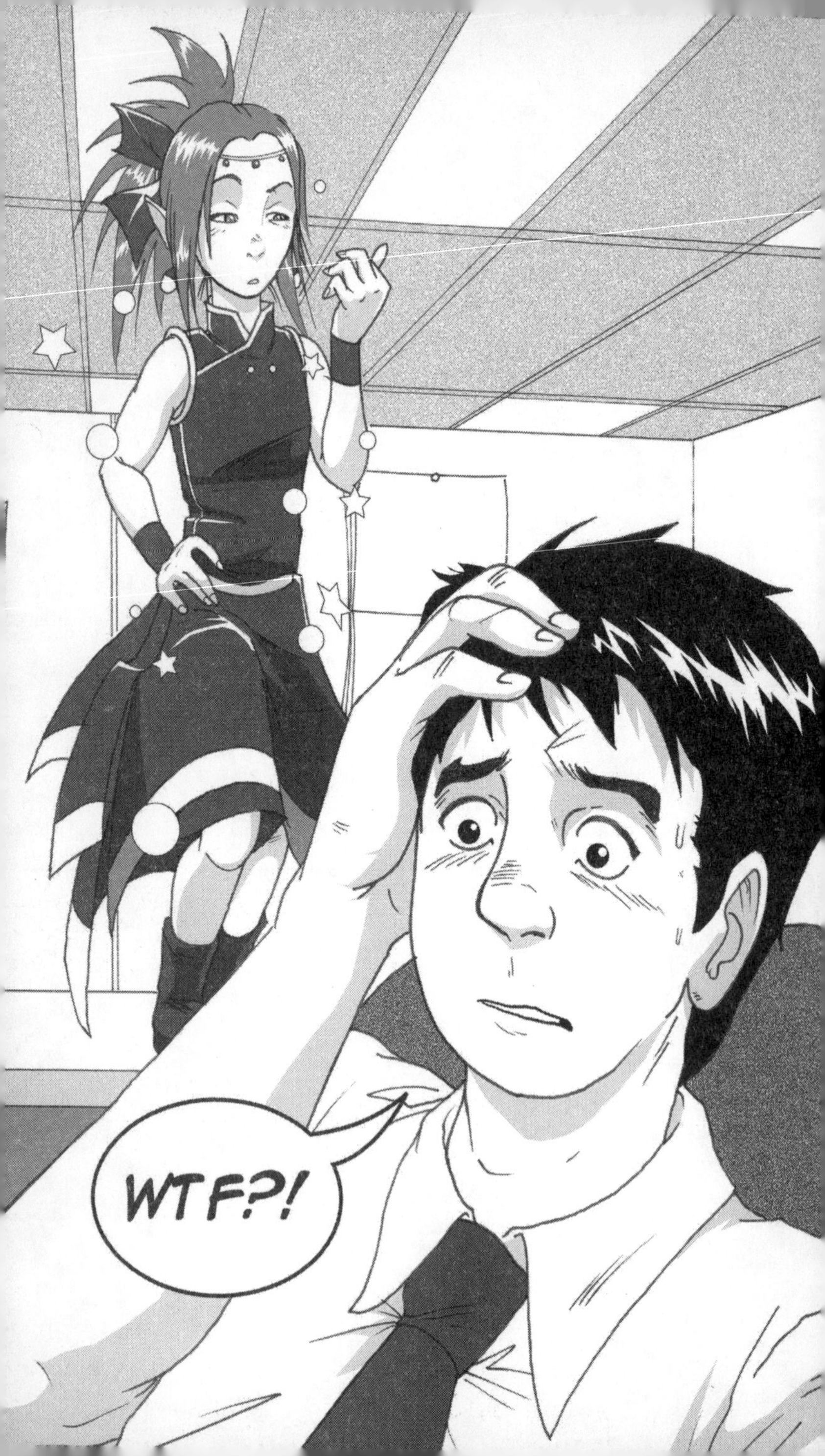
WTF?!

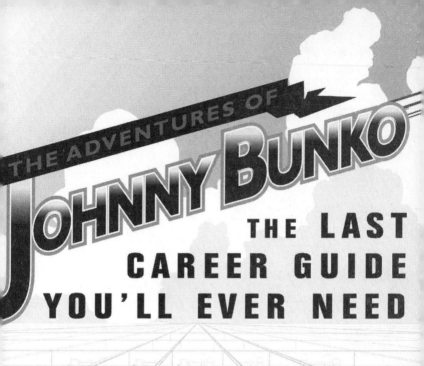

THE ADVENTURES OF
JOHNNY BUNKO

THE LAST CAREER GUIDE YOU'LL EVER NEED

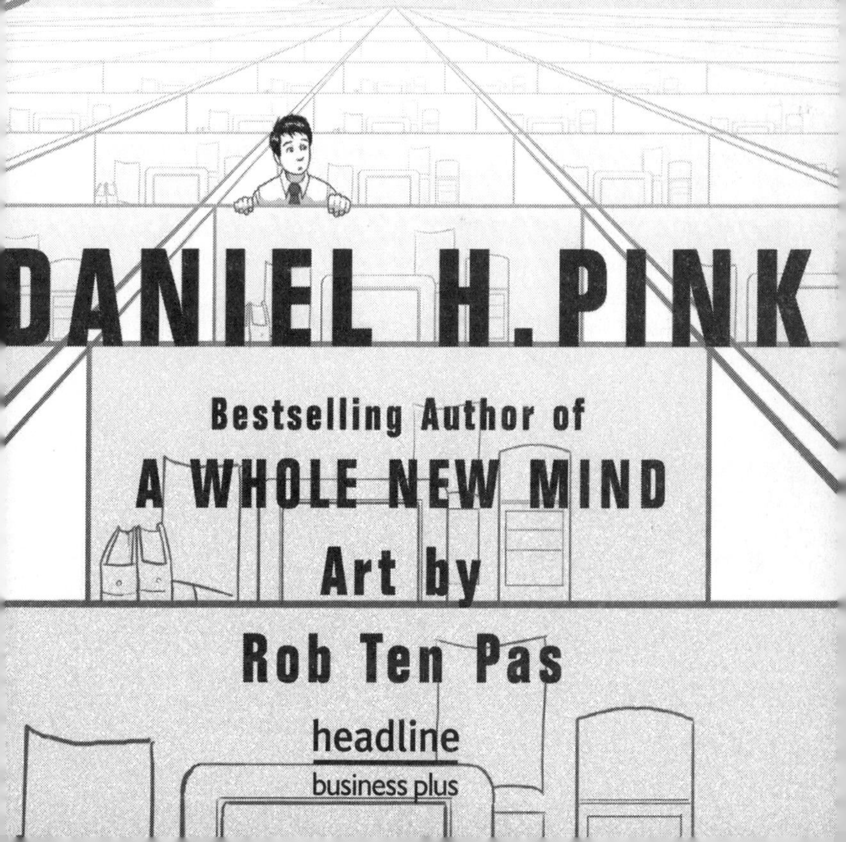

DANIEL H. PINK

Bestselling Author of
A WHOLE NEW MIND

Art by

Rob Ten Pas

headline
business plus

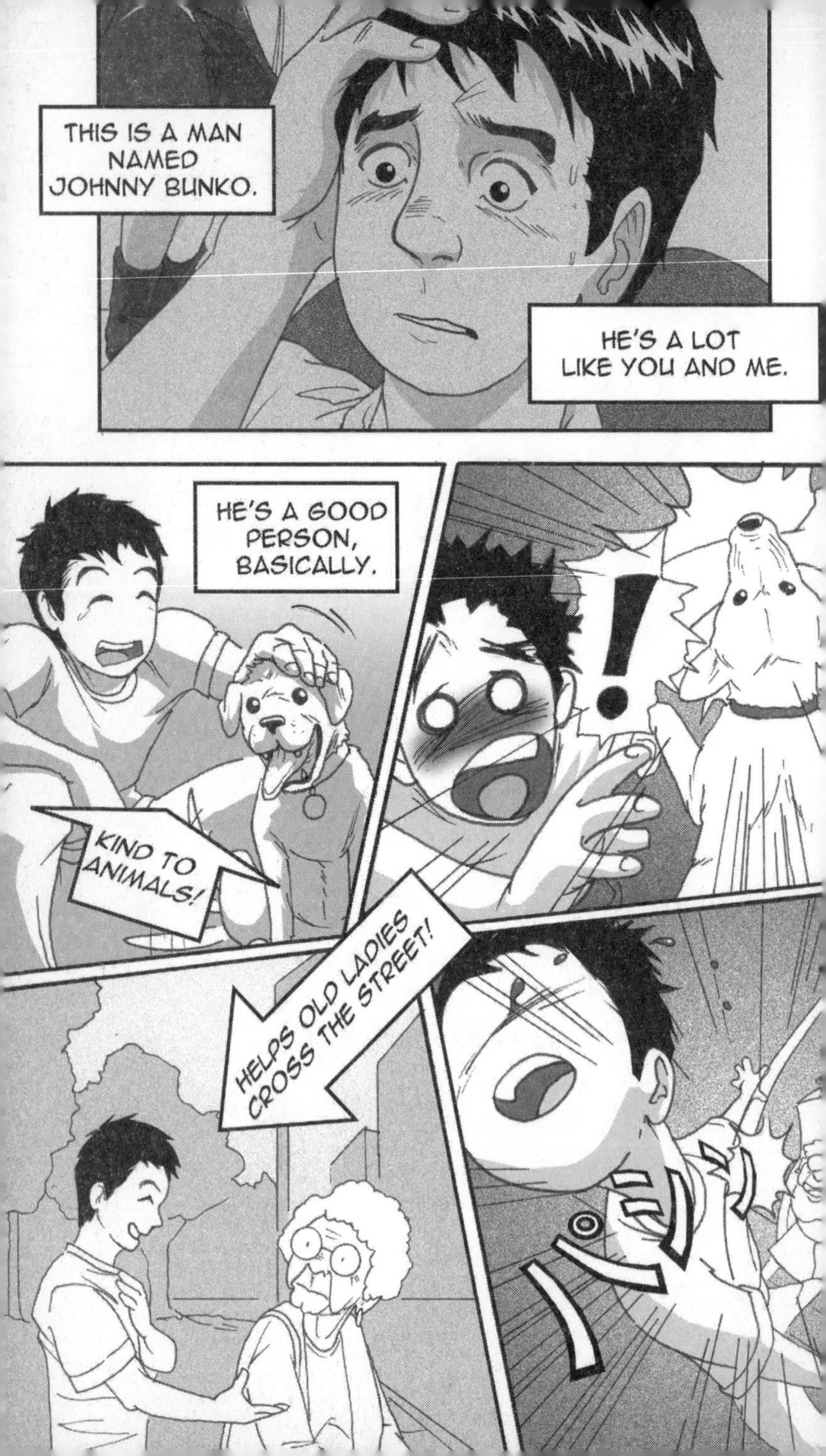
THIS IS A MAN NAMED JOHNNY BUNKO.
HE'S A LOT LIKE YOU AND ME.
HE'S A GOOD PERSON, BASICALLY.
KIND TO ANIMALS!
!
HELPS OLD LADIES CROSS THE STREET!

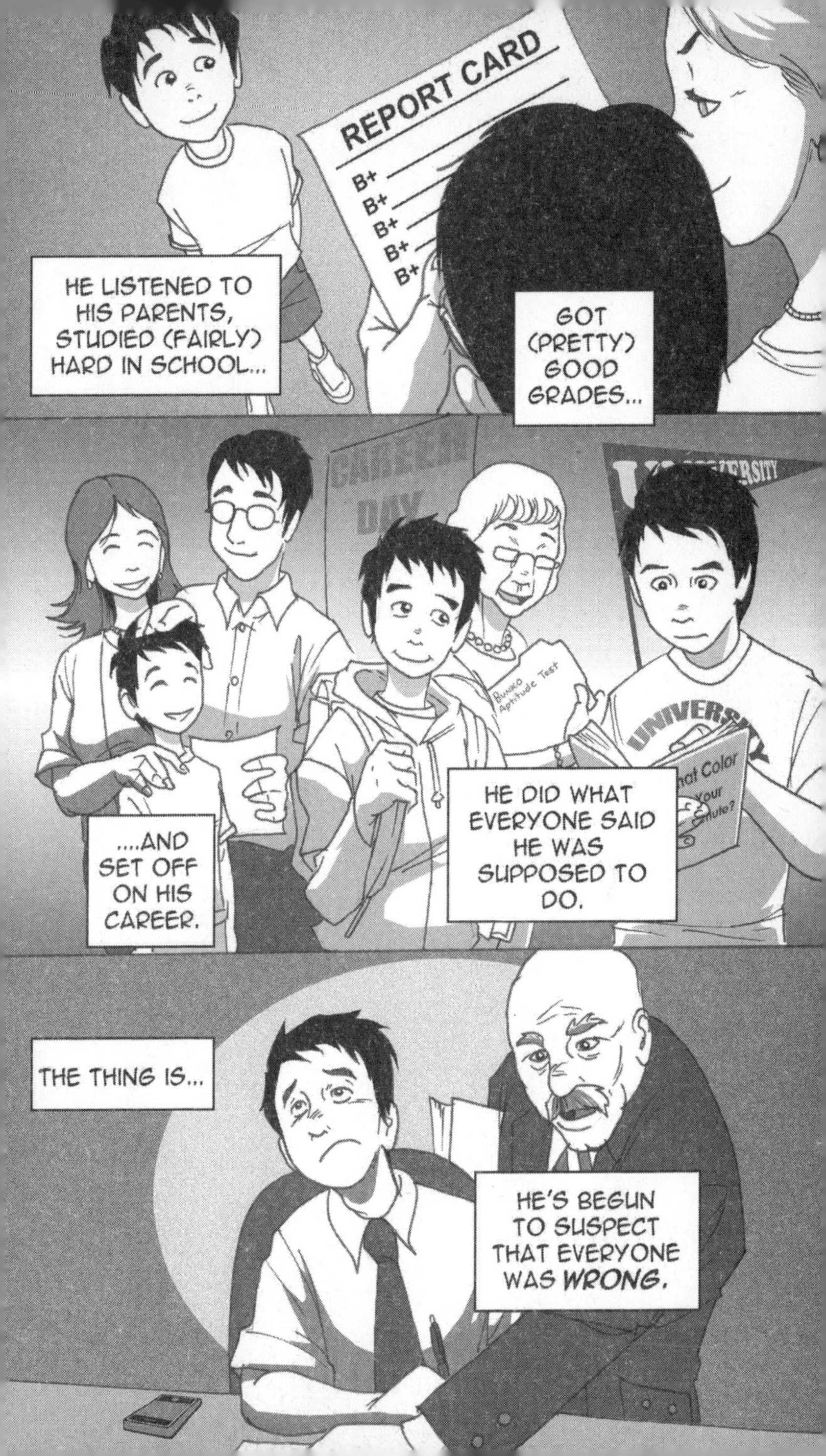
REPORT CARD
B+
B+
B+
B+
B+
HE LISTENED TO HIS PARENTS, STUDIED (FAIRLY) HARD IN SCHOOL...
GOT (PRETTY) GOOD GRADES...
....AND SET OFF ON HIS CAREER.
HE DID WHAT EVERYONE SAID HE WAS SUPPOSED TO DO.
THE THING IS...
HE'S BEGUN TO SUSPECT THAT EVERYONE WAS *WRONG*.

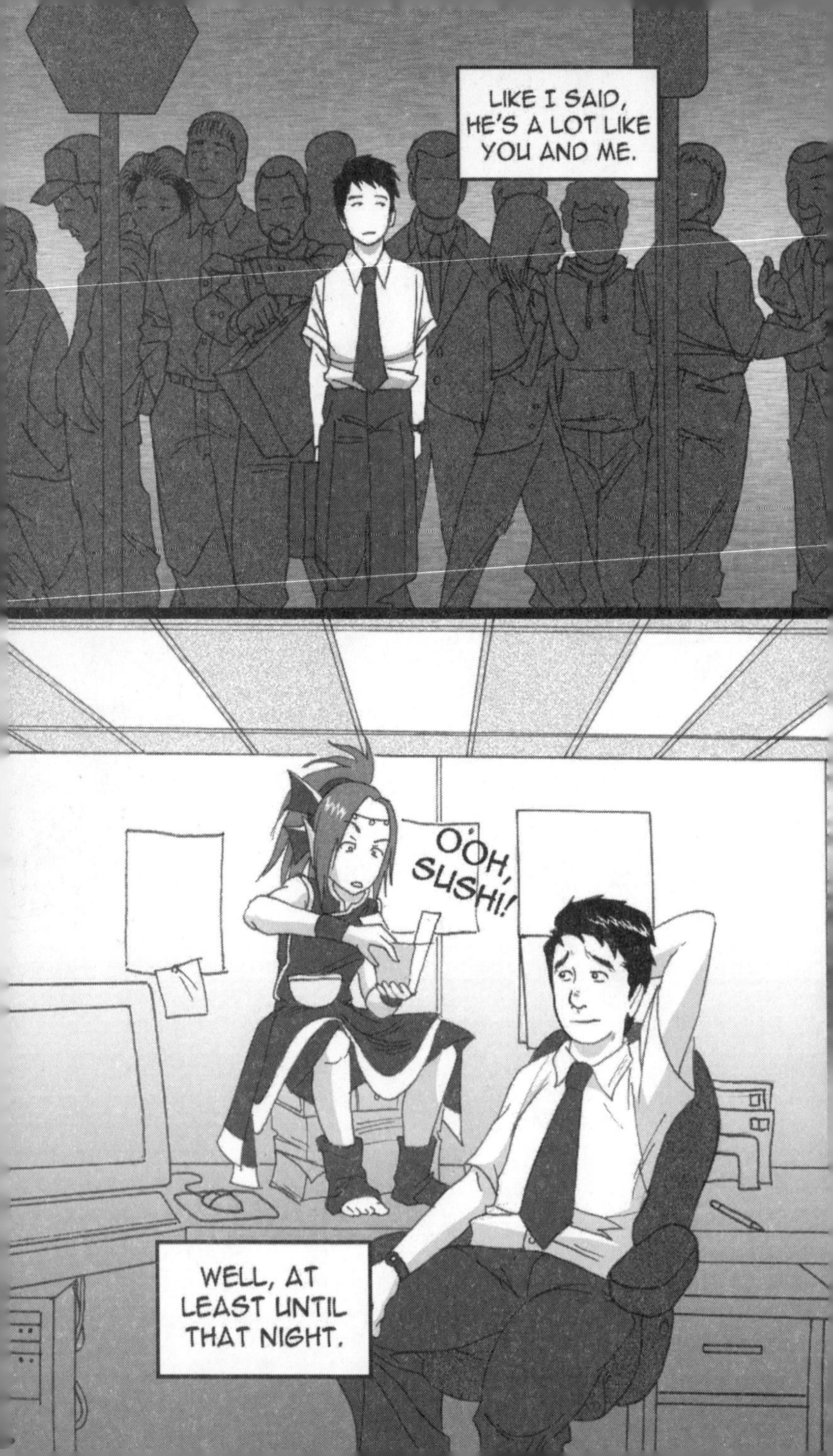
LIKE I SAID, HE'S A LOT LIKE YOU AND ME.
OOOH, SUSHI!
WELL, AT LEAST UNTIL THAT NIGHT.

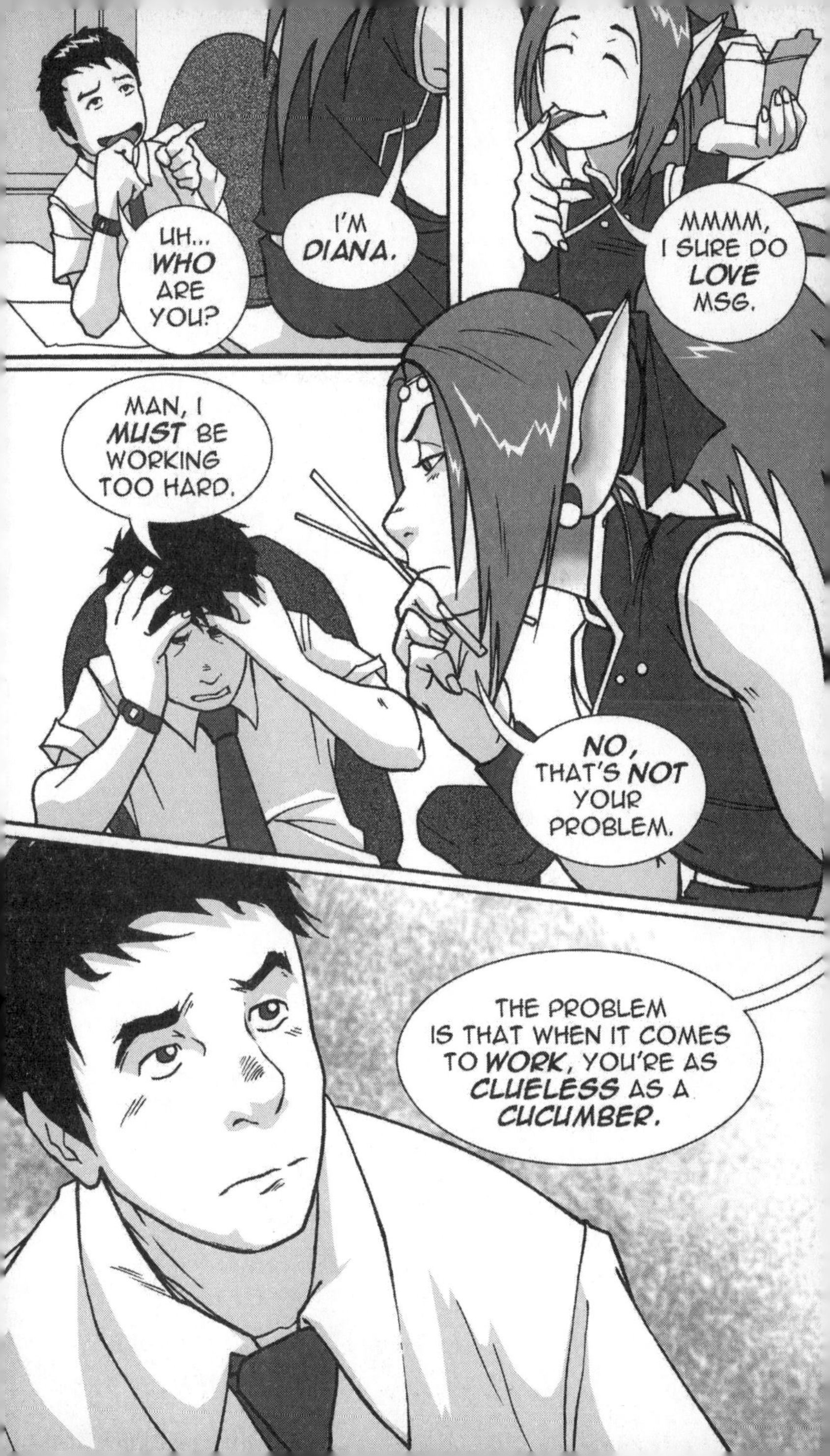
UH... **WHO** ARE YOU?
I'M **DIANA.**
MMMM, I SURE DO **LOVE** MSG.
MAN, I **MUST** BE WORKING TOO HARD.
NO, THAT'S **NOT** YOUR PROBLEM.
THE PROBLEM IS THAT WHEN IT COMES TO **WORK**, YOU'RE AS **CLUELESS** AS A **CUCUMBER.**

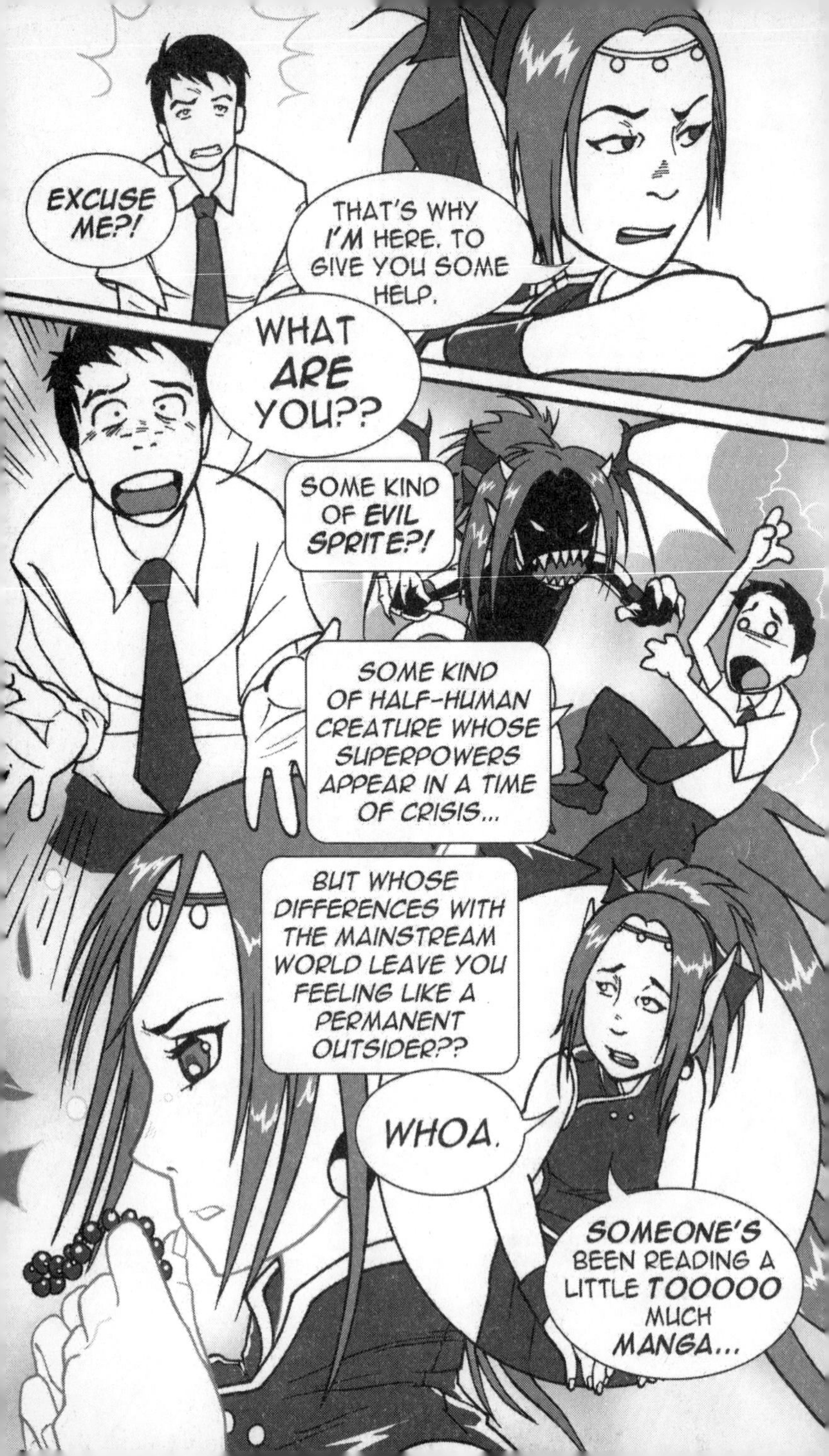
EXCUSE ME?!
THAT'S WHY I'M HERE. TO GIVE YOU SOME HELP.
WHAT ARE YOU??
SOME KIND OF EVIL SPRITE?!
SOME KIND OF HALF-HUMAN CREATURE WHOSE SUPERPOWERS APPEAR IN A TIME OF CRISIS...
BUT WHOSE DIFFERENCES WITH THE MAINSTREAM WORLD LEAVE YOU FEELING LIKE A PERMANENT OUTSIDER??
WHOA.
SOMEONE'S BEEN READING A LITTLE TOOOOO MUCH MANGA...

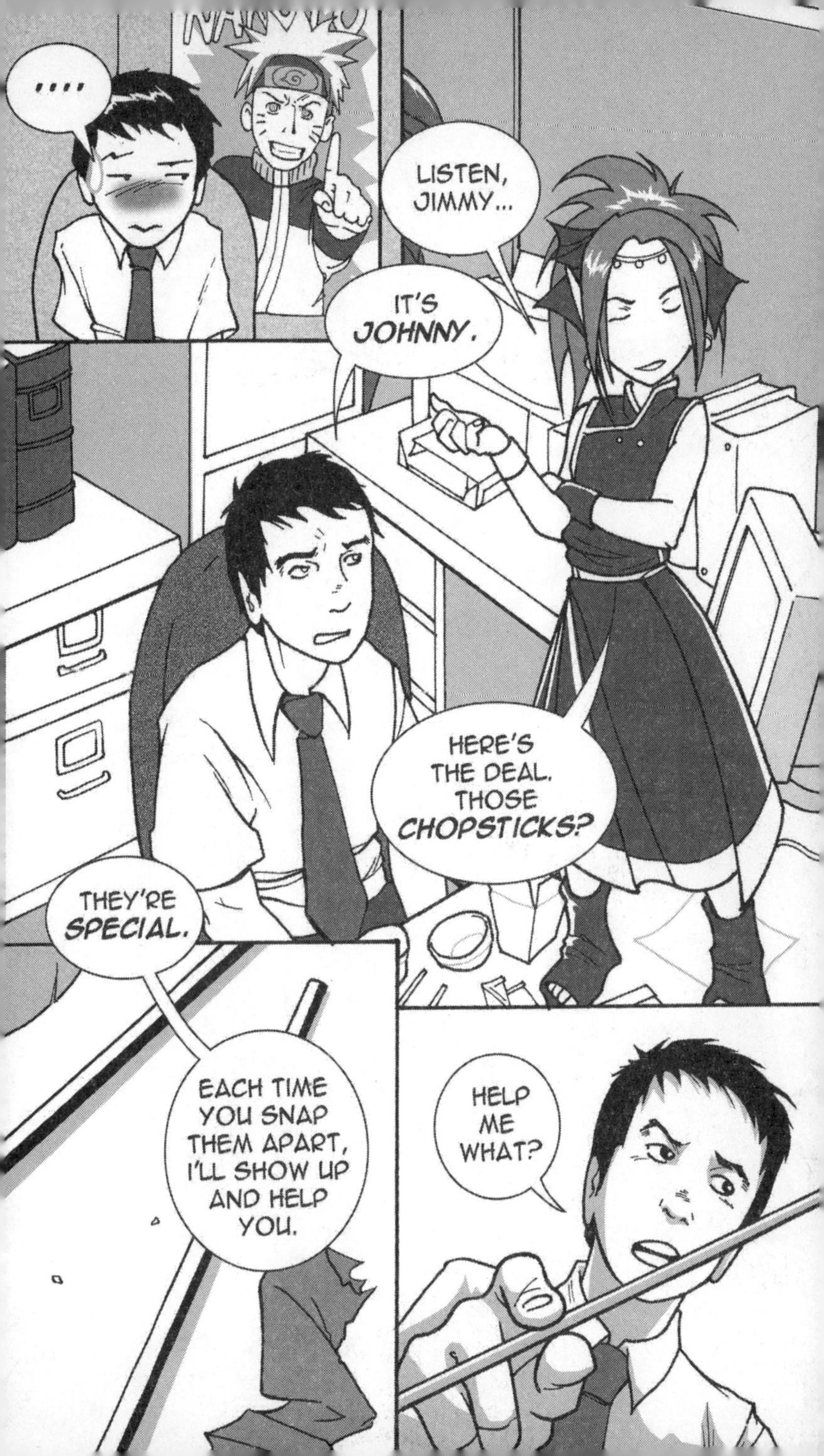
....
LISTEN, JIMMY...
IT'S JOHNNY.
HERE'S THE DEAL. THOSE CHOPSTICKS?
THEY'RE SPECIAL.
EACH TIME YOU SNAP THEM APART, I'LL SHOW UP AND HELP YOU.
HELP ME WHAT?

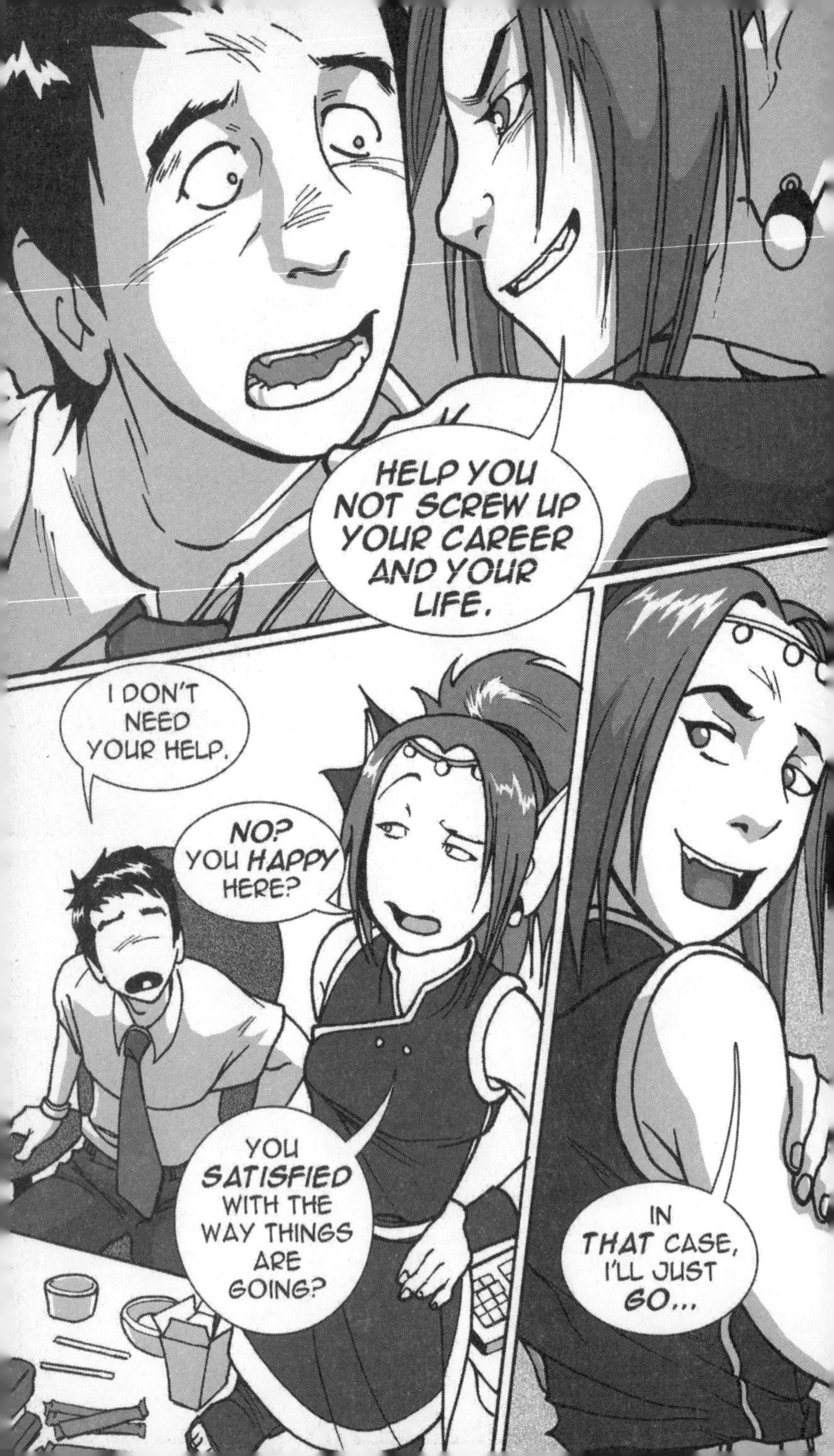
HELP YOU NOT SCREW UP YOUR CAREER AND YOUR LIFE.
I DON'T NEED YOUR HELP.
NO? YOU HAPPY HERE?
YOU SATISFIED WITH THE WAY THINGS ARE GOING?
IN THAT CASE, I'LL JUST GO...

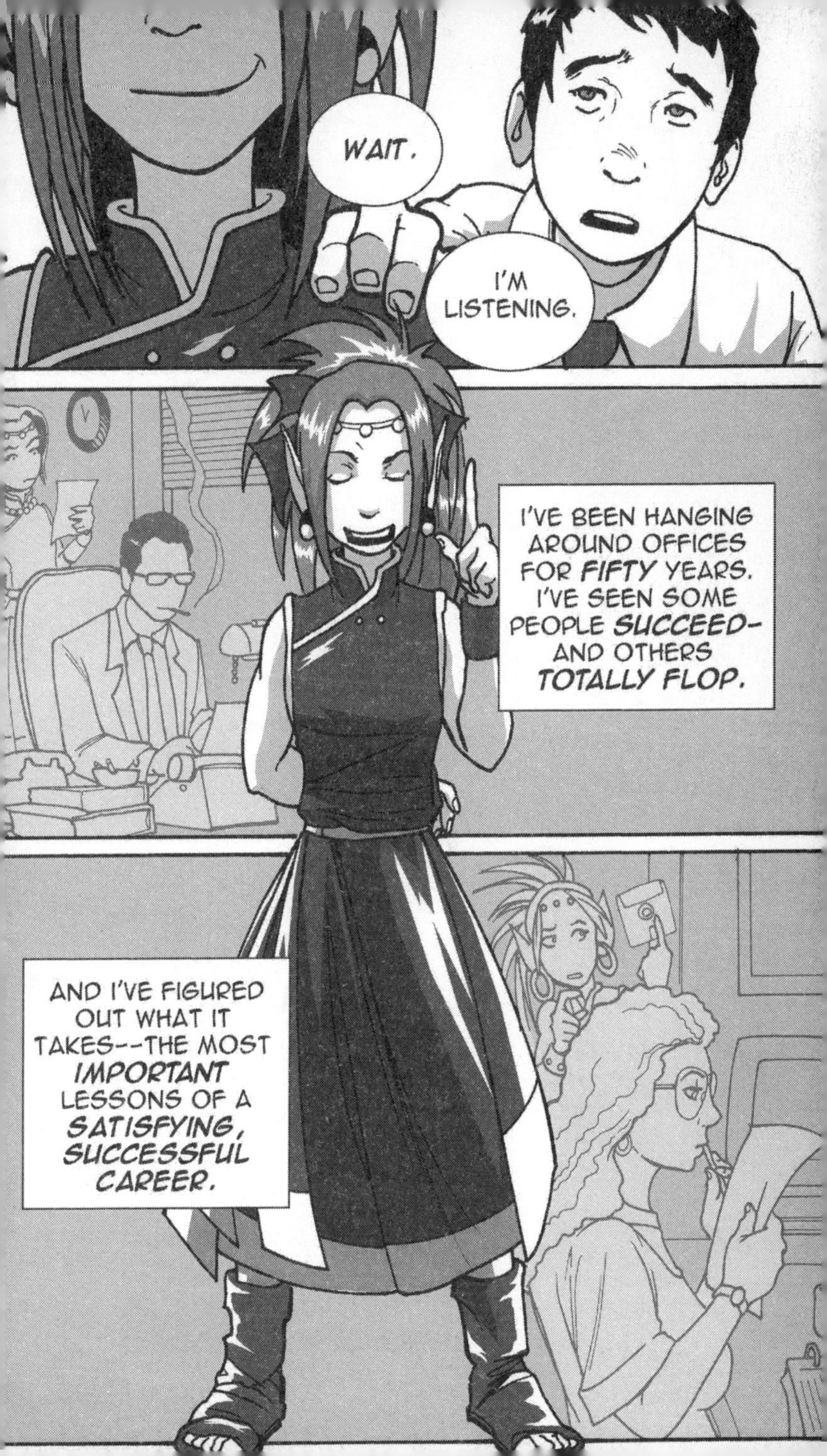
WAIT.
I'M LISTENING.
I'VE BEEN HANGING AROUND OFFICES FOR FIFTY YEARS. I'VE SEEN SOME PEOPLE SUCCEED-AND OTHERS TOTALLY FLOP.
AND I'VE FIGURED OUT WHAT IT TAKES--THE MOST IMPORTANT LESSONS OF A SATISFYING, SUCCESSFUL CAREER.

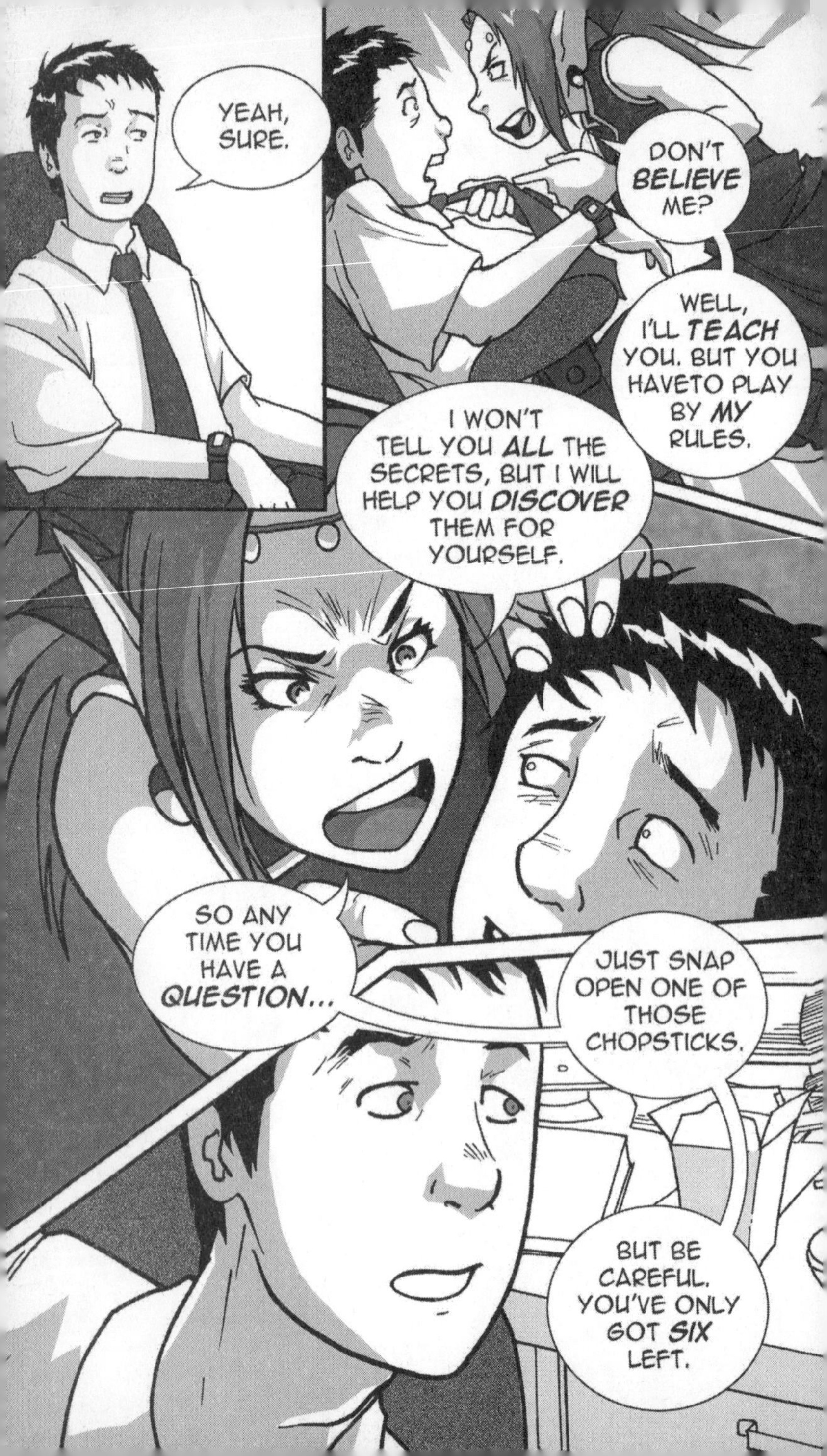
YEAH, SURE.
DON'T BELIEVE ME?
WELL, I'LL TEACH YOU. BUT YOU HAVETO PLAY BY MY RULES.
I WON'T TELL YOU ALL THE SECRETS, BUT I WILL HELP YOU DISCOVER THEM FOR YOURSELF.
SO ANY TIME YOU HAVE A QUESTION...
JUST SNAP OPEN ONE OF THOSE CHOPSTICKS.
BUT BE CAREFUL. YOU'VE ONLY GOT SIX LEFT.

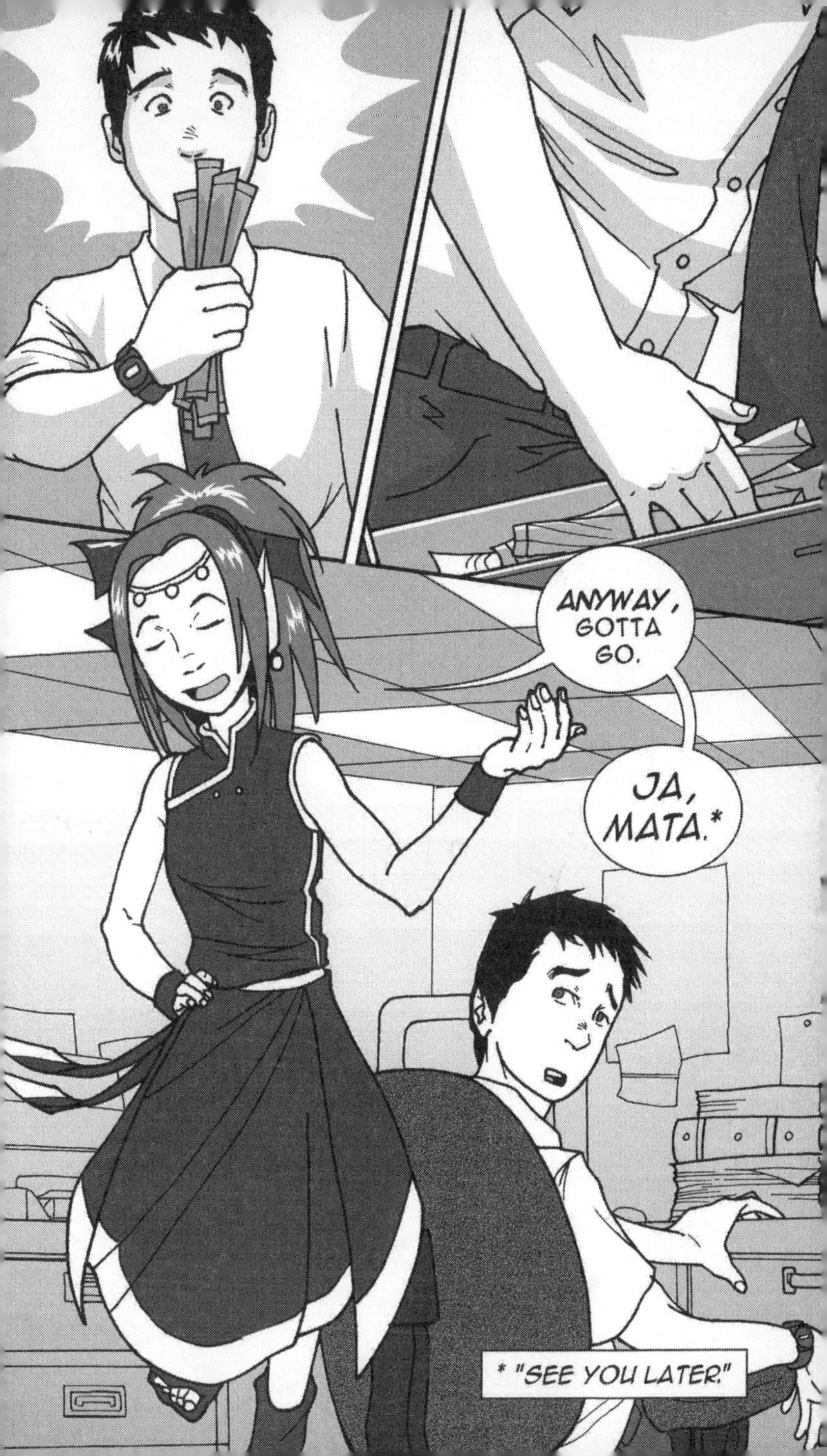
ANYWAY, GOTTA GO.
JA, MATA.*
* "SEE YOU LATER."

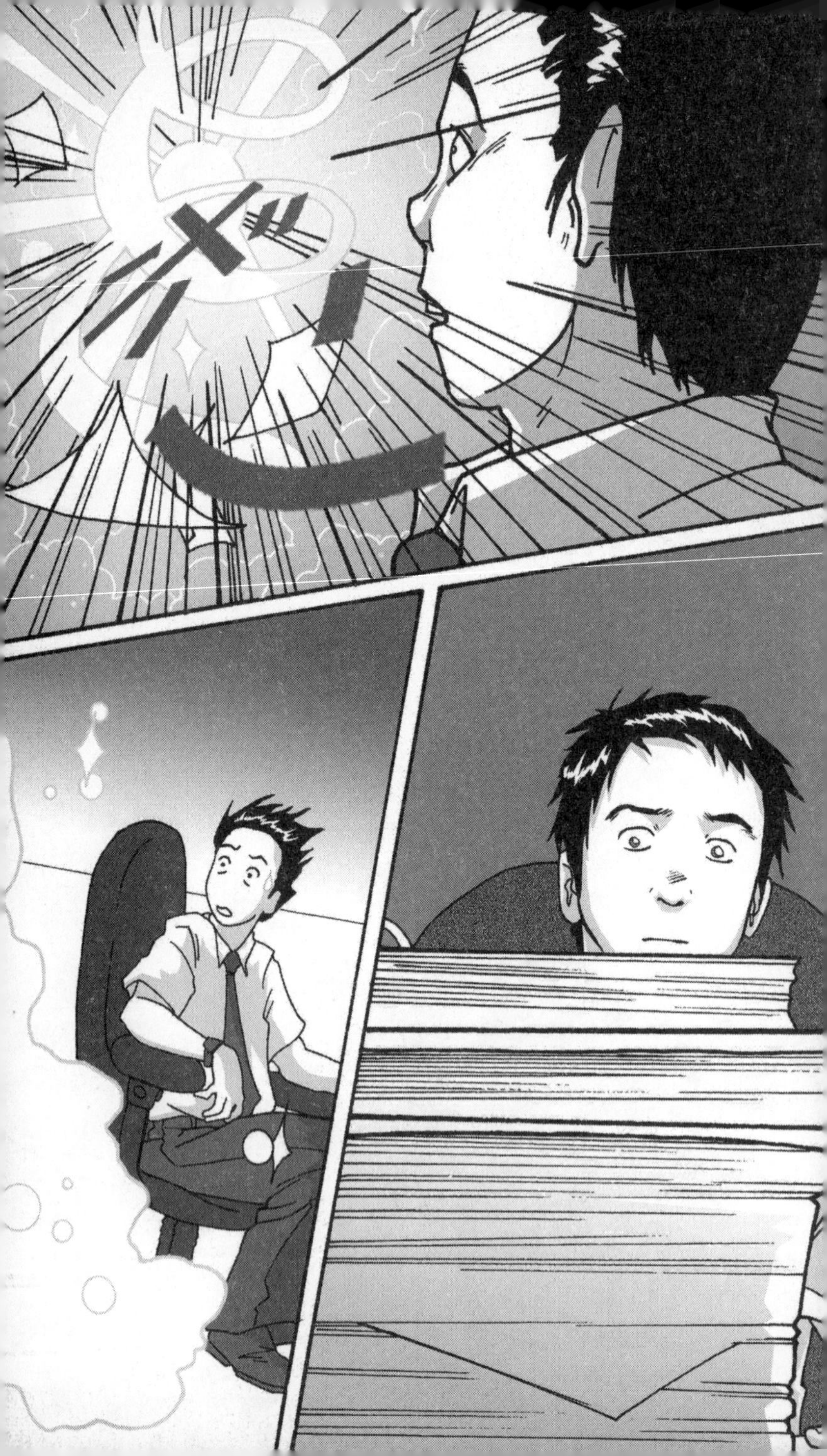

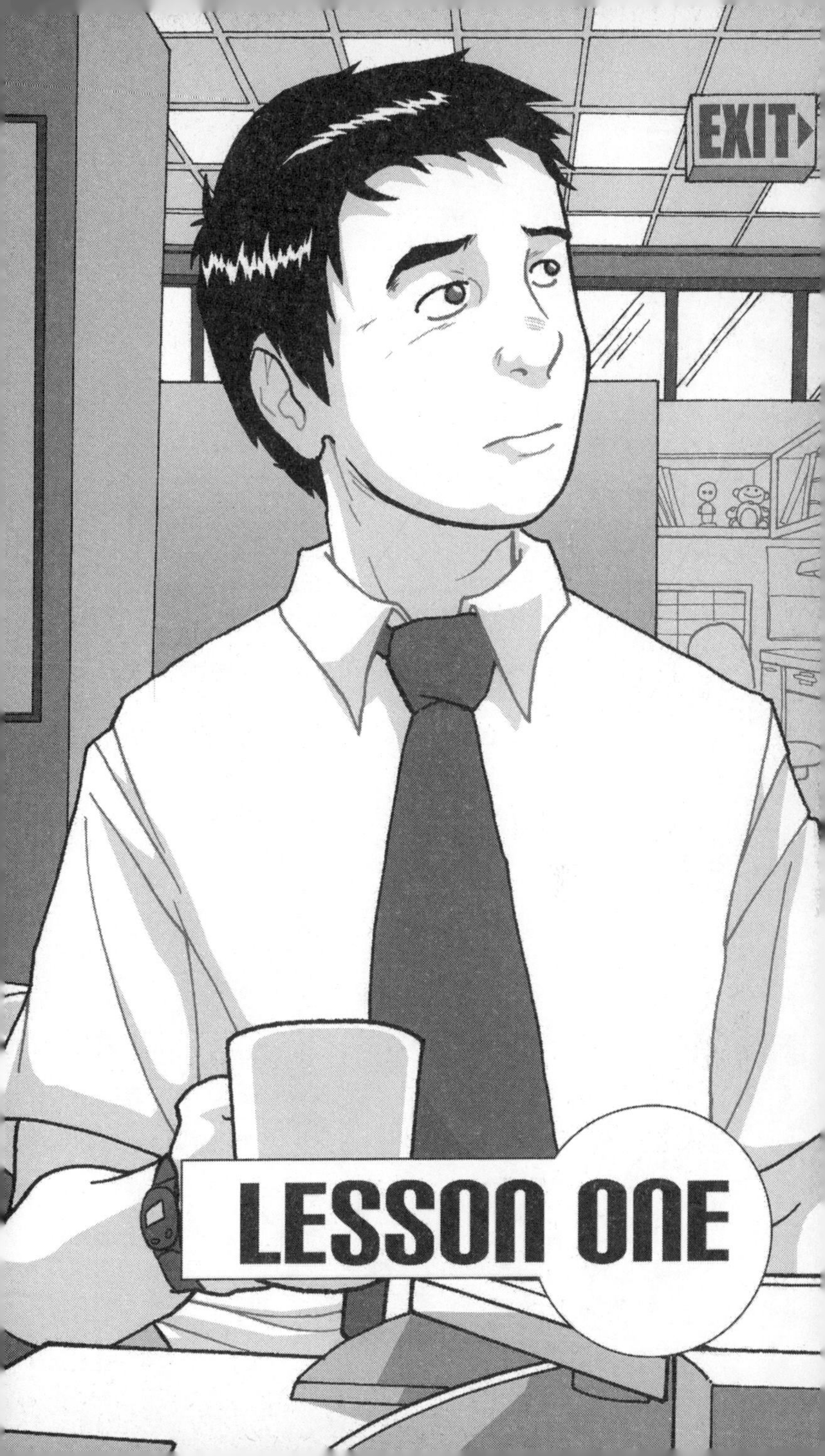
EXIT
LESSON ONE

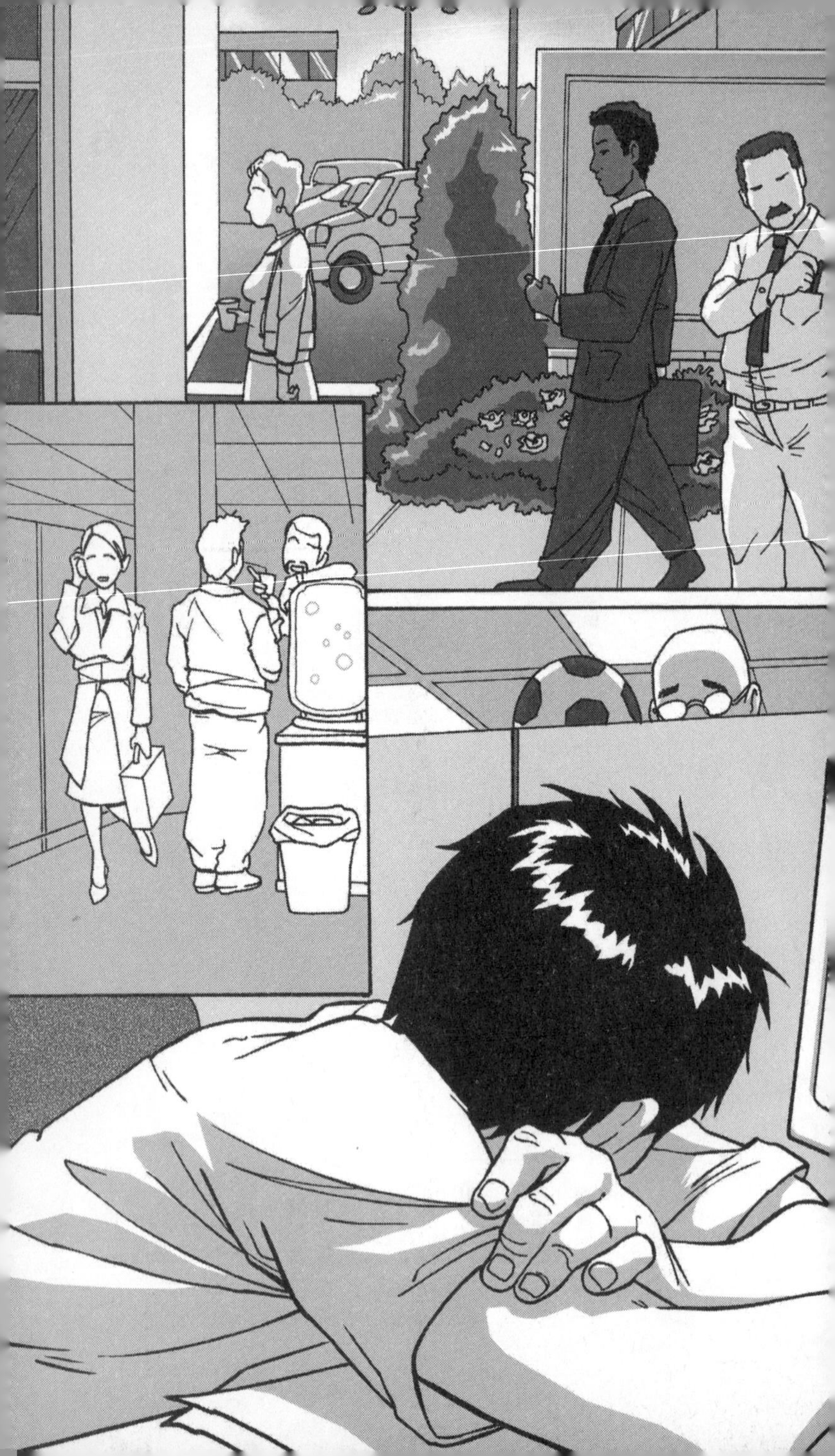

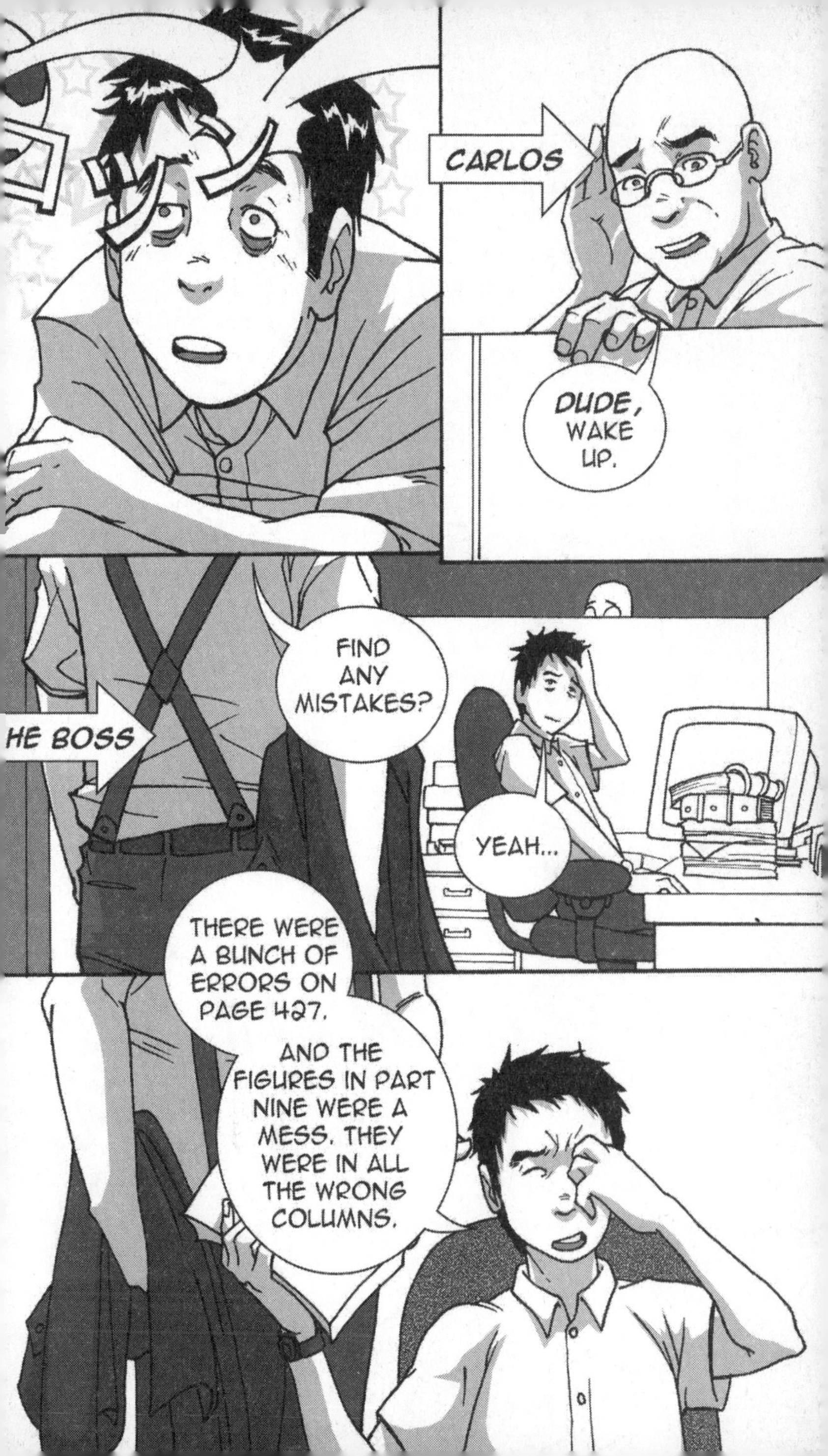
CARLOS
DUDE, WAKE UP.
HE BOSS
FIND ANY MISTAKES?
YEAH...
THERE WERE A BUNCH OF ERRORS ON PAGE 427.
AND THE FIGURES IN PART NINE WERE A MESS. THEY WERE IN ALL THE WRONG COLUMNS.

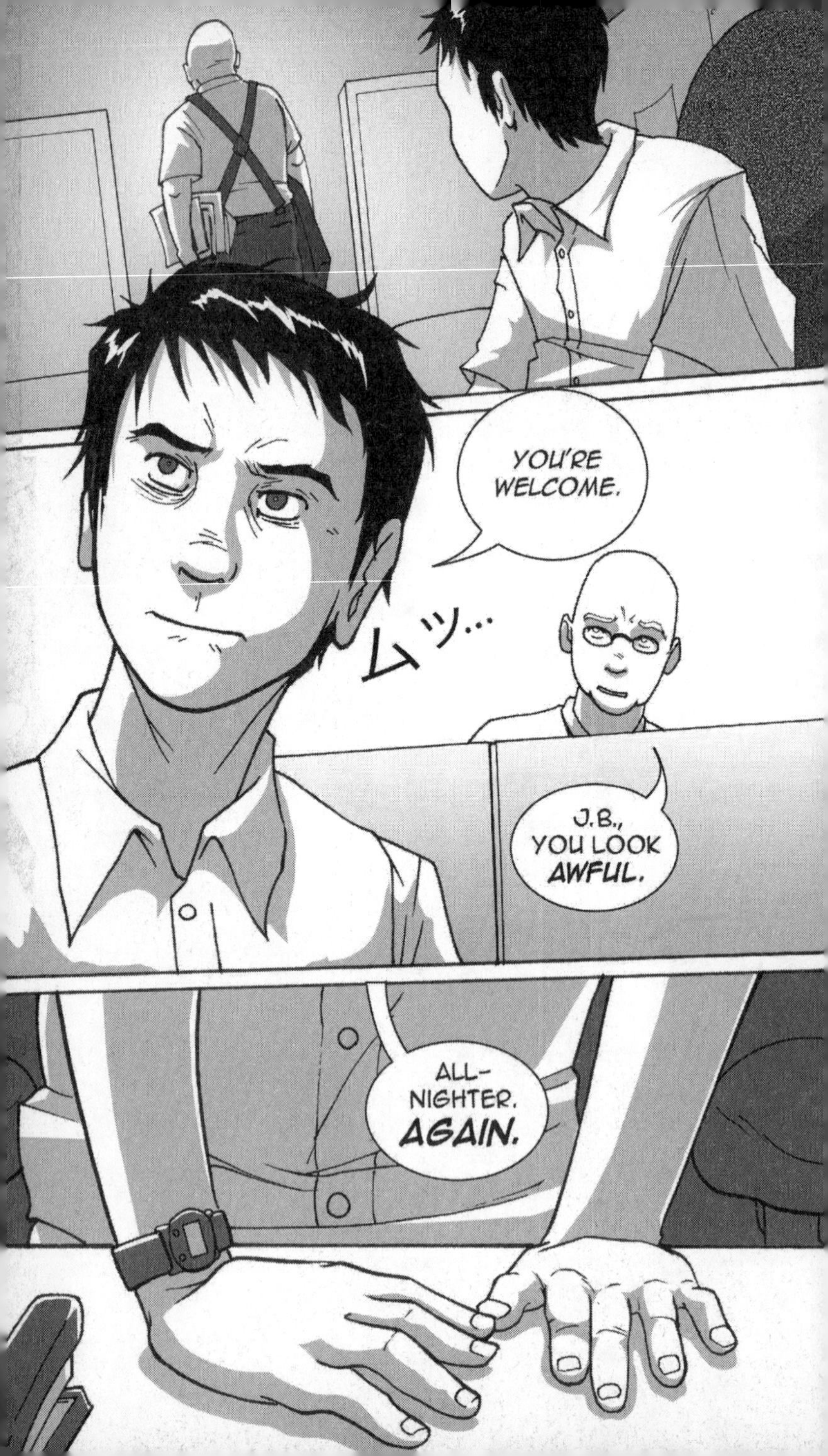
YOU'RE WELCOME.
ムッ...
J.B., YOU LOOK AWFUL.
ALL-NIGHTER. AGAIN.

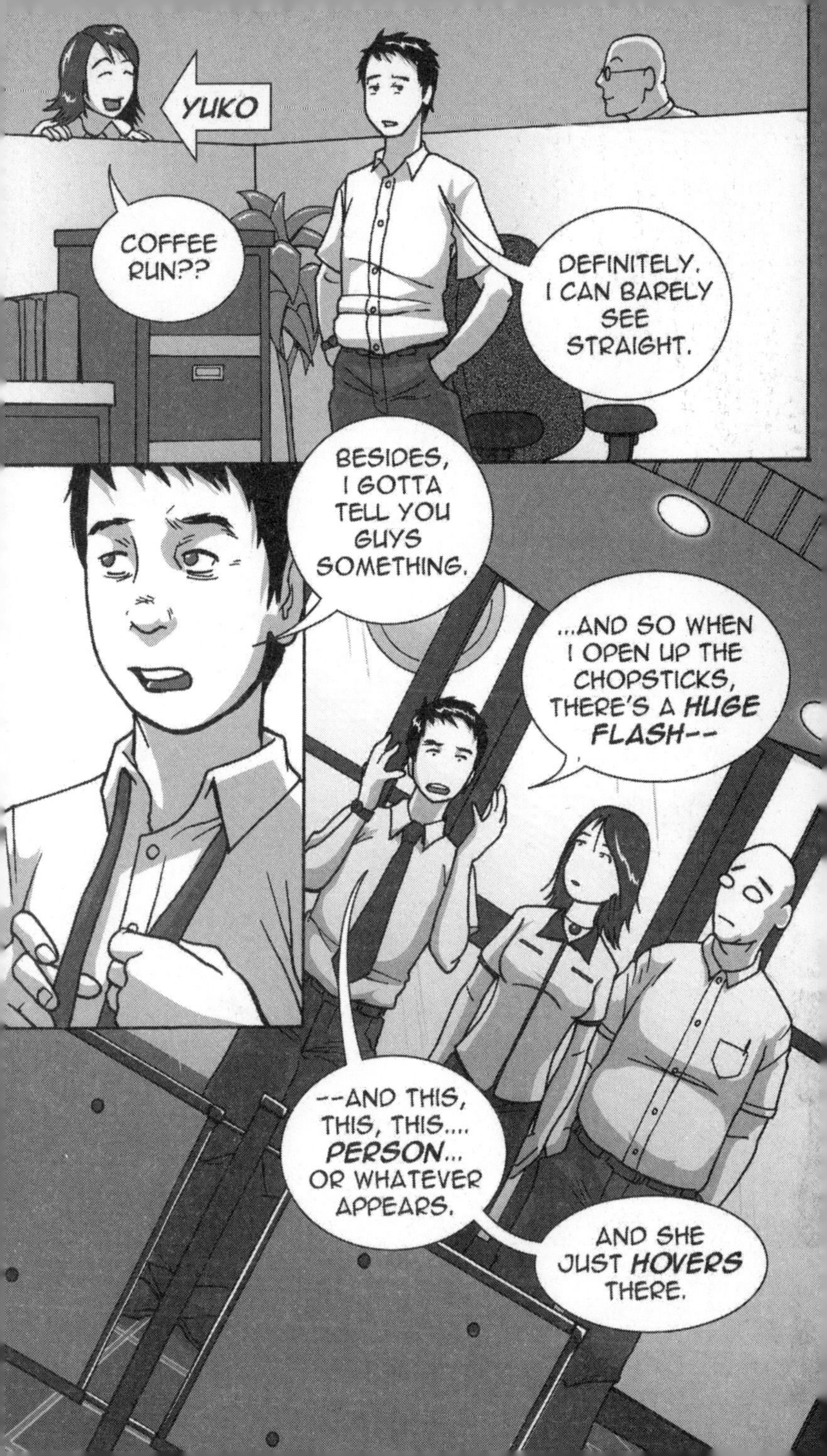
YUKO
COFFEE RUN??
DEFINITELY. I CAN BARELY SEE STRAIGHT.
BESIDES, I GOTTA TELL YOU GUYS SOMETHING.
...AND SO WHEN I OPEN UP THE CHOPSTICKS, THERE'S A HUGE FLASH--
--AND THIS, THIS, THIS.... PERSON... OR WHATEVER APPEARS.
AND SHE JUST HOVERS THERE.

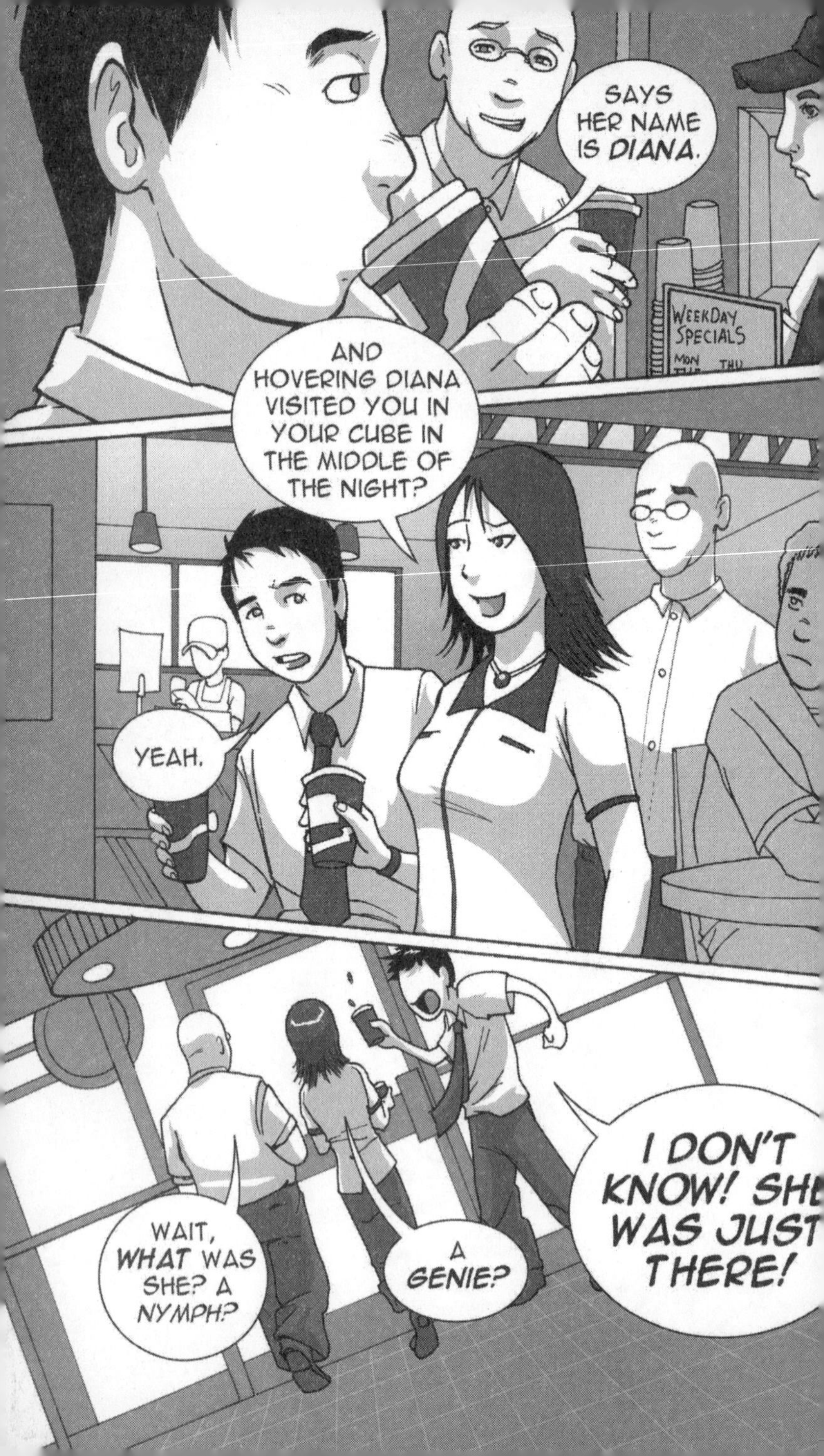
SAYS HER NAME IS DIANA.
WEEKDAY SPECIALS
AND HOVERING DIANA VISITED YOU IN YOUR CUBE IN THE MIDDLE OF THE NIGHT?
YEAH.
I DON'T KNOW! SHE WAS JUST THERE!
WAIT, WHAT WAS SHE? A NYMPH?
A GENIE?

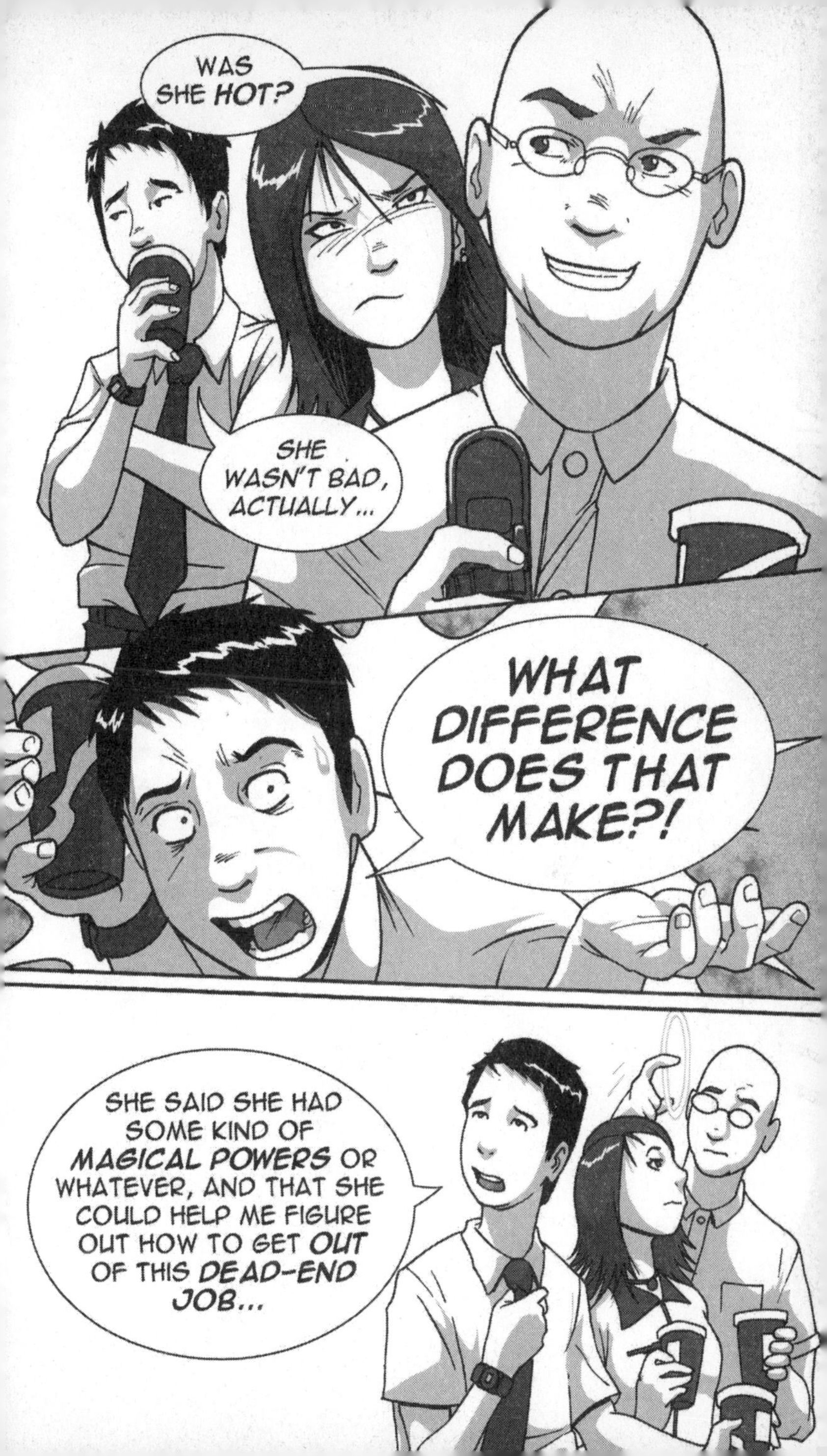
WAS SHE HOT?
SHE WASN'T BAD, ACTUALLY...
WHAT DIFFERENCE DOES THAT MAKE?!
SHE SAID SHE HAD SOME KIND OF MAGICAL POWERS OR WHATEVER, AND THAT SHE COULD HELP ME FIGURE OUT HOW TO GET OUT OF THIS DEAD-END JOB...

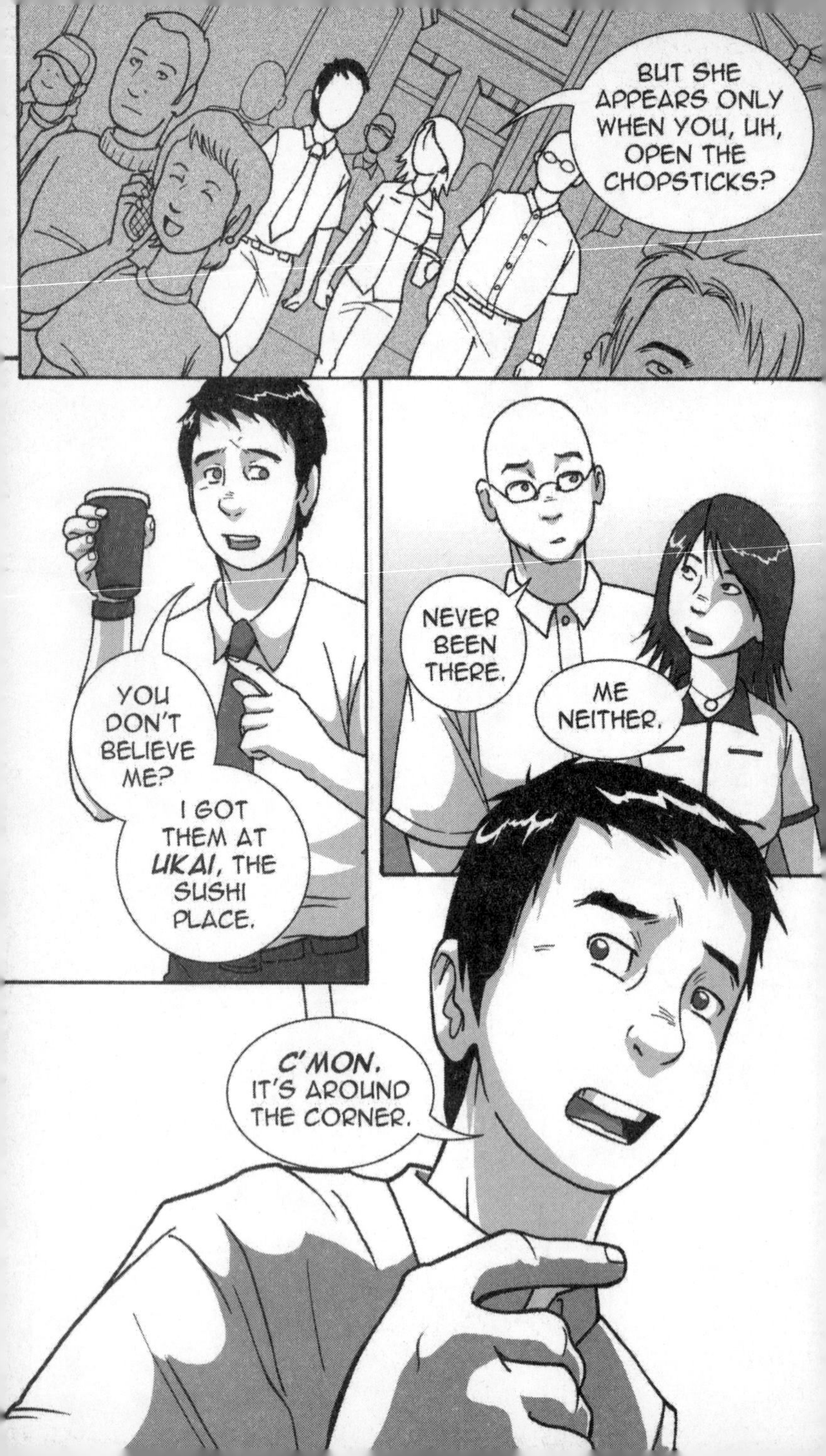
BUT SHE APPEARS ONLY WHEN YOU, UH, OPEN THE CHOPSTICKS?
YOU DON'T BELIEVE ME?
I GOT THEM AT *UKAI*, THE SUSHI PLACE.
NEVER BEEN THERE.
ME NEITHER.
C'MON. IT'S AROUND THE CORNER.

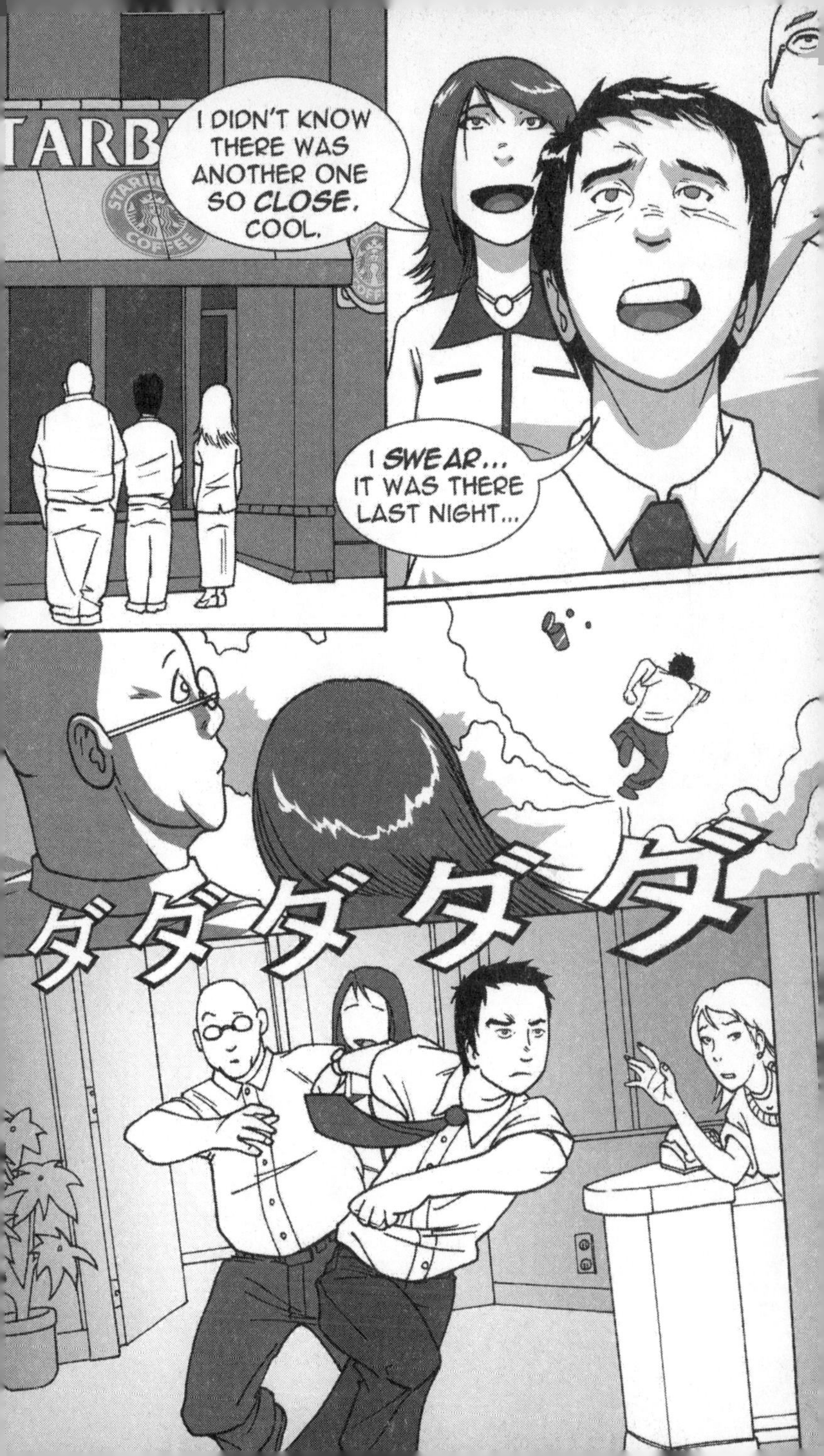
I DIDN'T KNOW THERE WAS ANOTHER ONE SO CLOSE. COOL.
I SWEAR... IT WAS THERE LAST NIGHT...
ダダダダダ

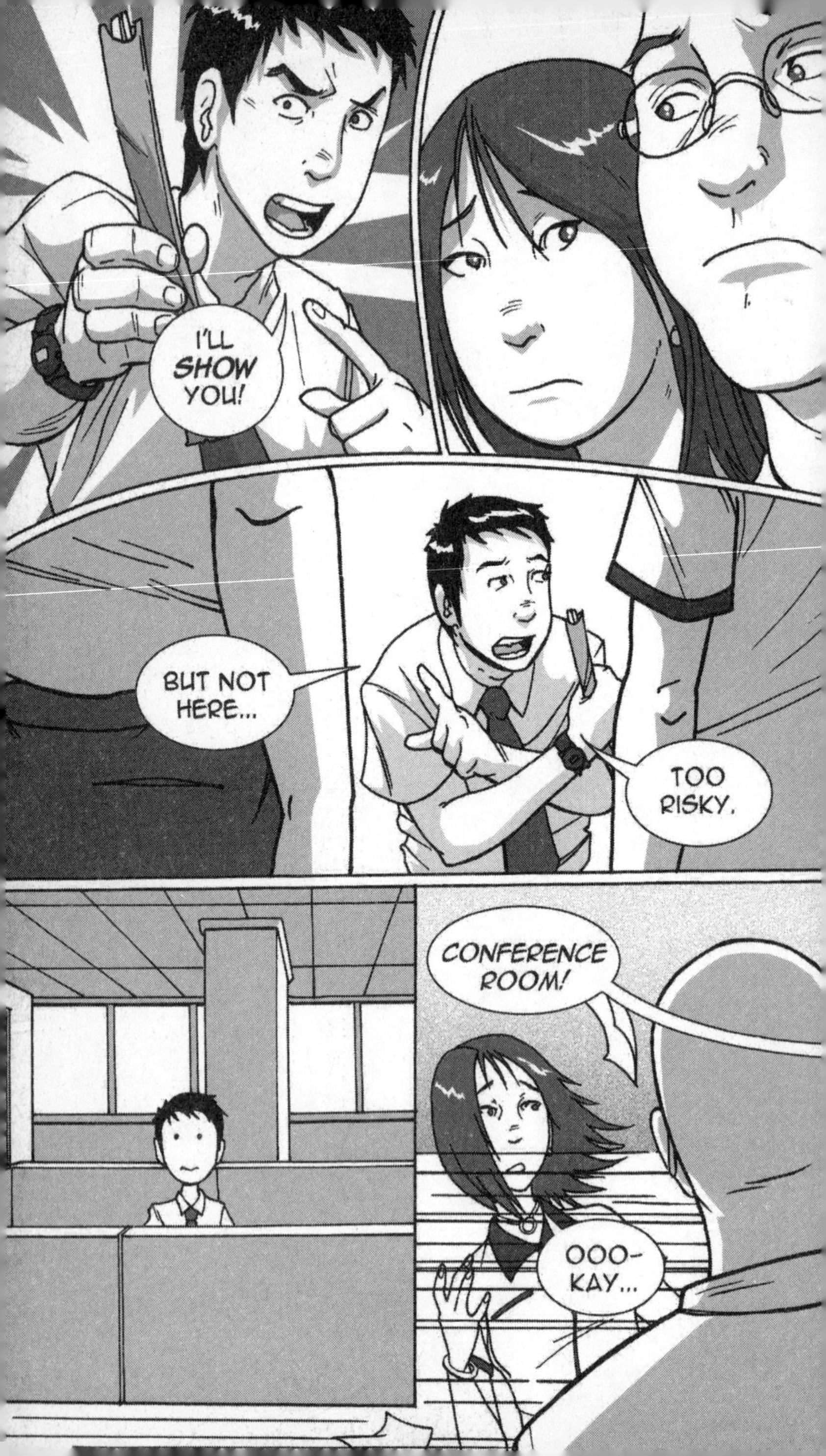
I'LL SHOW YOU!
BUT NOT HERE...
TOO RISKY.
CONFERENCE ROOM!
OOO-KAY...

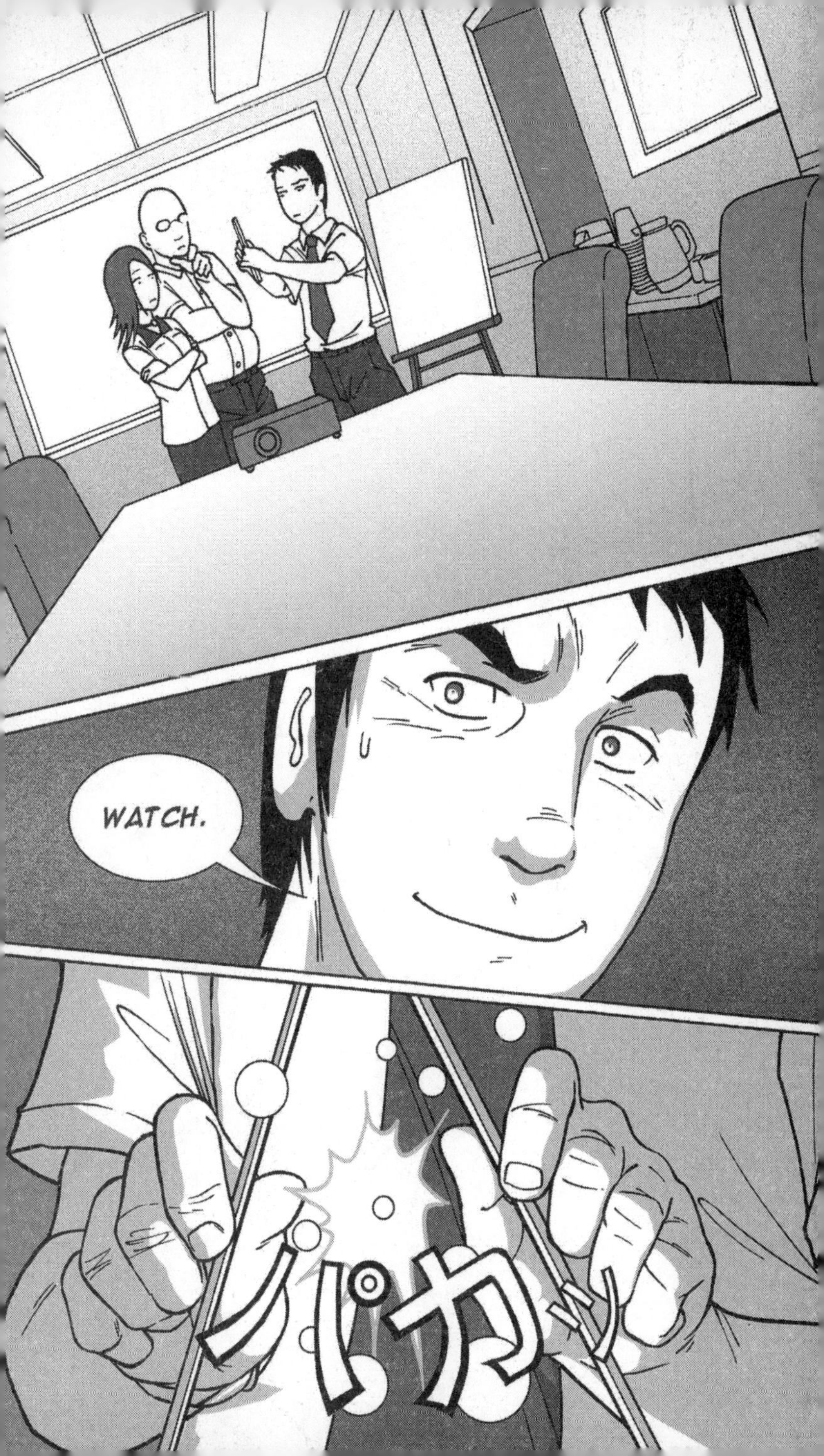
WATCH.
パカッ

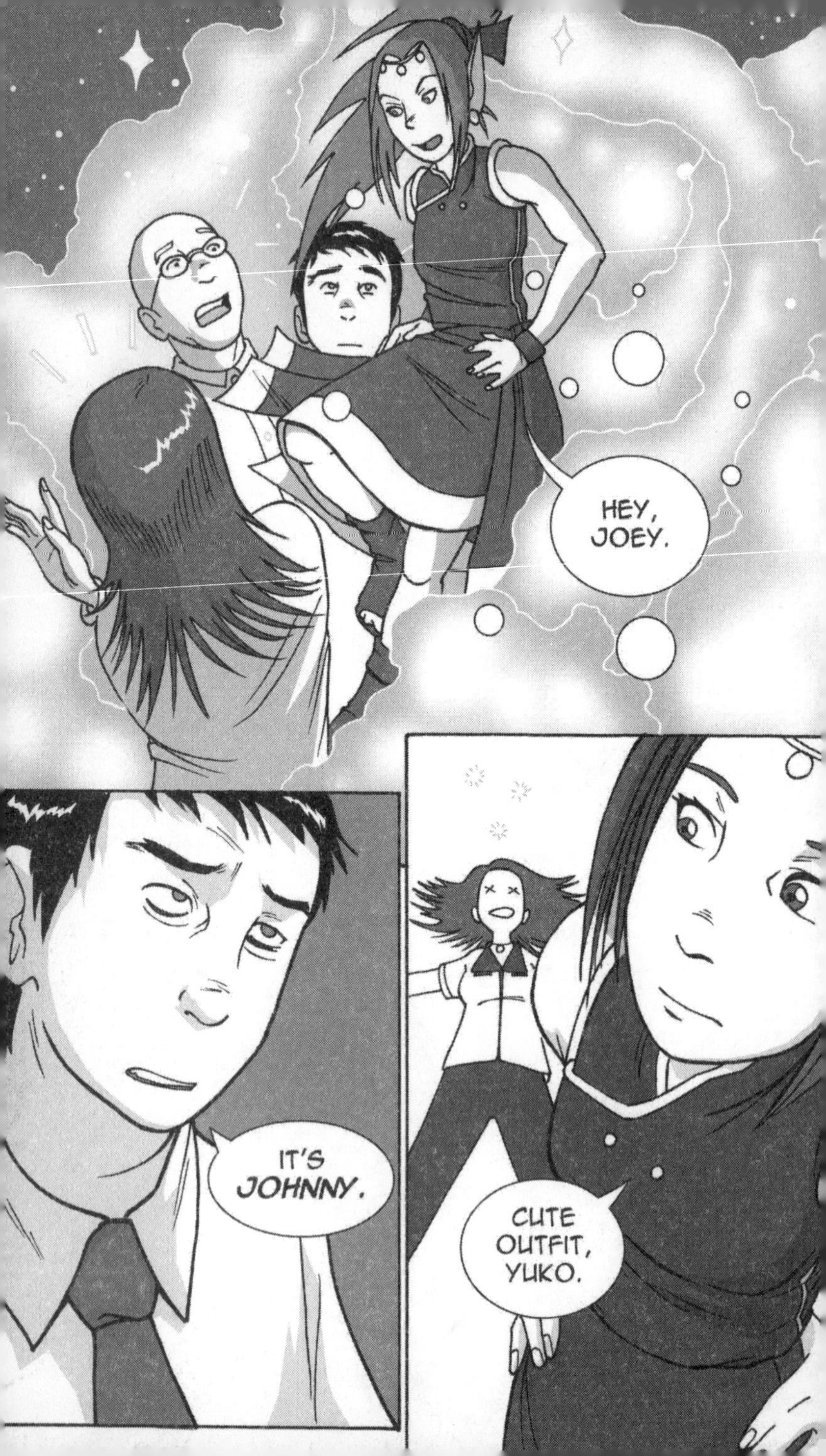
HEY, JOEY.
IT'S JOHNNY.
CUTE OUTFIT, YUKO.

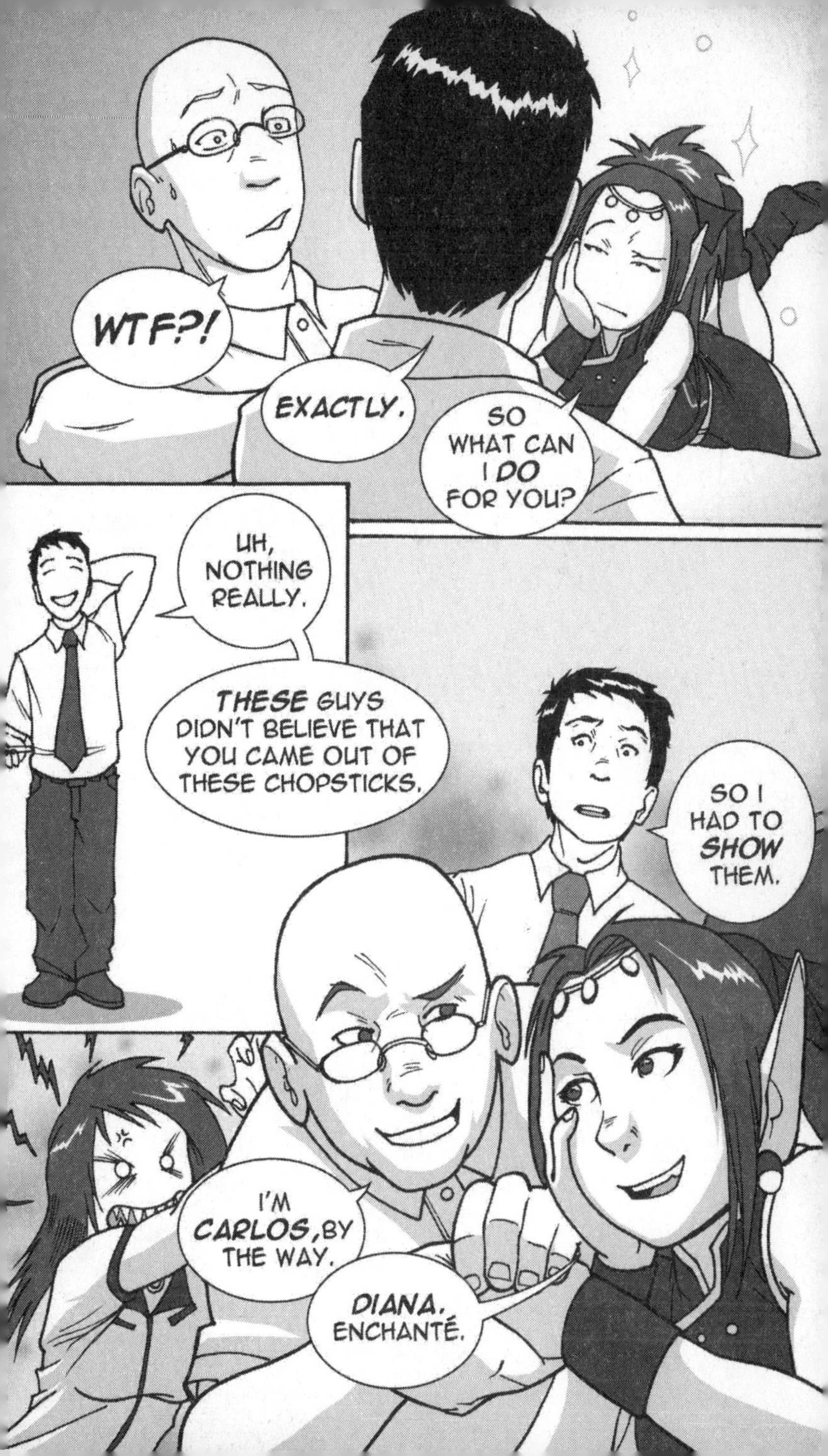
WTF?!
EXACTLY.
SO WHAT CAN I DO FOR YOU?
UH, NOTHING REALLY.
THESE GUYS DIDN'T BELIEVE THAT YOU CAME OUT OF THESE CHOPSTICKS.
SO I HAD TO SHOW THEM.
I'M CARLOS, BY THE WAY.
DIANA. ENCHANTÉ.

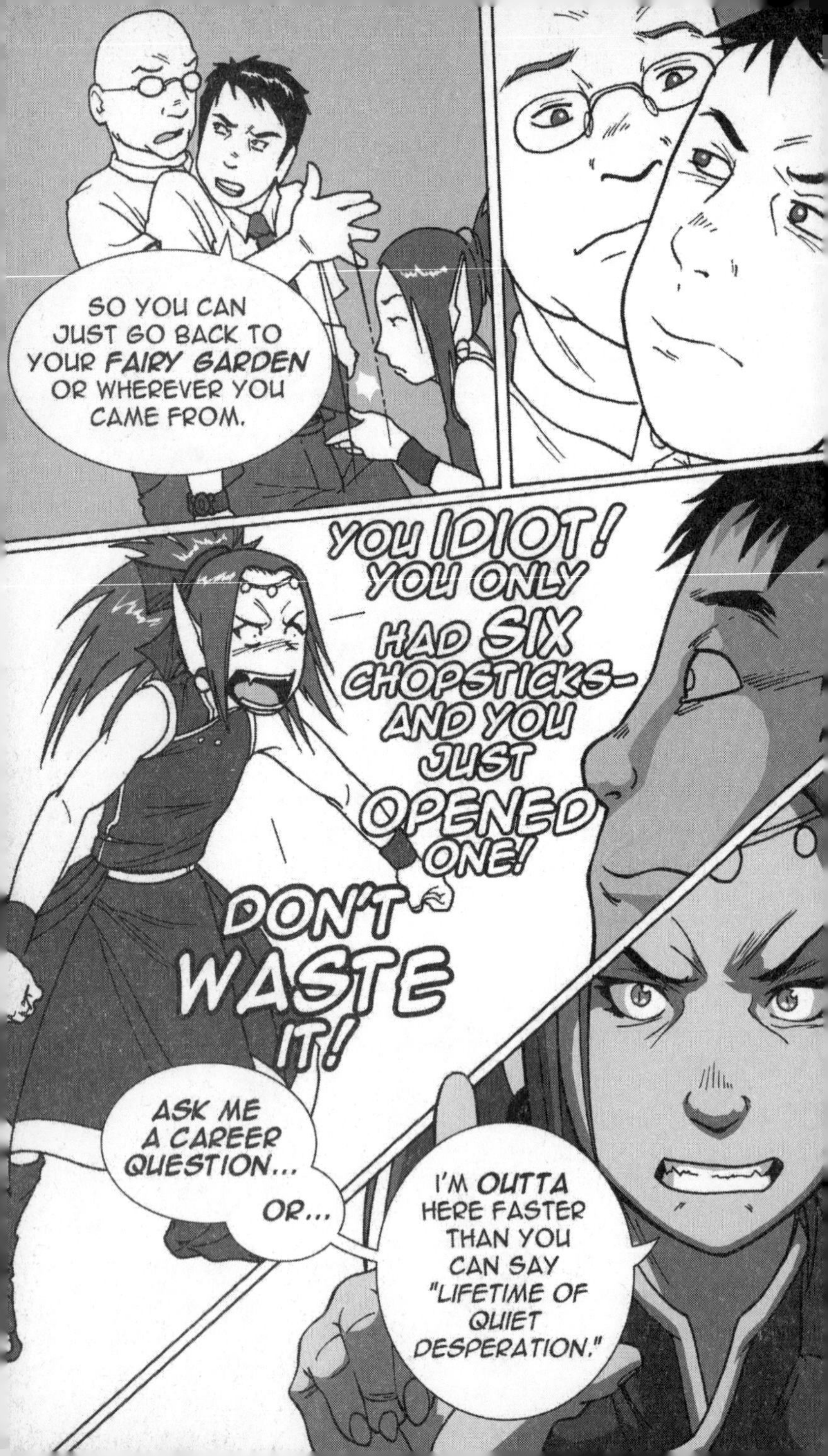
SO YOU CAN JUST GO BACK TO YOUR FAIRY GARDEN OR WHEREVER YOU CAME FROM.
YOU IDIOT! YOU ONLY HAD SIX CHOPSTICKS– AND YOU JUST OPENED ONE!
DON'T WASTE IT!
ASK ME A CAREER QUESTION...
OR...
I'M OUTTA HERE FASTER THAN YOU CAN SAY "LIFETIME OF QUIET DESPERATION."

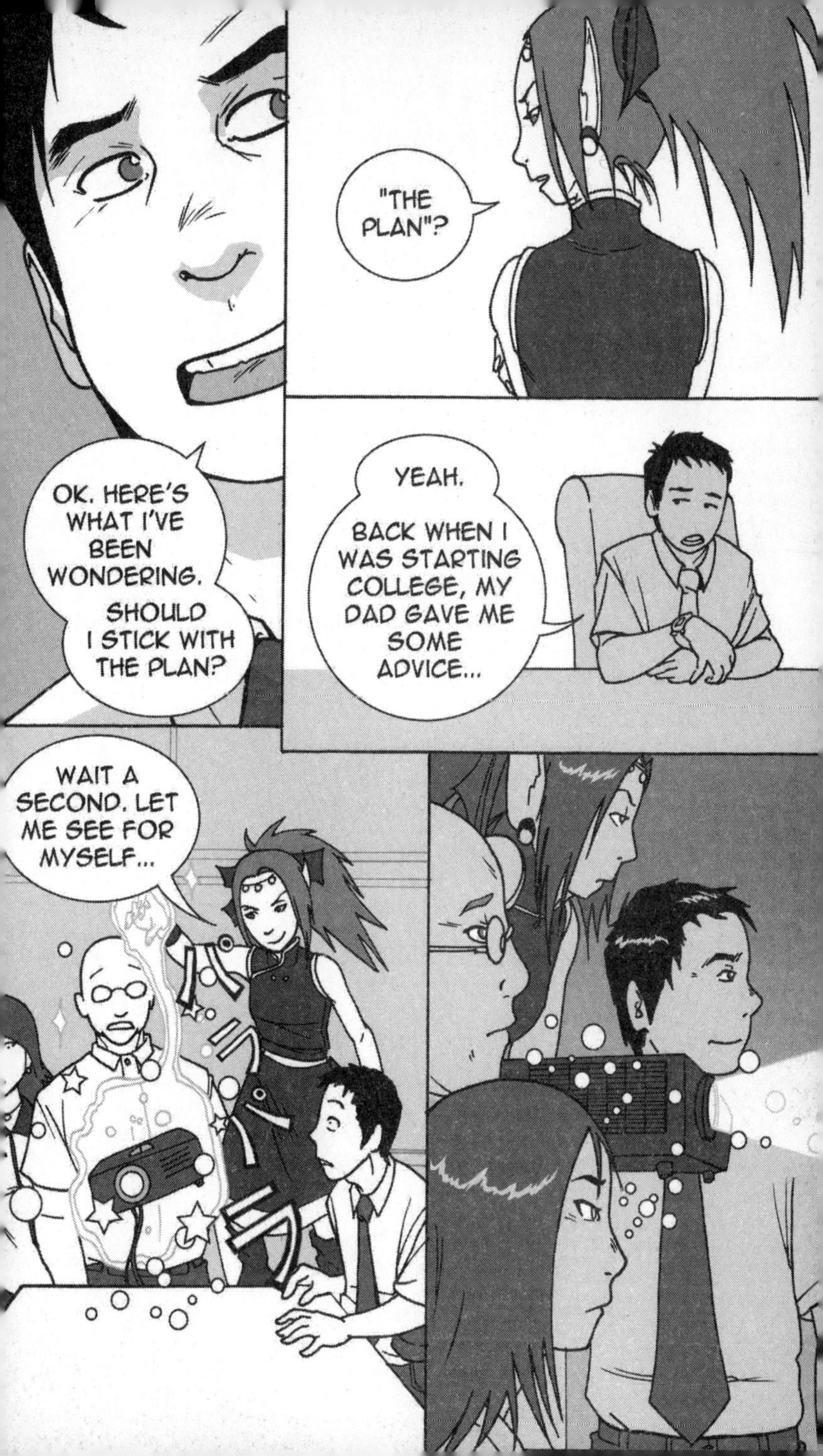
"THE PLAN"?
OK. HERE'S WHAT I'VE BEEN WONDERING.
SHOULD I STICK WITH THE PLAN?
YEAH.
BACK WHEN I WAS STARTING COLLEGE, MY DAD GAVE ME SOME ADVICE...
WAIT A SECOND. LET ME SEE FOR MYSELF...

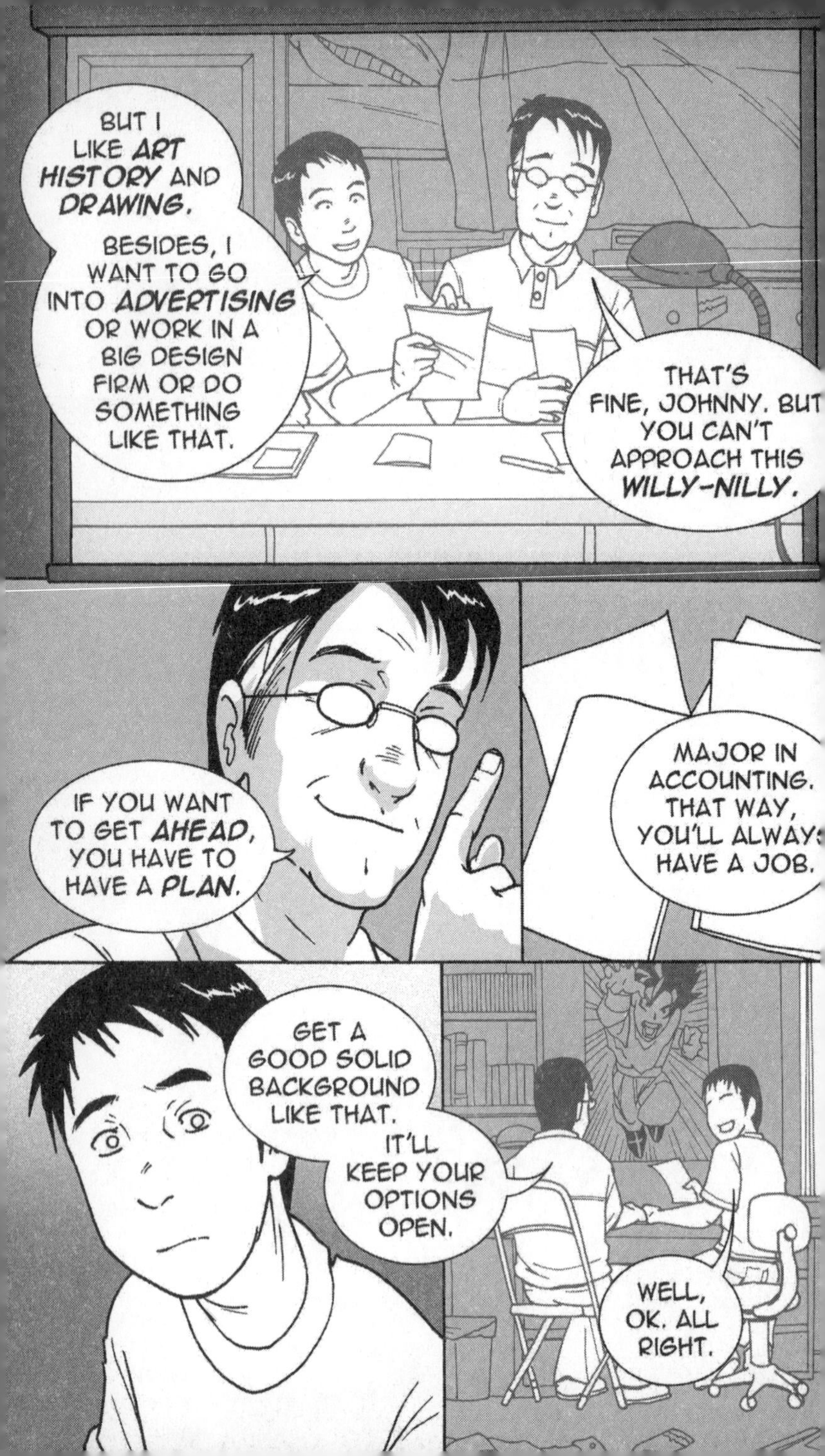
BUT I LIKE ART HISTORY AND DRAWING.
BESIDES, I WANT TO GO INTO ADVERTISING OR WORK IN A BIG DESIGN FIRM OR DO SOMETHING LIKE THAT.
THAT'S FINE, JOHNNY. BUT YOU CAN'T APPROACH THIS WILLY-NILLY.
IF YOU WANT TO GET AHEAD, YOU HAVE TO HAVE A PLAN.
MAJOR IN ACCOUNTING. THAT WAY, YOU'LL ALWAYS HAVE A JOB.
GET A GOOD SOLID BACKGROUND LIKE THAT.
IT'LL KEEP YOUR OPTIONS OPEN.
WELL, OK. ALL RIGHT.

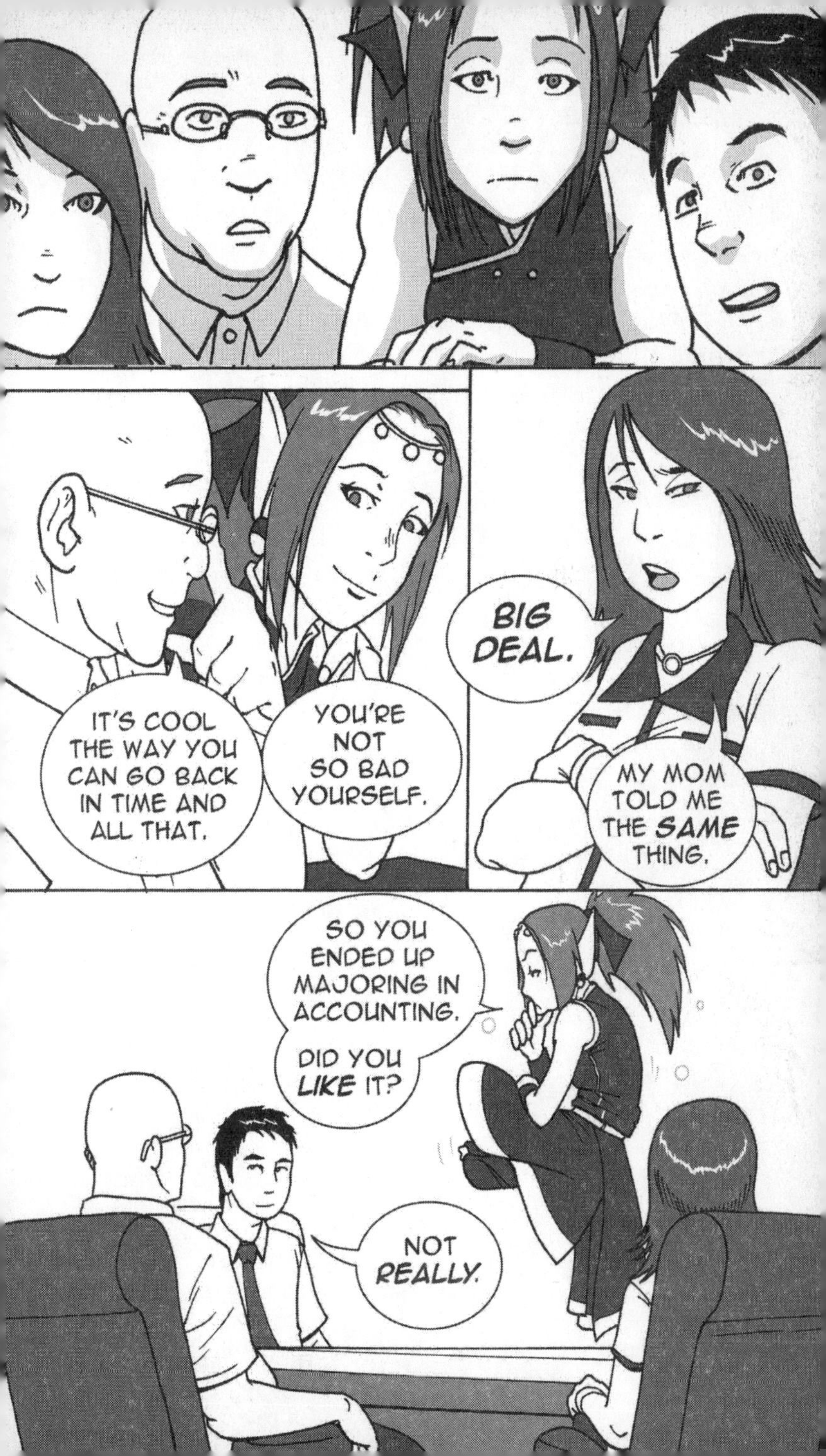
IT'S COOL THE WAY YOU CAN GO BACK IN TIME AND ALL THAT.
YOU'RE NOT SO BAD YOURSELF.
BIG DEAL.
MY MOM TOLD ME THE SAME THING.
SO YOU ENDED UP MAJORING IN ACCOUNTING.
DID YOU LIKE IT?
NOT REALLY.

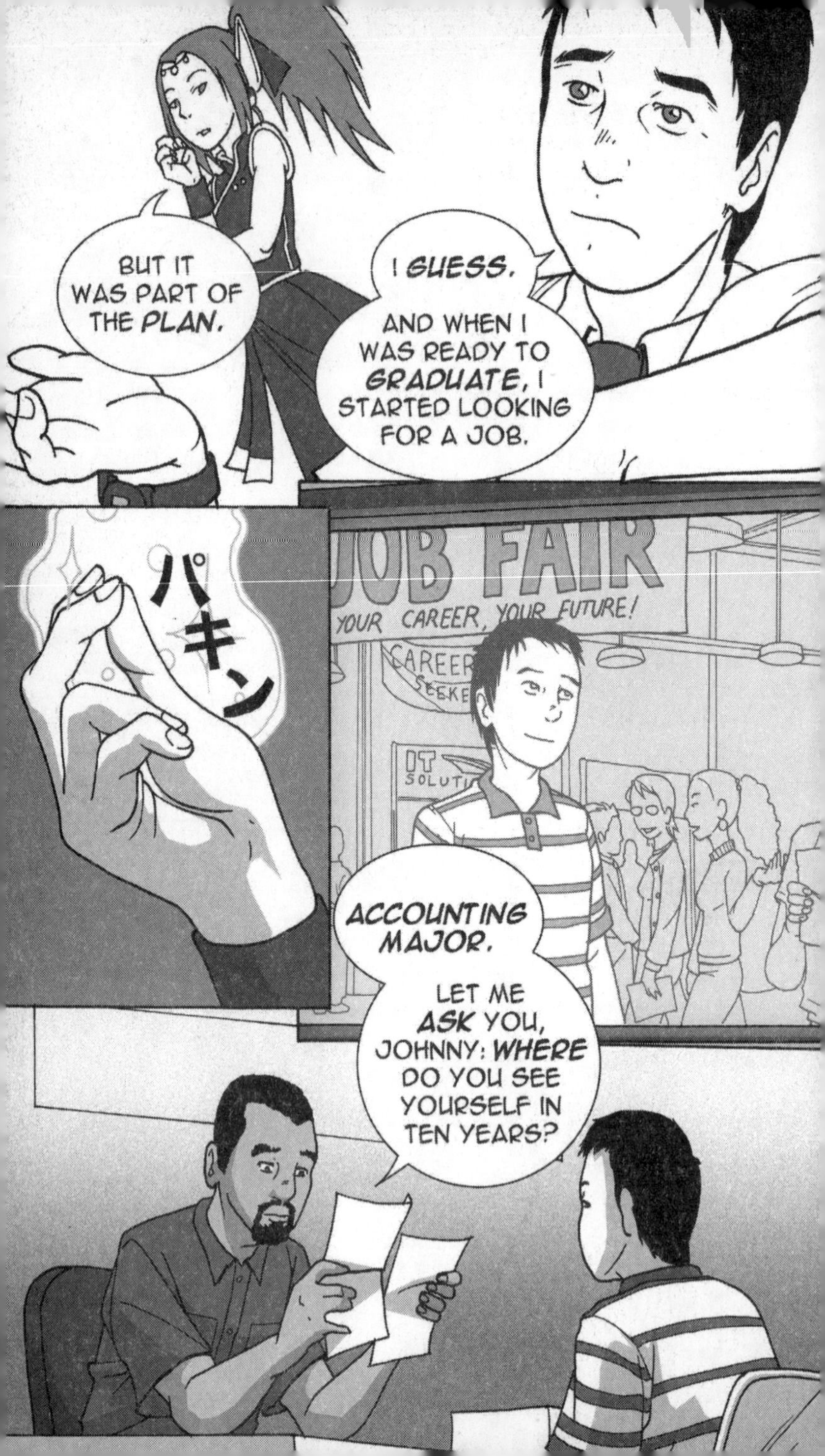
BUT IT WAS PART OF THE PLAN.
I GUESS.
AND WHEN I WAS READY TO GRADUATE, I STARTED LOOKING FOR A JOB.
パキン
JOB FAIR
YOUR CAREER, YOUR FUTURE!
CAREER SEEKE
IT SOLUTI
ACCOUNTING MAJOR.
LET ME ASK YOU, JOHNNY: WHERE DO YOU SEE YOURSELF IN TEN YEARS?

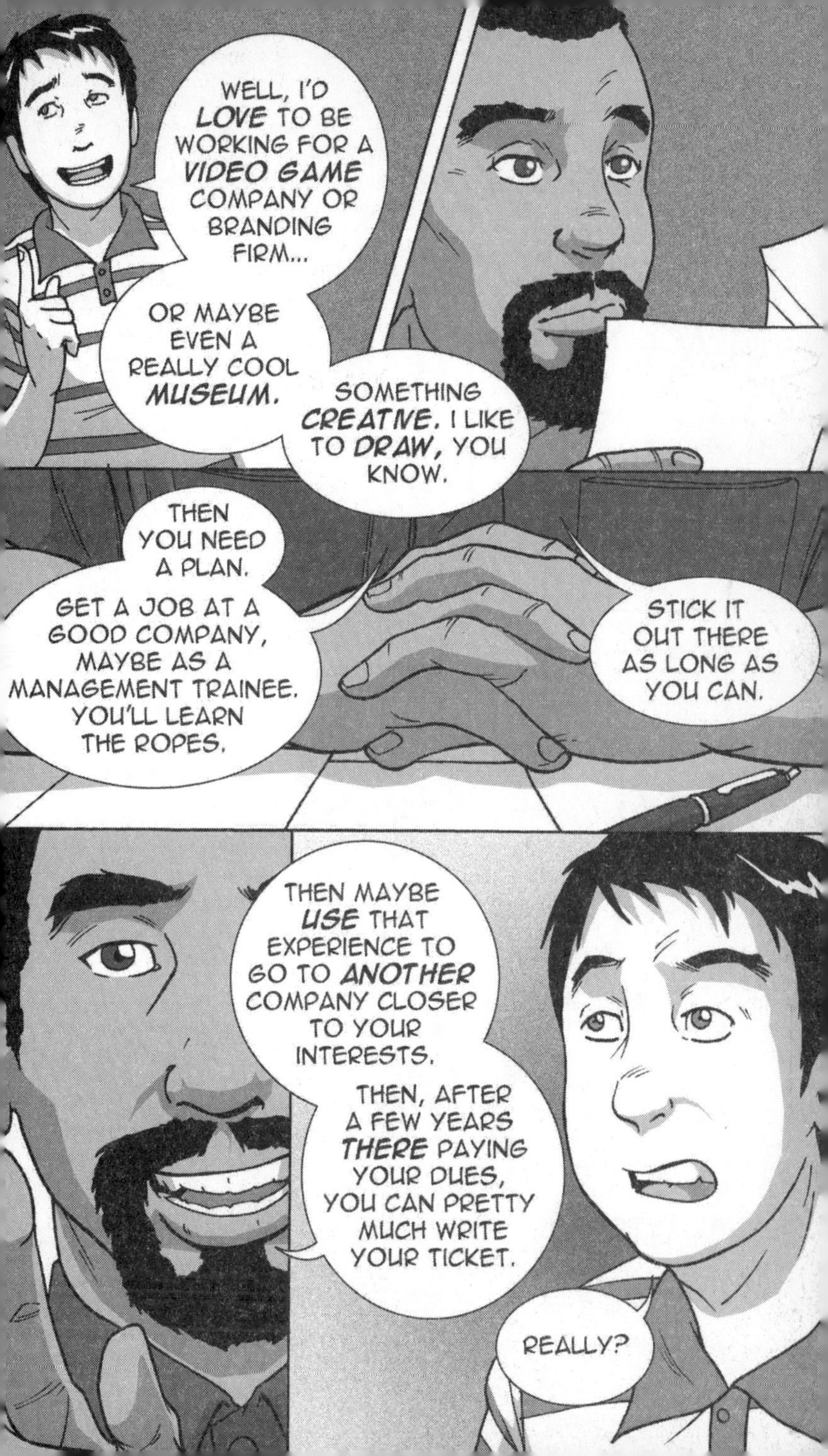
WELL, I'D LOVE TO BE WORKING FOR A VIDEO GAME COMPANY OR BRANDING FIRM...
OR MAYBE EVEN A REALLY COOL MUSEUM.
SOMETHING CREATIVE. I LIKE TO DRAW, YOU KNOW.
THEN YOU NEED A PLAN.
GET A JOB AT A GOOD COMPANY, MAYBE AS A MANAGEMENT TRAINEE. YOU'LL LEARN THE ROPES.
STICK IT OUT THERE AS LONG AS YOU CAN.
THEN MAYBE USE THAT EXPERIENCE TO GO TO ANOTHER COMPANY CLOSER TO YOUR INTERESTS.
THEN, AFTER A FEW YEARS THERE PAYING YOUR DUES, YOU CAN PRETTY MUCH WRITE YOUR TICKET.
REALLY?

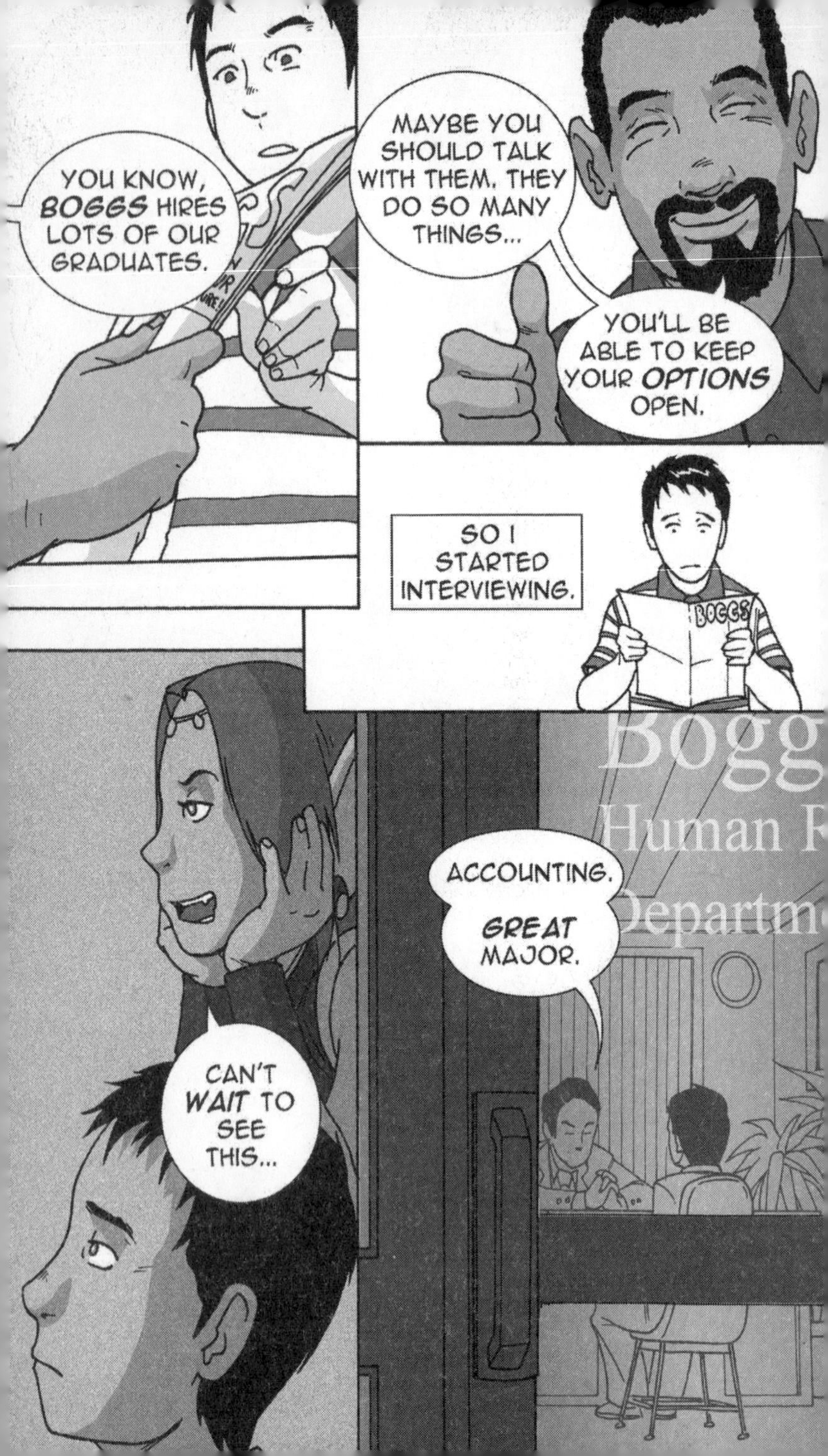
YOU KNOW, BOGGS HIRES LOTS OF OUR GRADUATES.
MAYBE YOU SHOULD TALK WITH THEM. THEY DO SO MANY THINGS...
YOU'LL BE ABLE TO KEEP YOUR OPTIONS OPEN.
SO I STARTED INTERVIEWING.
BOGGS
Bogg
Human R
Departm
ACCOUNTING.
GREAT MAJOR.
CAN'T WAIT TO SEE THIS...

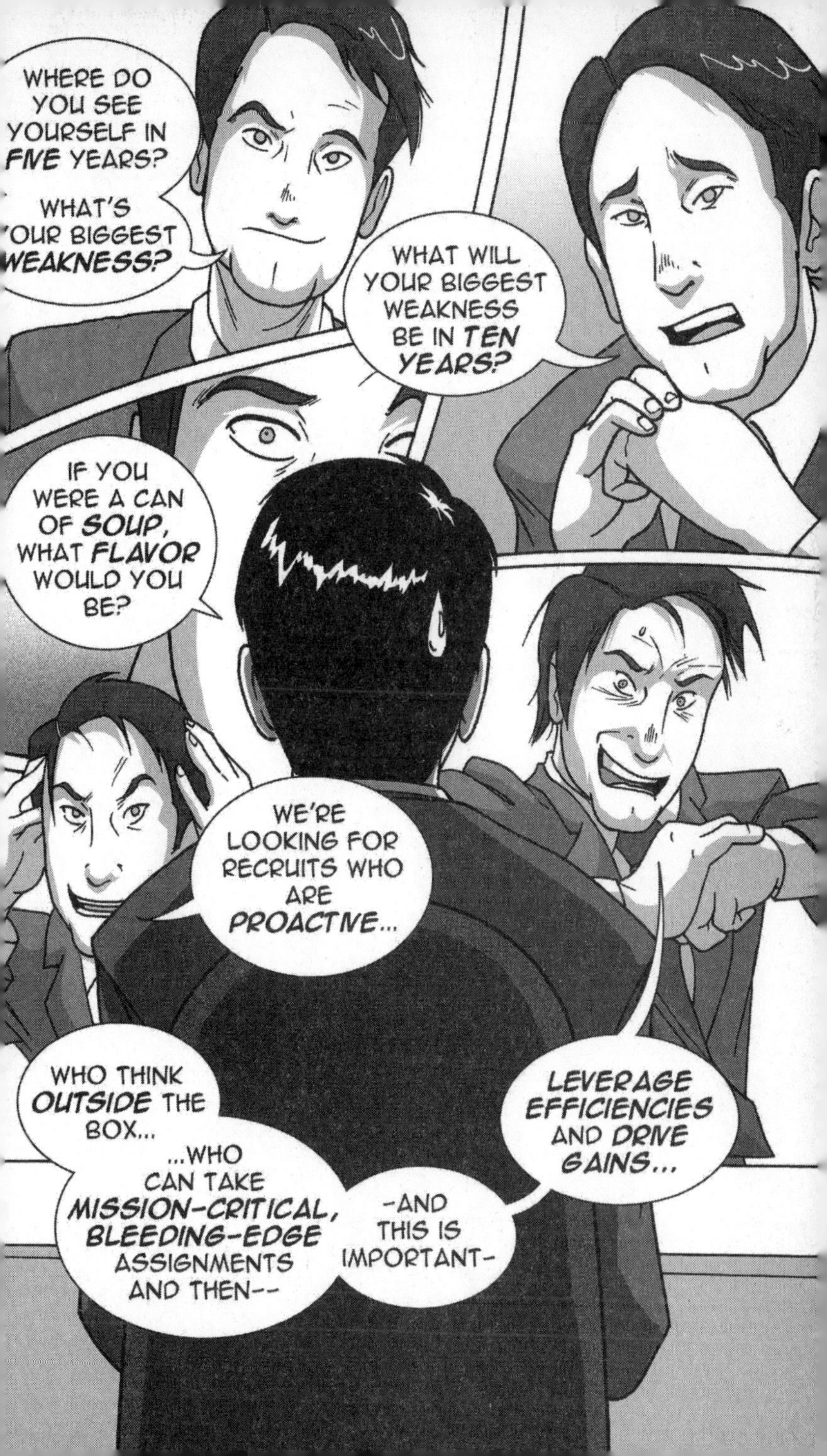
WHERE DO YOU SEE YOURSELF IN FIVE YEARS?
WHAT'S YOUR BIGGEST WEAKNESS?
WHAT WILL YOUR BIGGEST WEAKNESS BE IN TEN YEARS?
IF YOU WERE A CAN OF SOUP, WHAT FLAVOR WOULD YOU BE?
WE'RE LOOKING FOR RECRUITS WHO ARE PROACTIVE...
WHO THINK OUTSIDE THE BOX...
...WHO CAN TAKE MISSION-CRITICAL, BLEEDING-EDGE ASSIGNMENTS AND THEN--
-AND THIS IS IMPORTANT-
LEVERAGE EFFICIENCIES AND DRIVE GAINS...

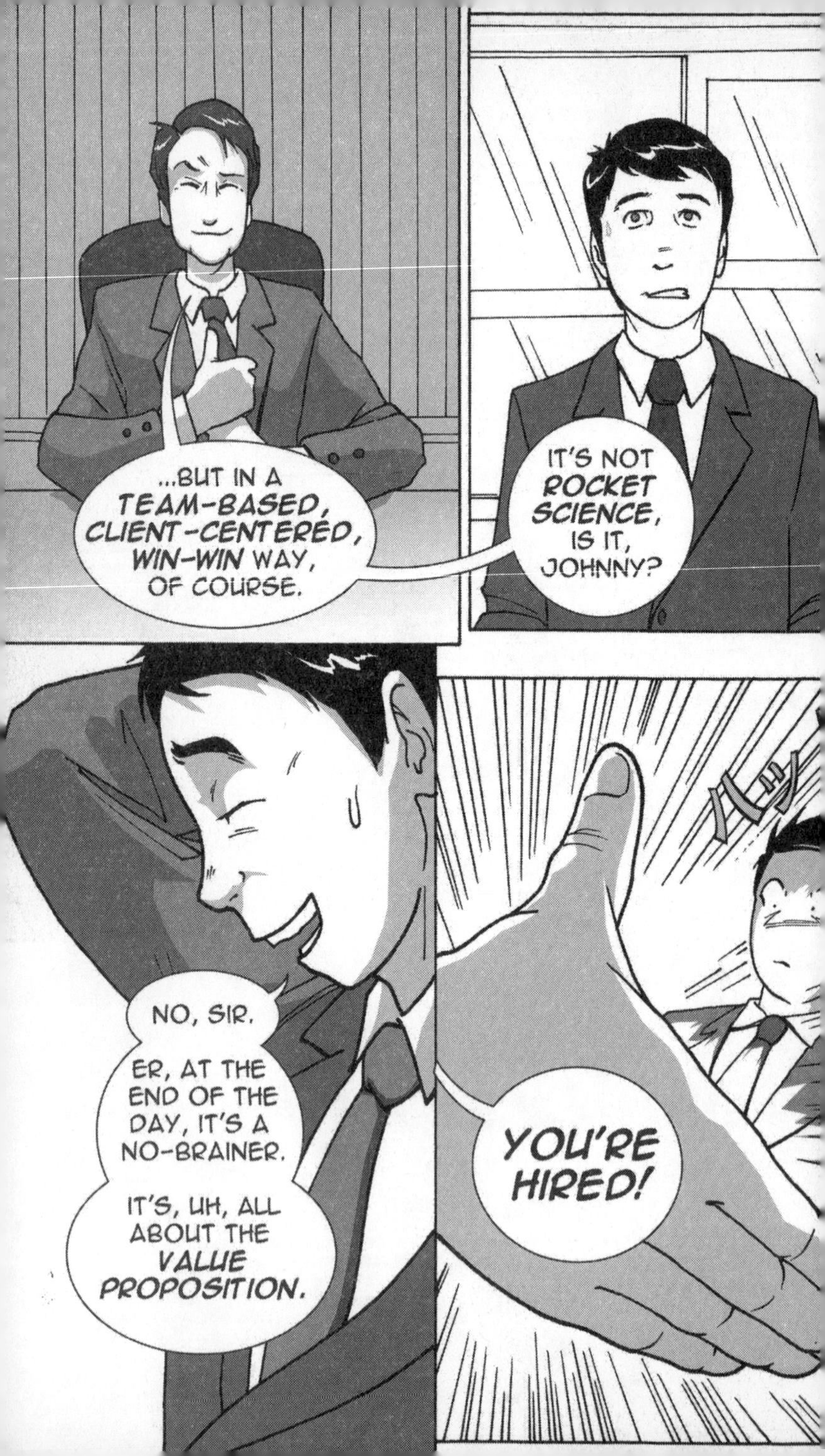
...BUT IN A TEAM-BASED, CLIENT-CENTERED, WIN-WIN WAY, OF COURSE.
IT'S NOT ROCKET SCIENCE, IS IT, JOHNNY?
NO, SIR.
ER, AT THE END OF THE DAY, IT'S A NO-BRAINER.
IT'S, UH, ALL ABOUT THE VALUE PROPOSITION.
YOU'RE HIRED!

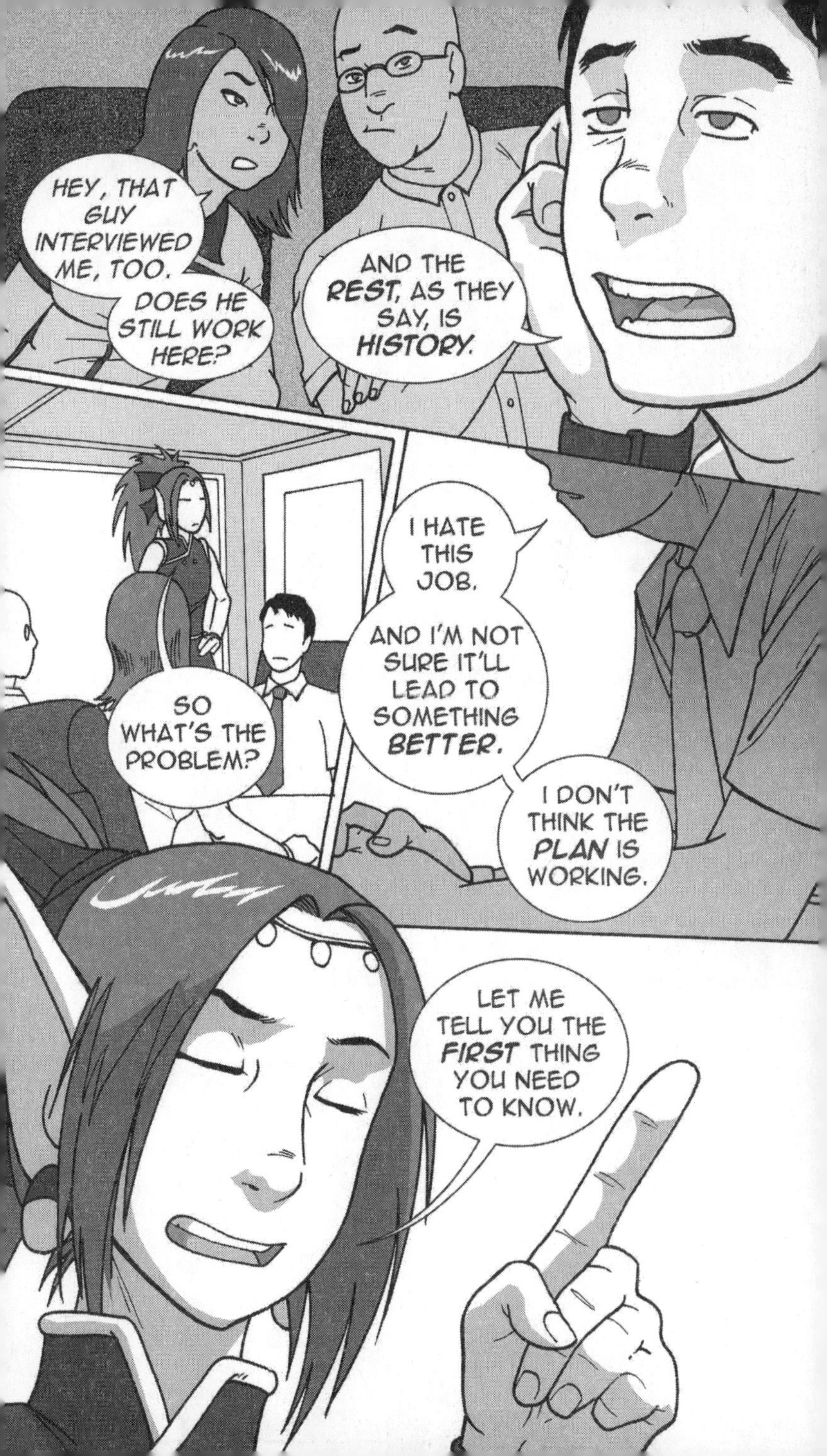
HEY, THAT GUY INTERVIEWED ME, TOO.
DOES HE STILL WORK HERE?
AND THE *REST*, AS THEY SAY, IS *HISTORY*.
I HATE THIS JOB.
AND I'M NOT SURE IT'LL LEAD TO SOMETHING *BETTER*.
SO WHAT'S THE PROBLEM?
I DON'T THINK THE *PLAN* IS WORKING.
LET ME TELL YOU THE *FIRST* THING YOU NEED TO KNOW.

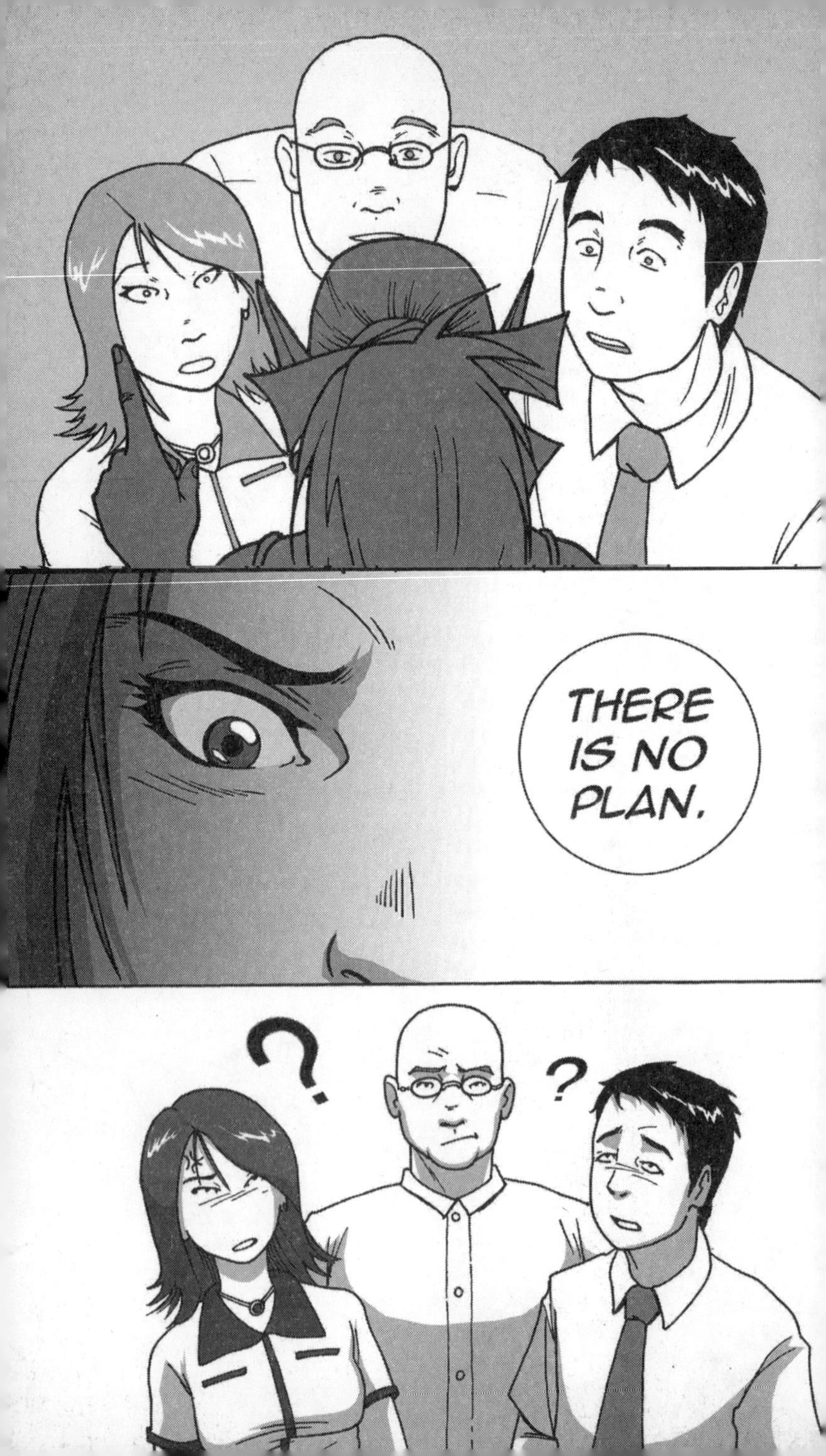
THERE IS NO PLAN.

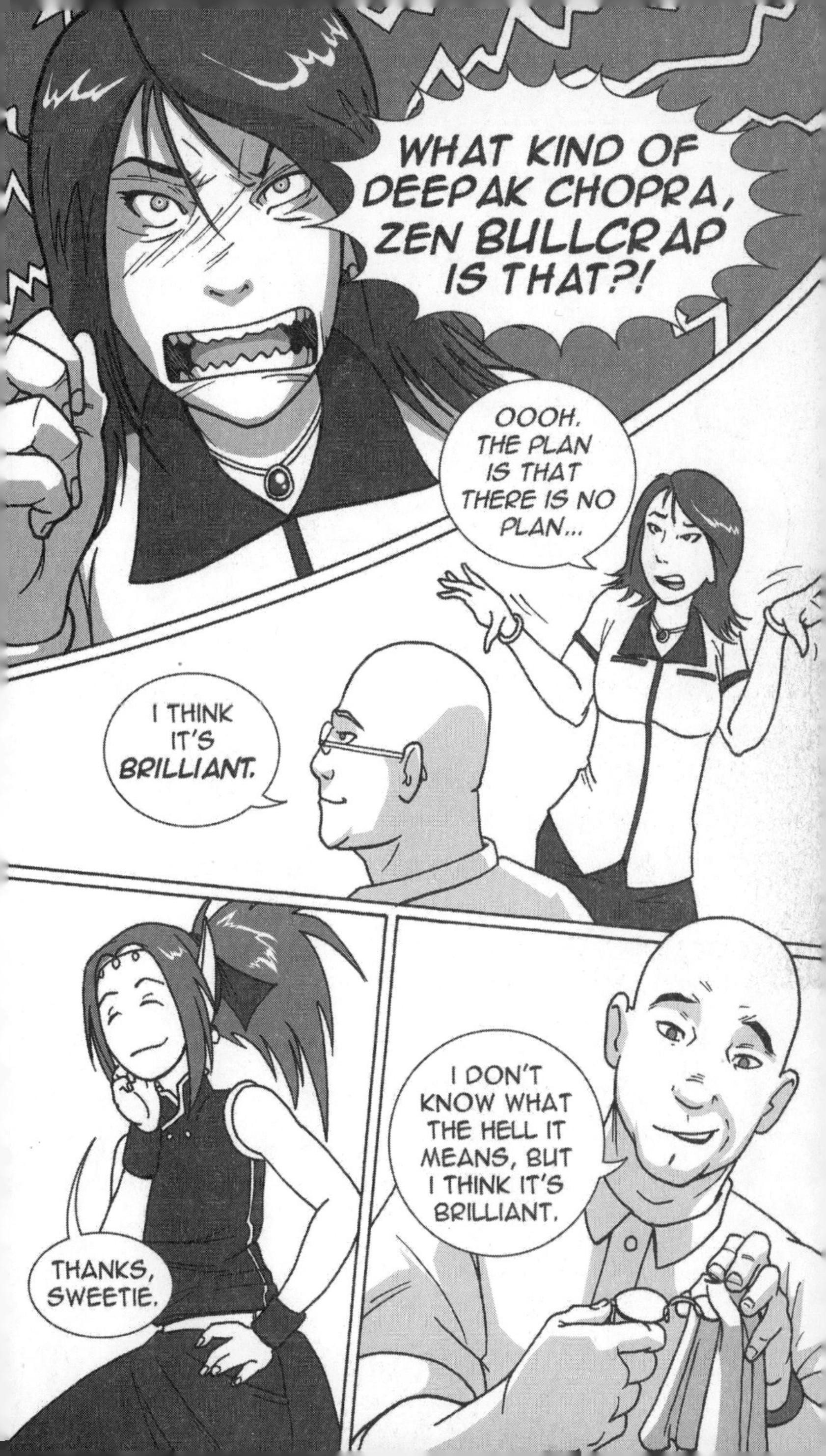
WHAT KIND OF DEEPAK CHOPRA, ZEN BULLCRAP IS THAT?!
OOOH. THE PLAN IS THAT THERE IS NO PLAN...
I THINK IT'S BRILLIANT.
I DON'T KNOW WHAT THE HELL IT MEANS, BUT I THINK IT'S BRILLIANT.
THANKS, SWEETIE.

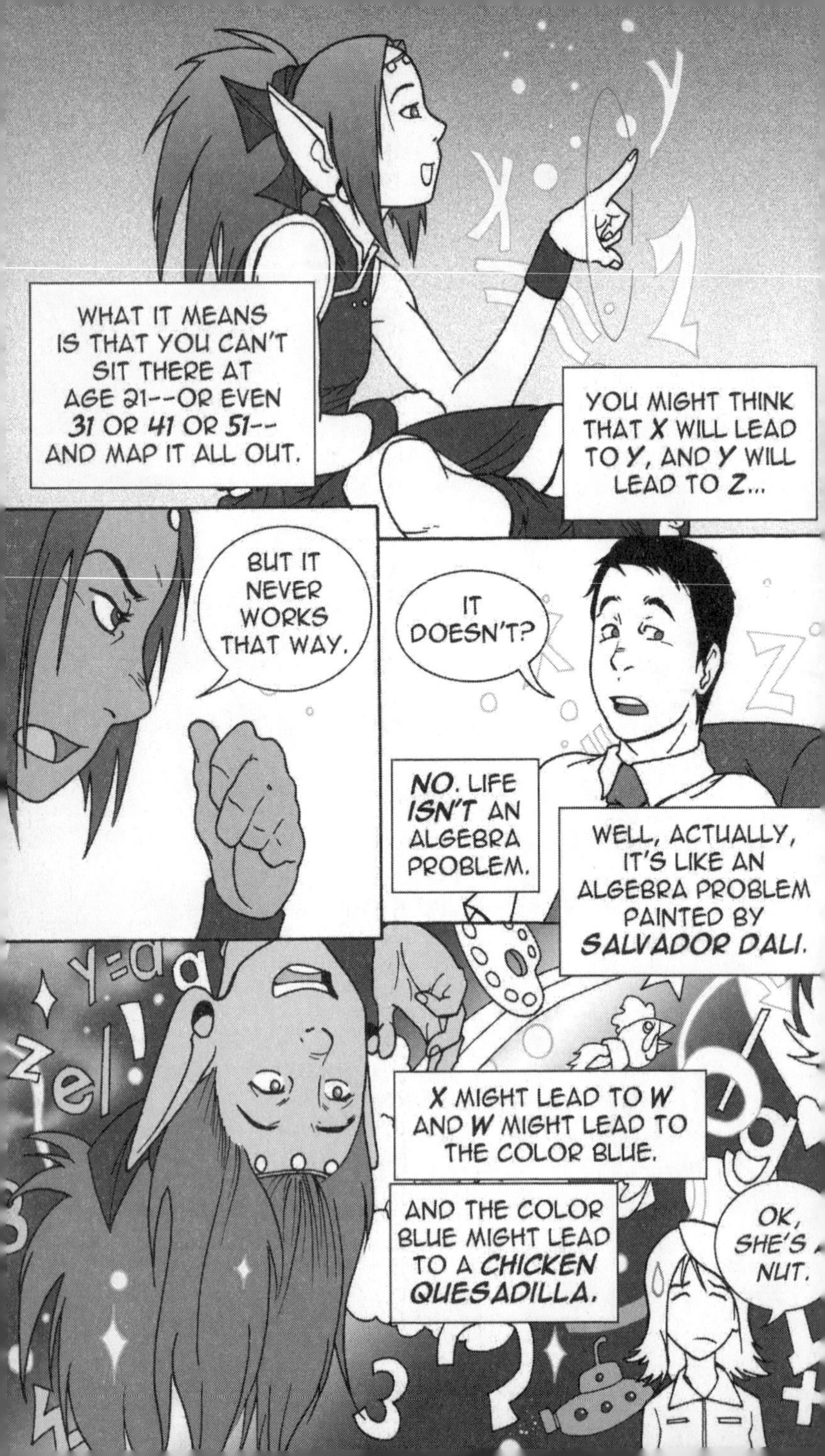
WHAT IT MEANS IS THAT YOU CAN'T SIT THERE AT AGE 21--OR EVEN 31 OR 41 OR 51-- AND MAP IT ALL OUT.
YOU MIGHT THINK THAT X WILL LEAD TO Y, AND Y WILL LEAD TO Z...
BUT IT NEVER WORKS THAT WAY.
IT DOESN'T?
NO. LIFE ISN'T AN ALGEBRA PROBLEM.
WELL, ACTUALLY, IT'S LIKE AN ALGEBRA PROBLEM PAINTED BY SALVADOR DALI.
X MIGHT LEAD TO W AND W MIGHT LEAD TO THE COLOR BLUE.
AND THE COLOR BLUE MIGHT LEAD TO A CHICKEN QUESADILLA.
OK, SHE'S NUT.

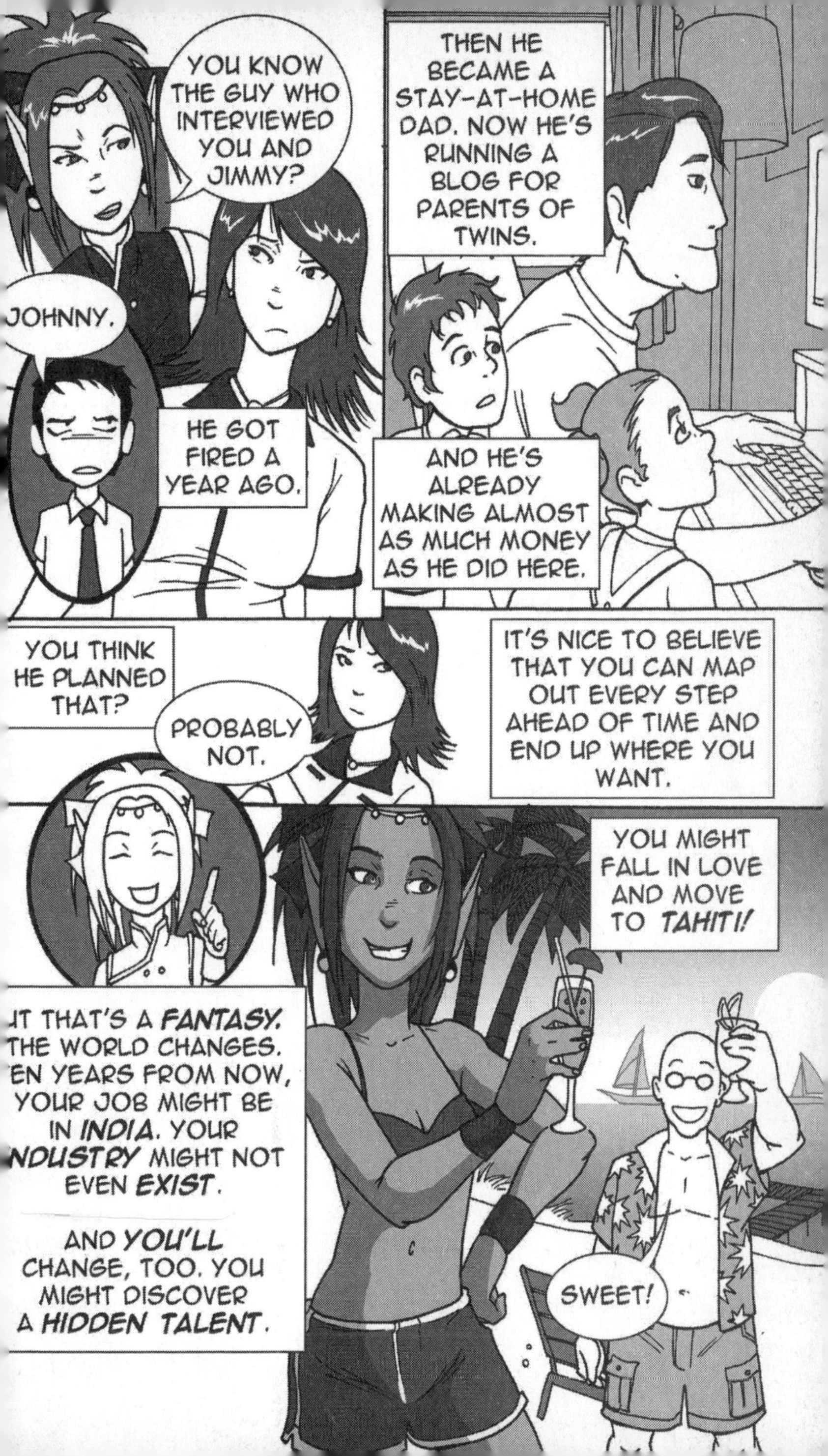

YOU KNOW THE GUY WHO INTERVIEWED YOU AND JIMMY?
JOHNNY.
HE GOT FIRED A YEAR AGO.
THEN HE BECAME A STAY-AT-HOME DAD. NOW HE'S RUNNING A BLOG FOR PARENTS OF TWINS.
AND HE'S ALREADY MAKING ALMOST AS MUCH MONEY AS HE DID HERE.
YOU THINK HE PLANNED THAT?
PROBABLY NOT.
IT'S NICE TO BELIEVE THAT YOU CAN MAP OUT EVERY STEP AHEAD OF TIME AND END UP WHERE YOU WANT.
YOU MIGHT FALL IN LOVE AND MOVE TO TAHITI!
SWEET!
THE WORLD CHANGES.
YEARS FROM NOW, YOUR JOB MIGHT BE IN INDIA. YOUR
MIGHT NOT EVEN EXIST.
AND YOU'LL CHANGE, TOO. YOU MIGHT DISCOVER A HIDDEN TALENT.

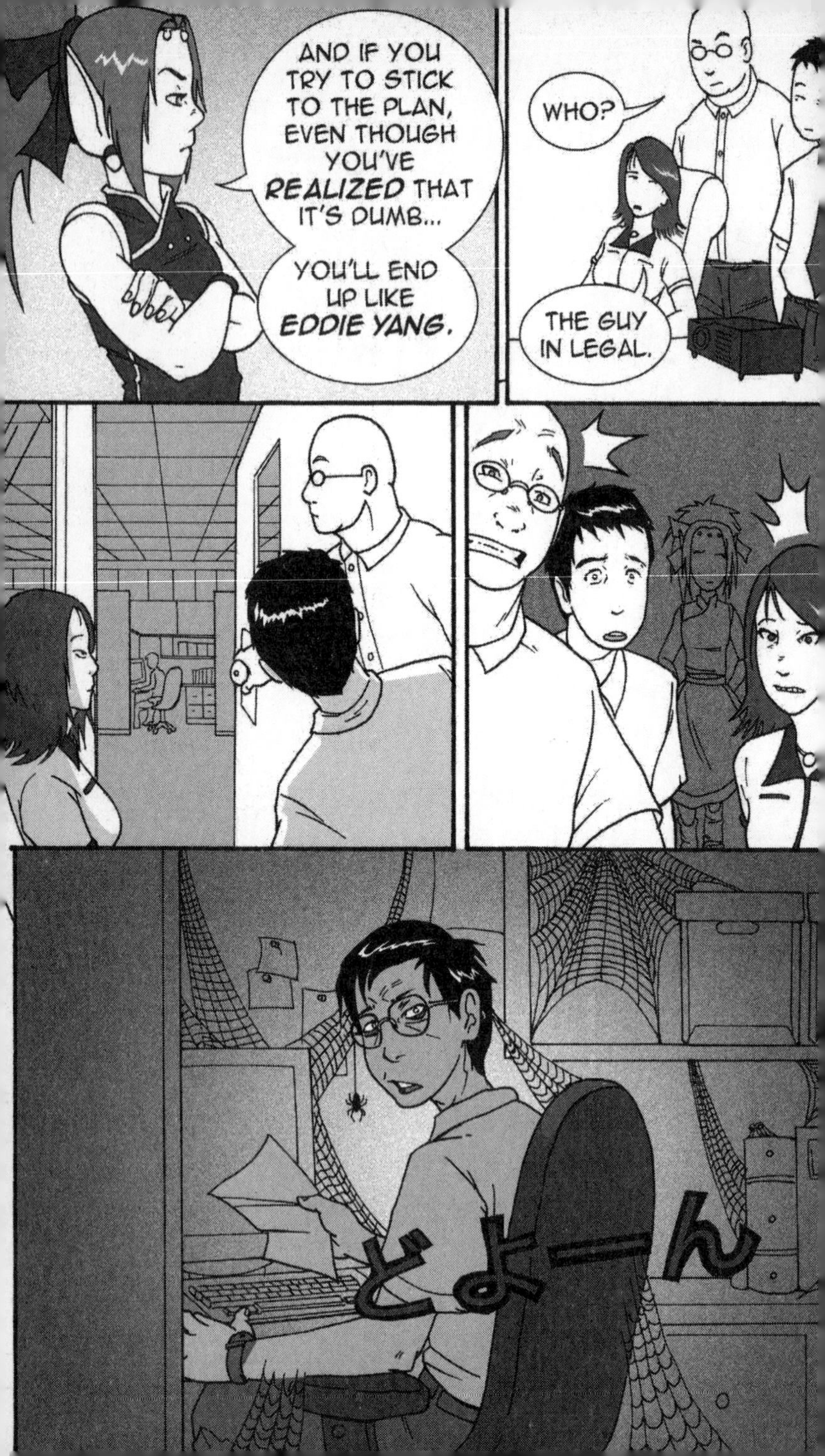

AND IF YOU TRY TO STICK TO THE PLAN, EVEN THOUGH YOU'VE REALIZED THAT IT'S DUMB...
YOU'LL END UP LIKE EDDIE YANG.
WHO?
THE GUY IN LEGAL.
どよーん

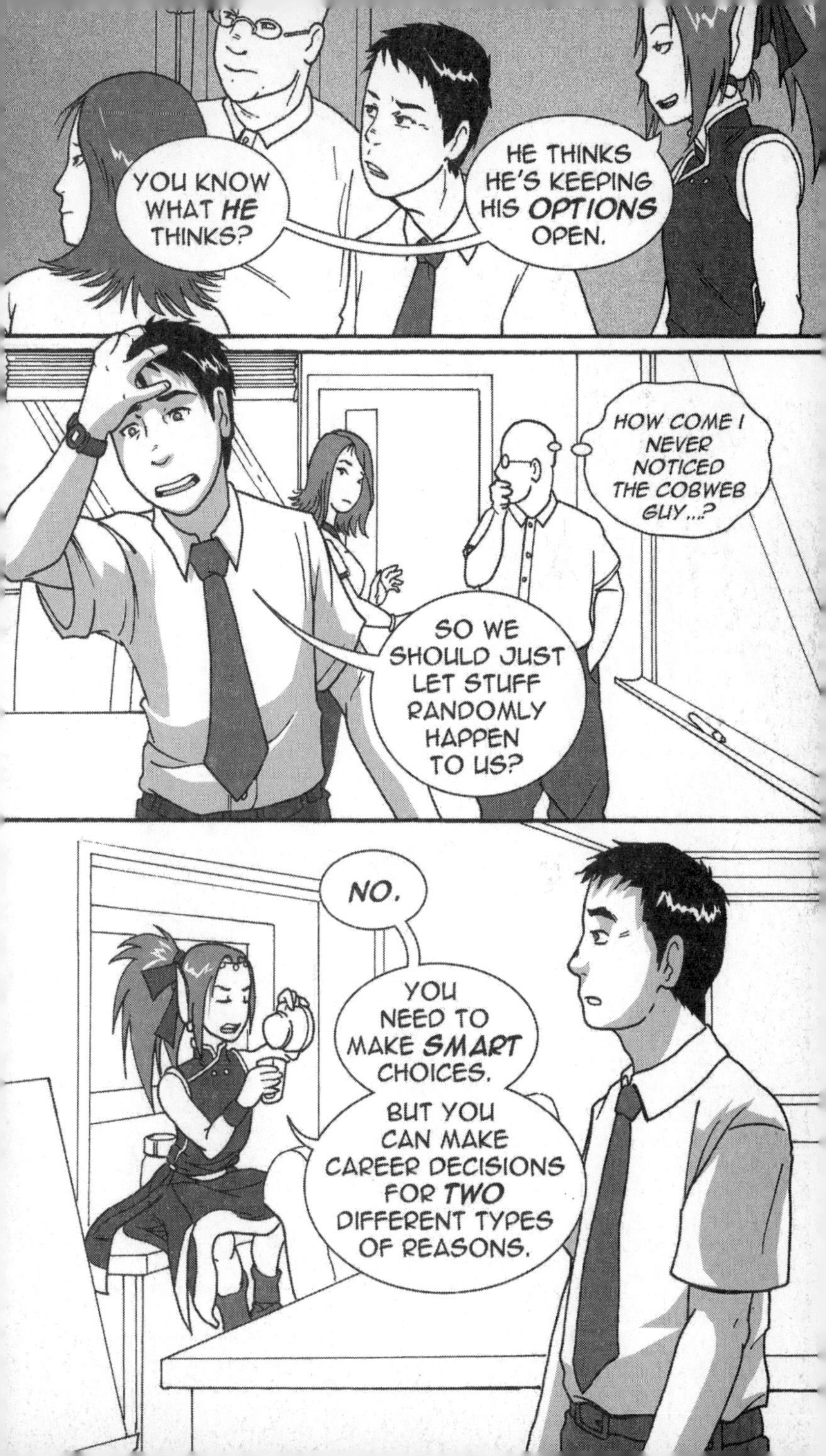
YOU KNOW WHAT **HE** THINKS?
HE THINKS HE'S KEEPING HIS **OPTIONS** OPEN.
HOW COME I NEVER NOTICED THE COBWEB GUY...?
SO WE SHOULD JUST LET STUFF RANDOMLY HAPPEN TO US?
NO.
YOU NEED TO MAKE **SMART** CHOICES.
BUT YOU CAN MAKE CAREER DECISIONS FOR **TWO** DIFFERENT TYPES OF REASONS.

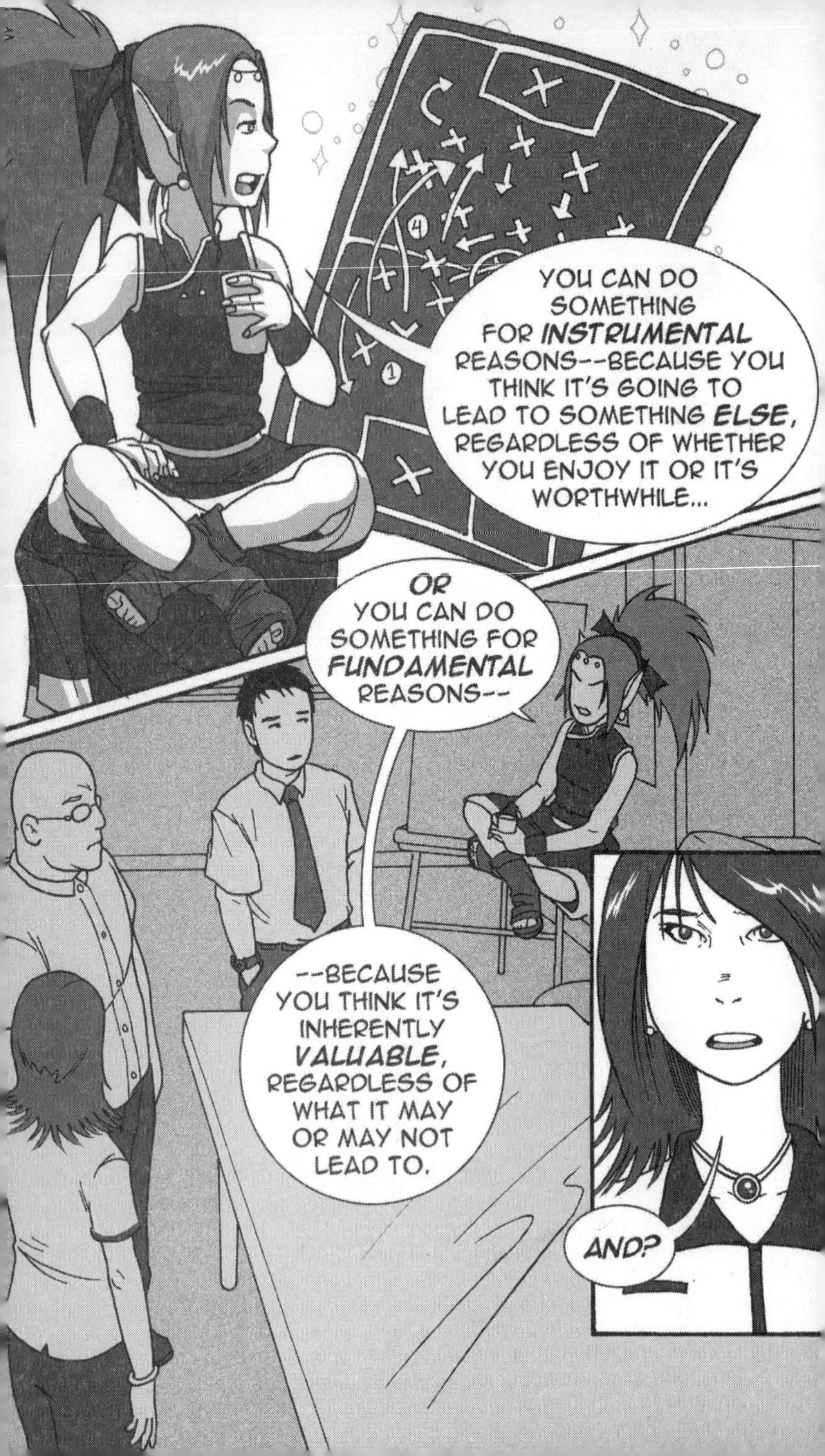
YOU CAN DO SOMETHING FOR INSTRUMENTAL REASONS--BECAUSE YOU THINK IT'S GOING TO LEAD TO SOMETHING ELSE, REGARDLESS OF WHETHER YOU ENJOY IT OR IT'S WORTHWHILE...
OR YOU CAN DO SOMETHING FOR FUNDAMENTAL REASONS--
--BECAUSE YOU THINK IT'S INHERENTLY VALUABLE, REGARDLESS OF WHAT IT MAY OR MAY NOT LEAD TO.
AND?

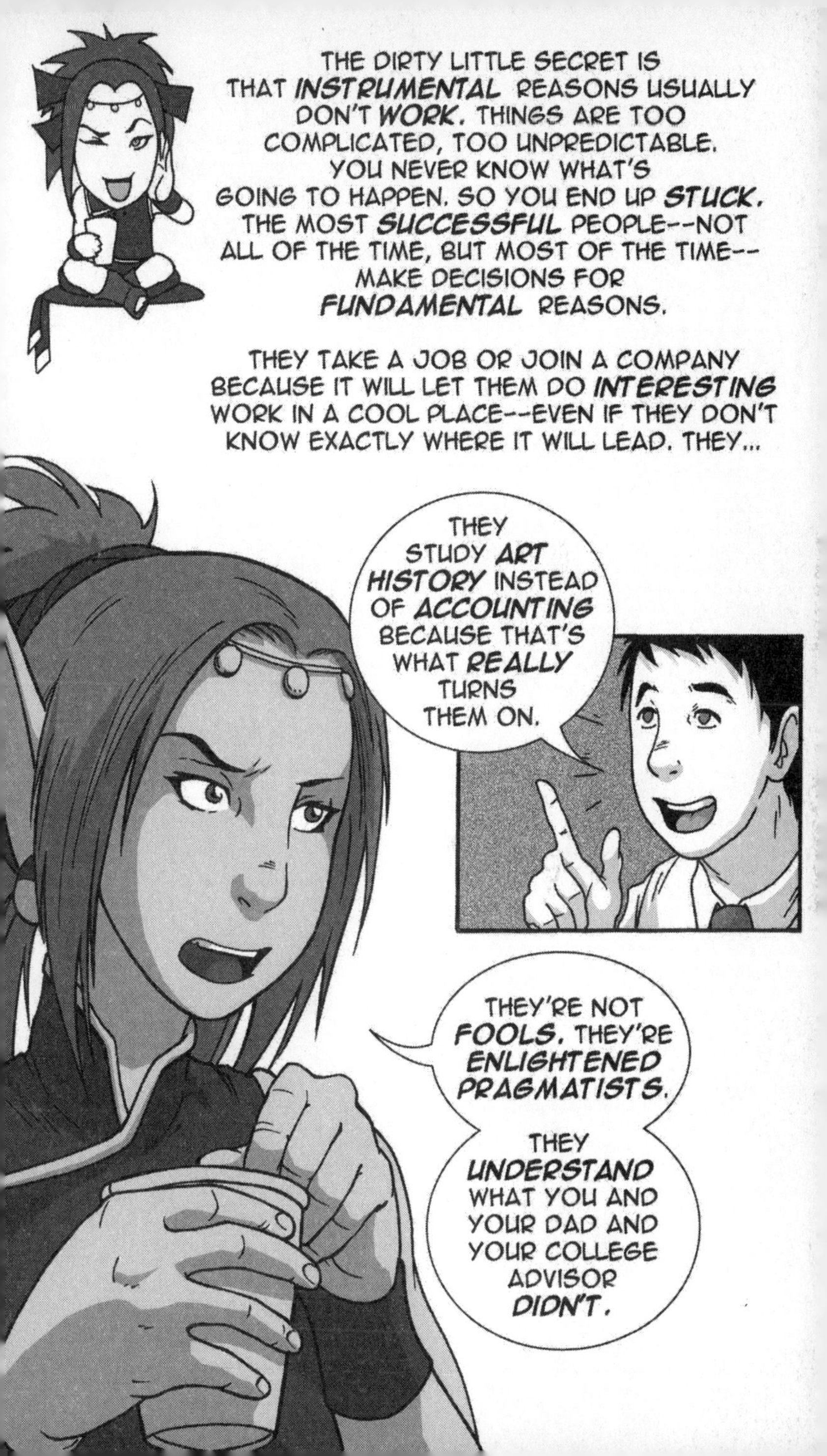
THE DIRTY LITTLE SECRET IS THAT INSTRUMENTAL REASONS USUALLY DON'T WORK. THINGS ARE TOO COMPLICATED, TOO UNPREDICTABLE. YOU NEVER KNOW WHAT'S GOING TO HAPPEN. SO YOU END UP STUCK. THE MOST SUCCESSFUL PEOPLE--NOT ALL OF THE TIME, BUT MOST OF THE TIME--MAKE DECISIONS FOR FUNDAMENTAL REASONS.
THEY TAKE A JOB OR JOIN A COMPANY BECAUSE IT WILL LET THEM DO INTERESTING WORK IN A COOL PLACE--EVEN IF THEY DON'T KNOW EXACTLY WHERE IT WILL LEAD. THEY...
THEY STUDY ART HISTORY INSTEAD OF ACCOUNTING BECAUSE THAT'S WHAT REALLY TURNS THEM ON.
THEY'RE NOT FOOLS. THEY'RE ENLIGHTENED PRAGMATISTS.
THEY UNDERSTAND WHAT YOU AND YOUR DAD AND YOUR COLLEGE ADVISOR DIDN'T.

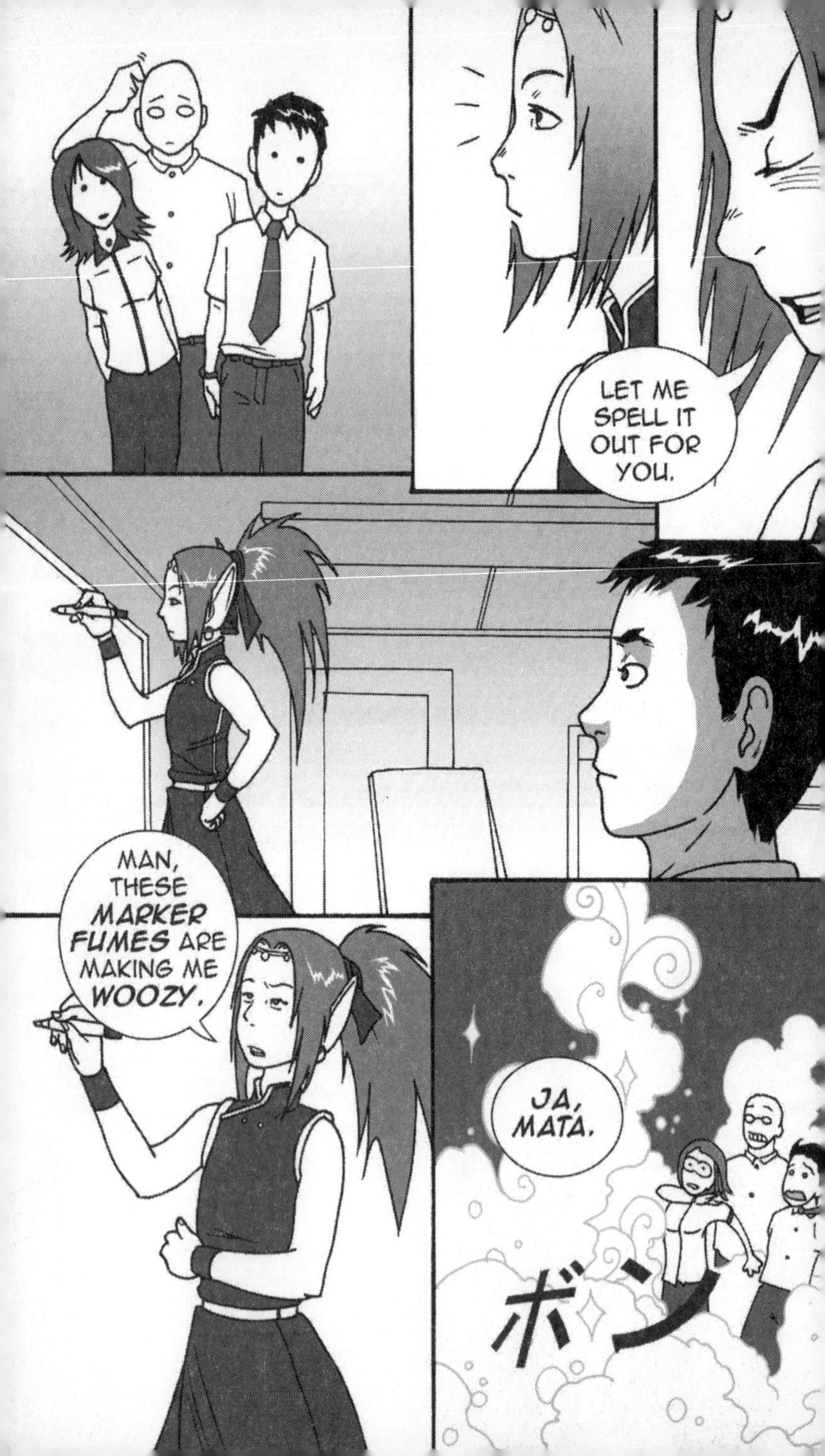
LET ME SPELL IT OUT FOR YOU.
MAN, THESE MARKER FUMES ARE MAKING ME WOOZY.
JA, MATA.
ボン

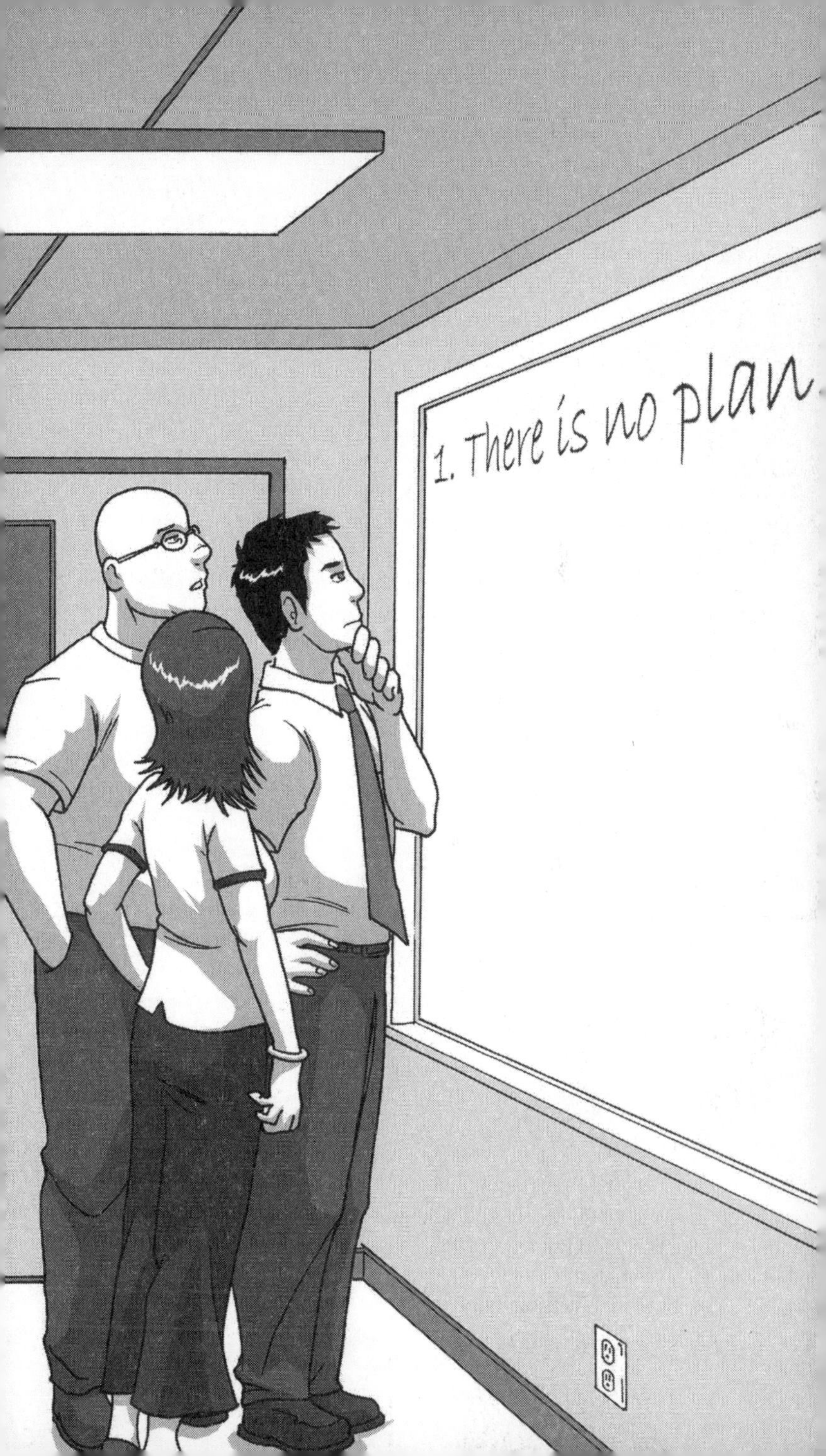
1. There is no plan

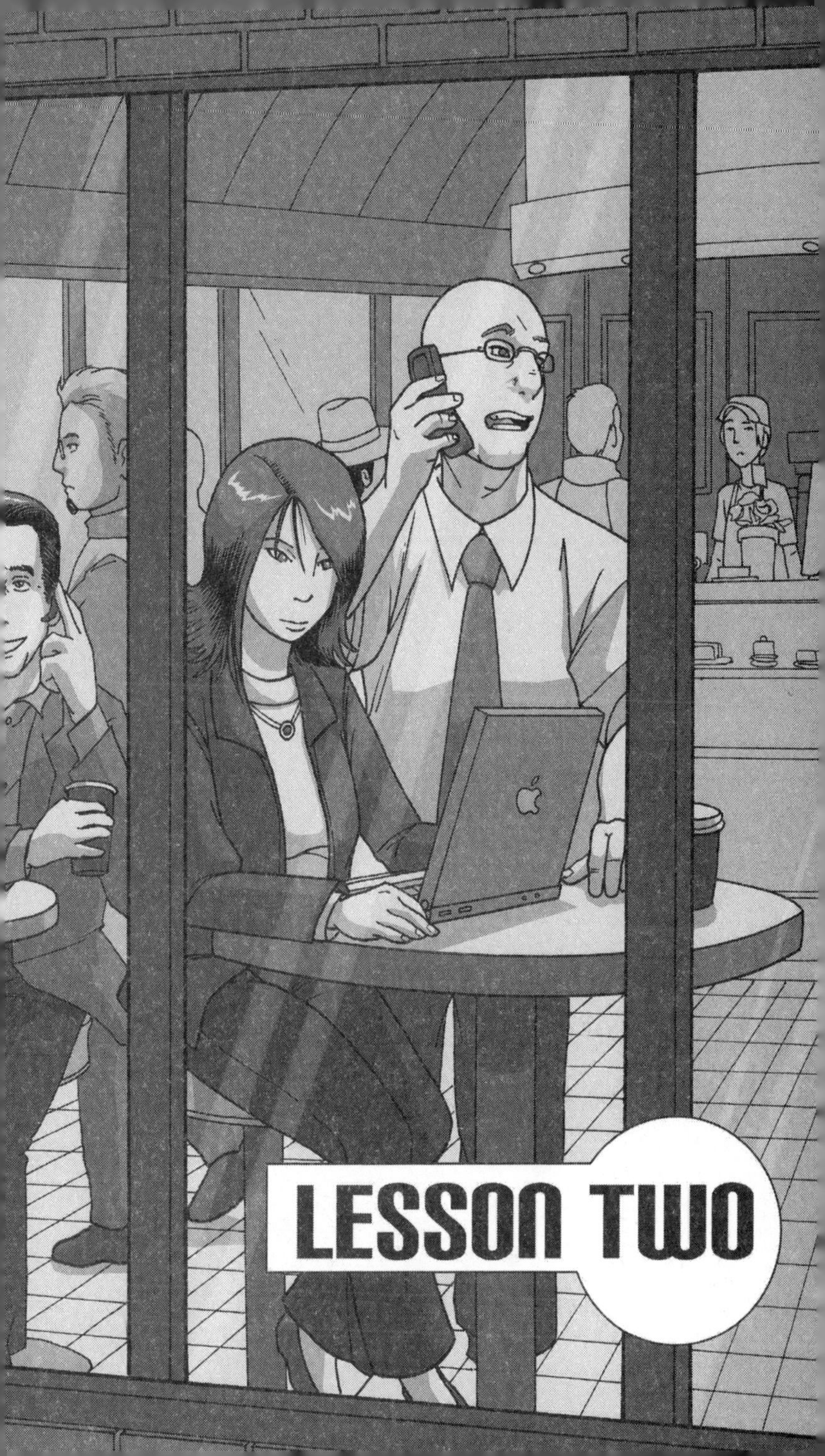
LESSON TWO

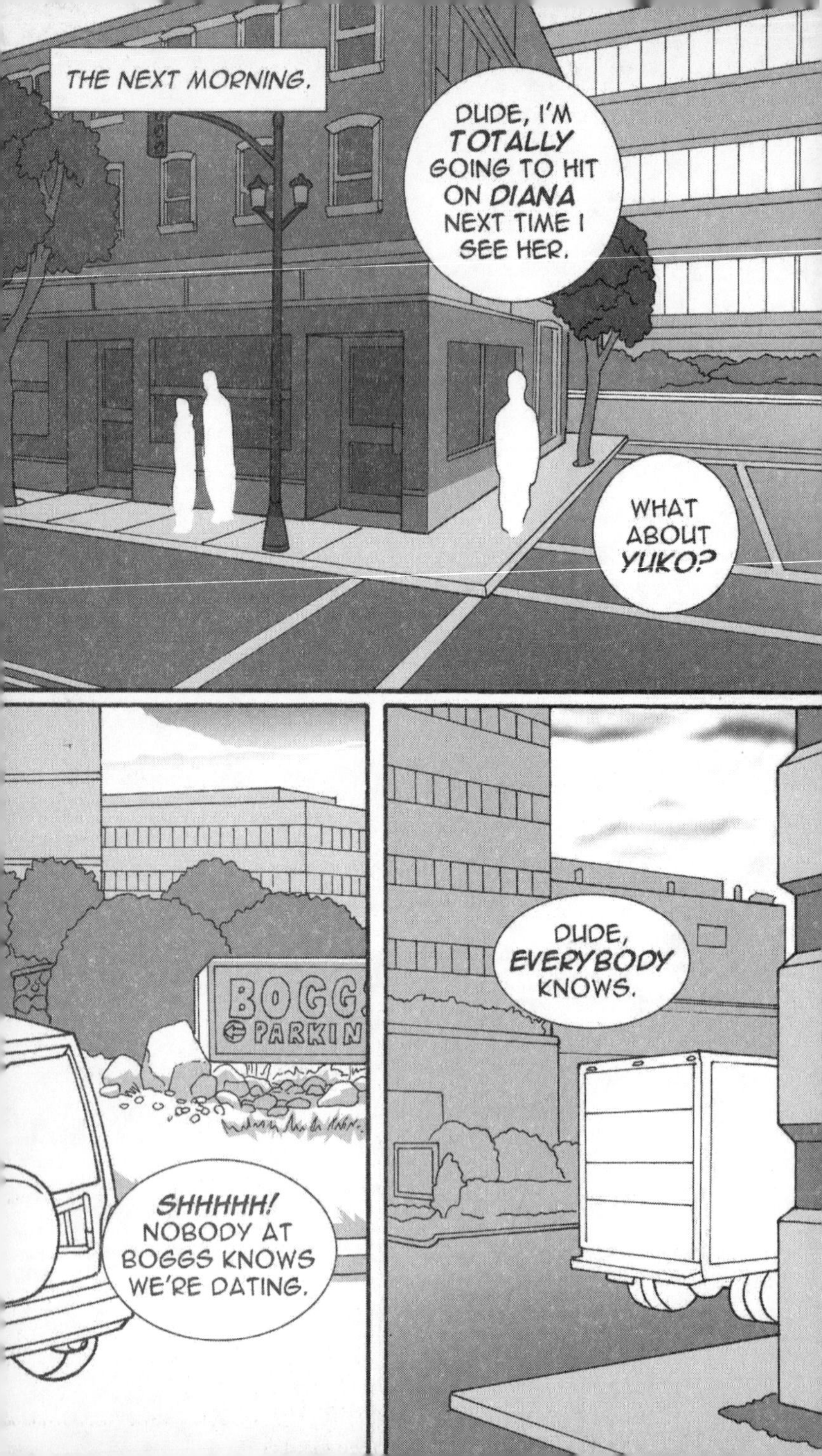
THE NEXT MORNING.
DUDE, I'M TOTALLY GOING TO HIT ON DIANA NEXT TIME I SEE HER.
WHAT ABOUT YUKO?
BOGGS PARKIN
SHHHHH! NOBODY AT BOGGS KNOWS WE'RE DATING.
DUDE, EVERYBODY KNOWS.

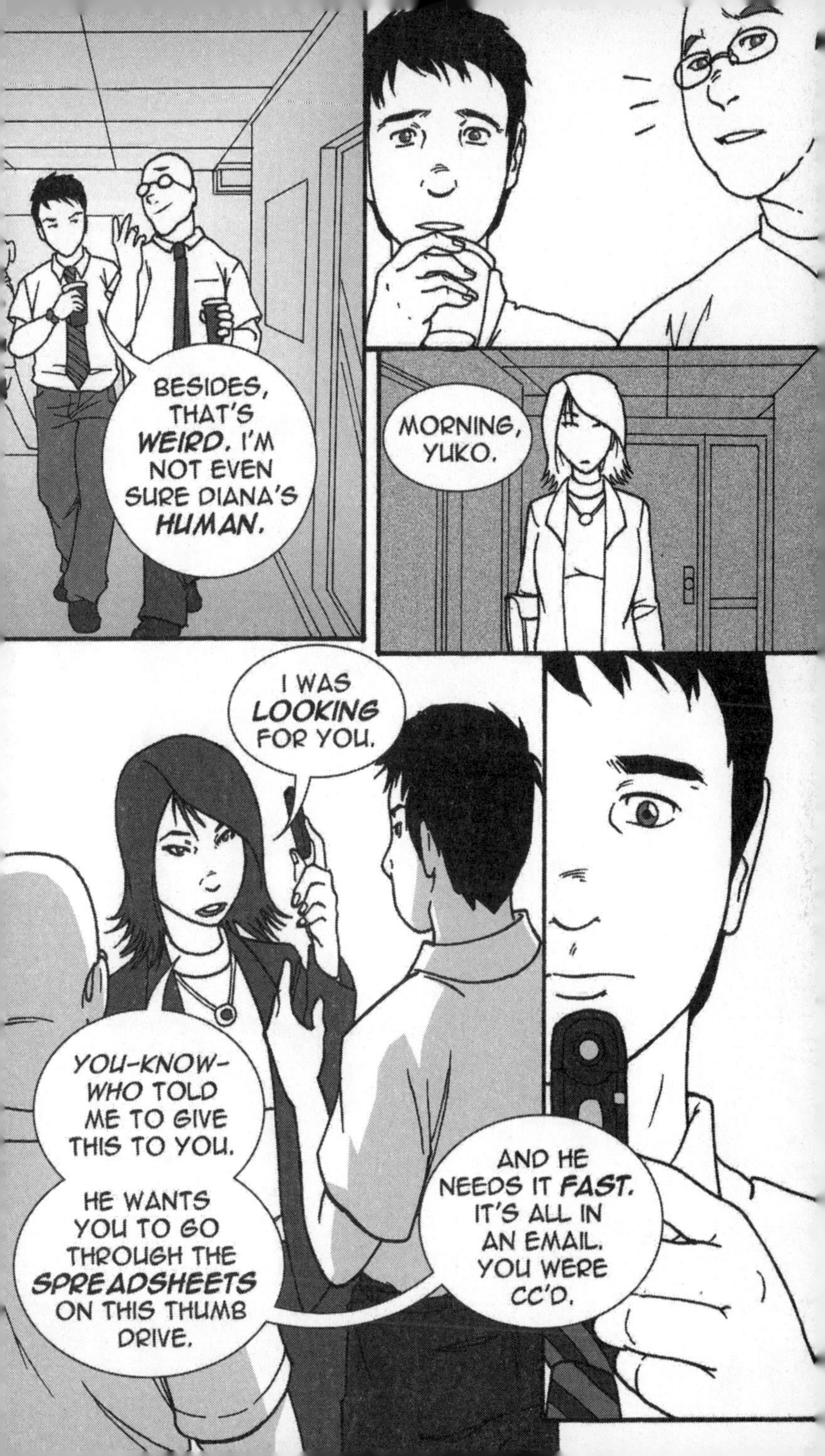
BESIDES, THAT'S WEIRD. I'M NOT EVEN SURE DIANA'S HUMAN.
MORNING, YUKO.
I WAS LOOKING FOR YOU.
YOU-KNOW-WHO TOLD ME TO GIVE THIS TO YOU.
HE WANTS YOU TO GO THROUGH THE SPREADSHEETS ON THIS THUMB DRIVE.
AND HE NEEDS IT FAST. IT'S ALL IN AN EMAIL. YOU WERE CC'D.

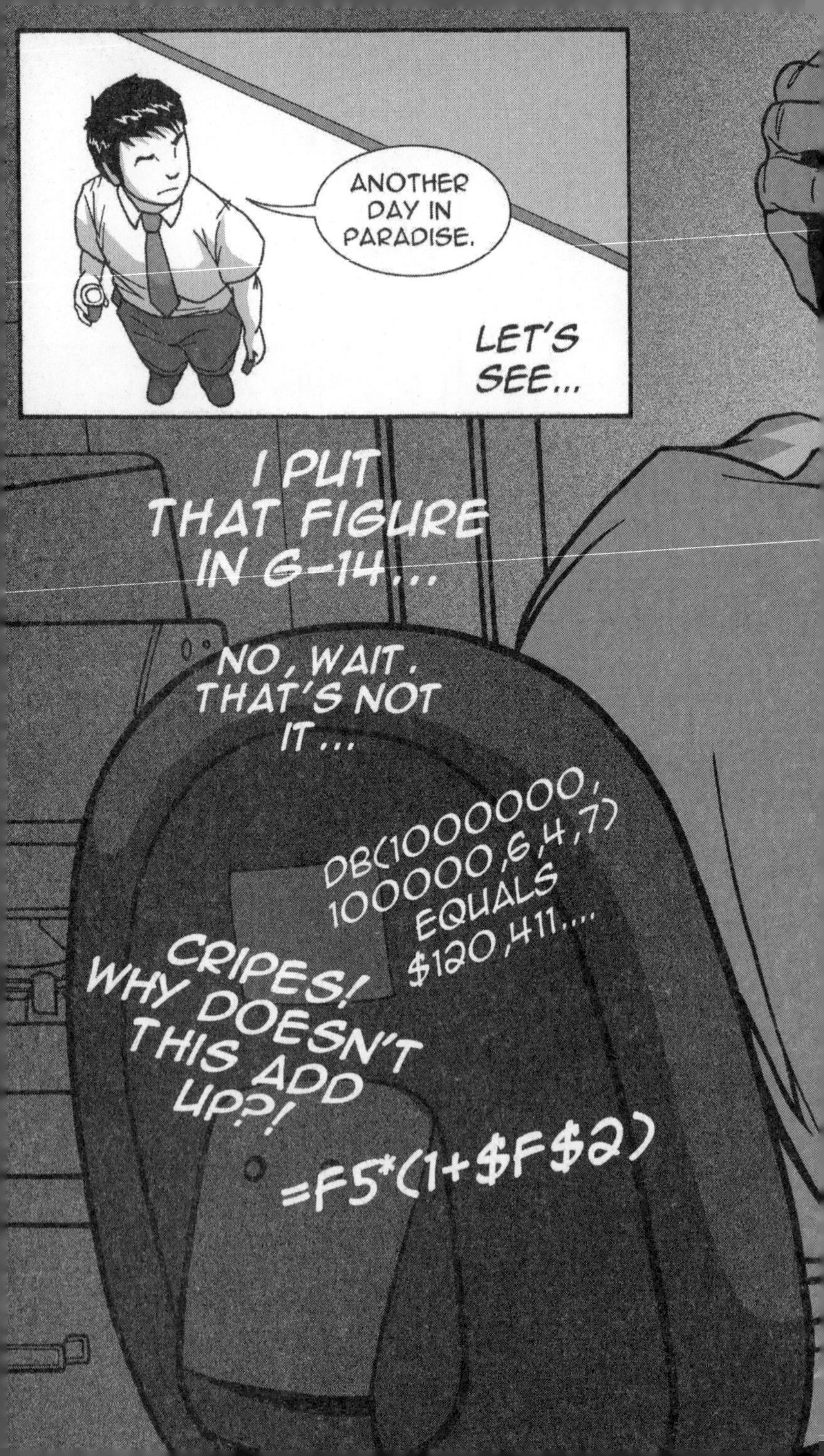
ANOTHER DAY IN PARADISE.
LET'S SEE...
I PUT THAT FIGURE IN G-14...
NO, WAIT. THAT'S NOT IT...
DB(1000000, 100000,6,4,7) EQUALS $120,411....
CRIPES! WHY DOESN'T THIS ADD UP?!
=F5*(1+F2)

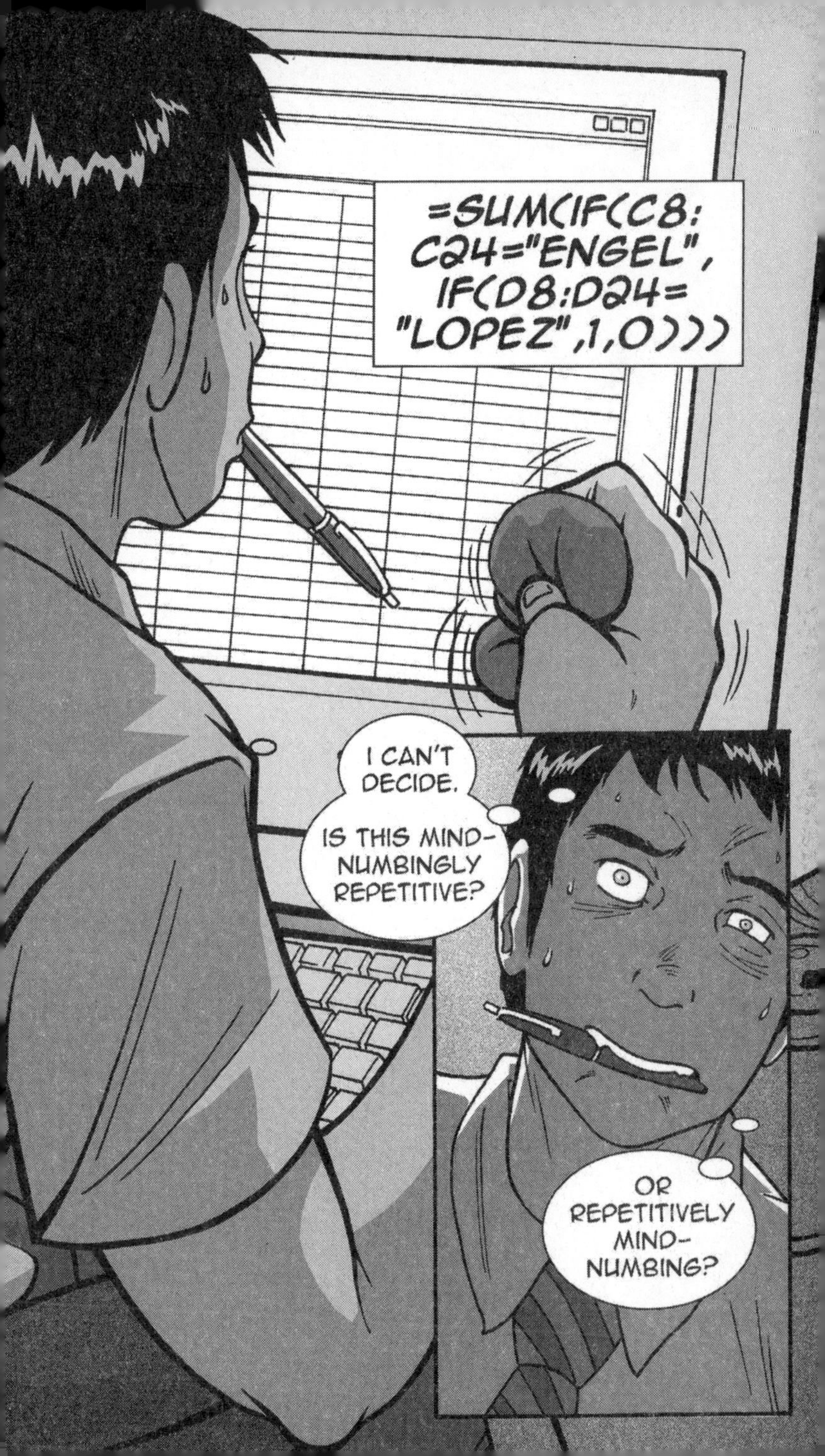

=SUM(IF(C8:C24="ENGEL", IF(D8:D24="LOPEZ",1,0)))
I CAN'T DECIDE.
IS THIS MIND-NUMBINGLY REPETITIVE?
OR REPETITIVELY MIND-NUMBING?

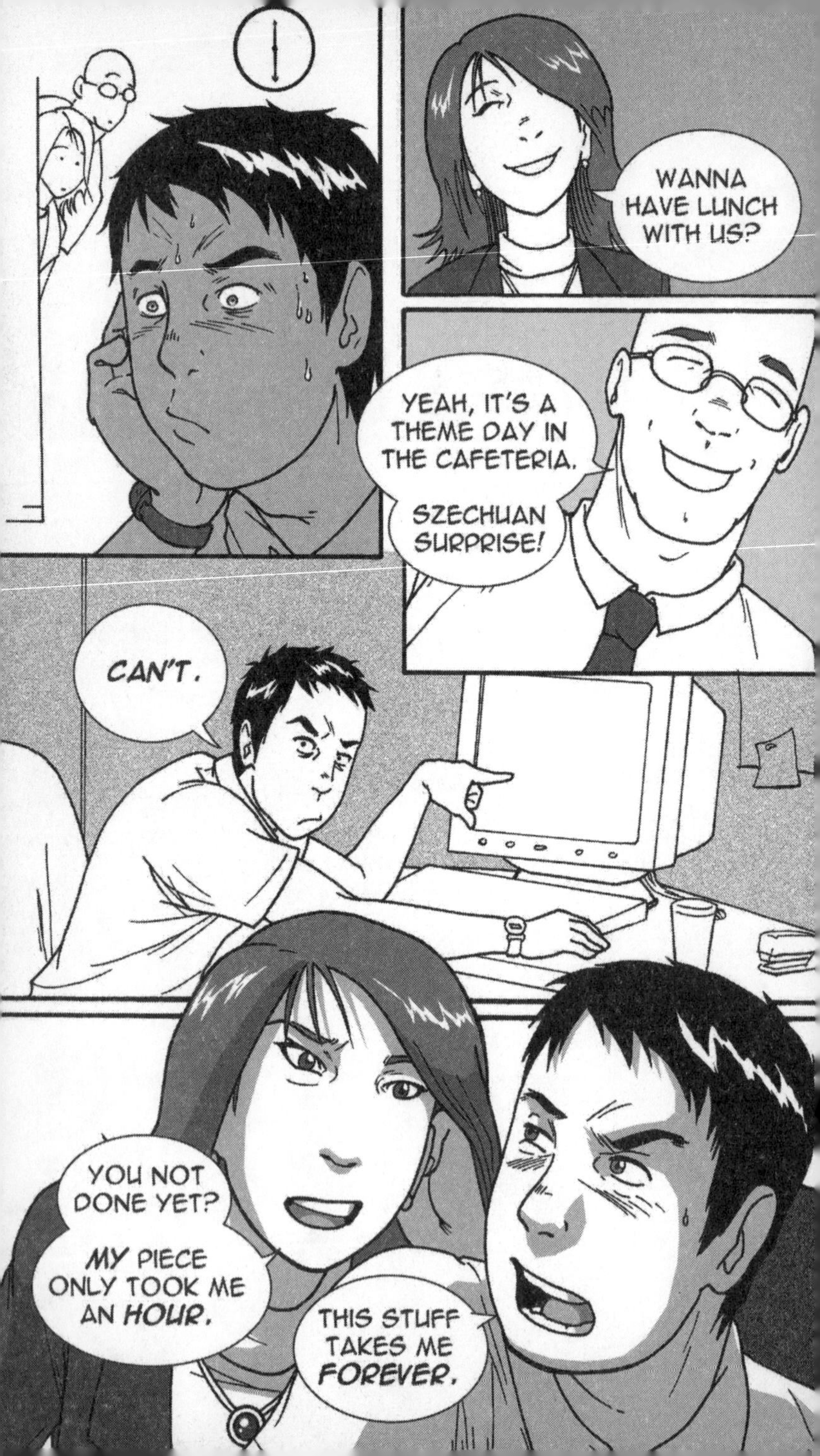
WANNA HAVE LUNCH WITH US?
YEAH, IT'S A THEME DAY IN THE CAFETERIA.
SZECHUAN SURPRISE!
CAN'T.
YOU NOT DONE YET?
MY PIECE ONLY TOOK ME AN HOUR.
THIS STUFF TAKES ME FOREVER.

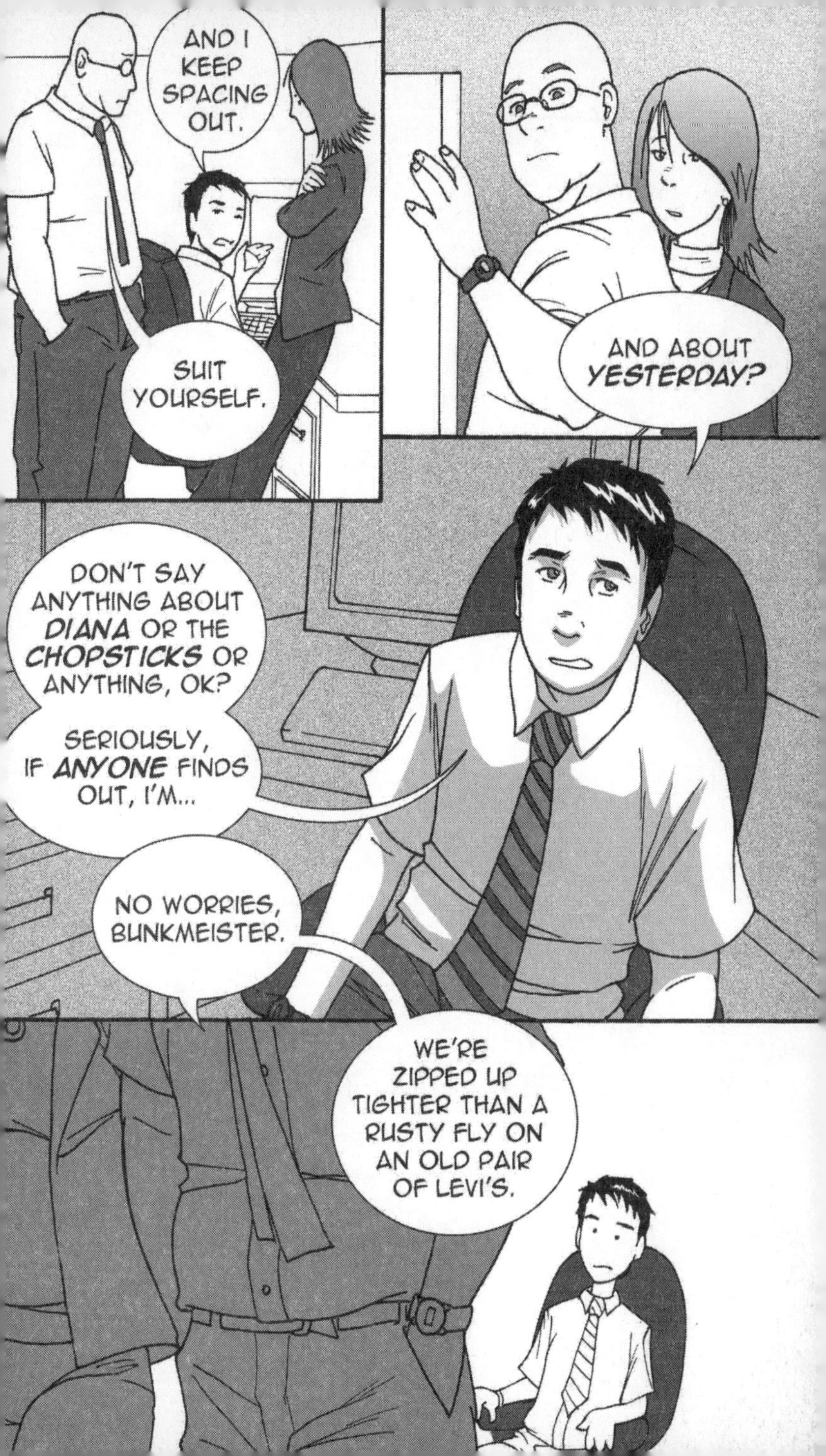
AND I KEEP SPACING OUT.
SUIT YOURSELF.
AND ABOUT *YESTERDAY?*
DON'T SAY ANYTHING ABOUT *DIANA* OR THE *CHOPSTICKS* OR ANYTHING, OK?
SERIOUSLY, IF *ANYONE* FINDS OUT, I'M...
NO WORRIES, BUNKMEISTER.
WE'RE ZIPPED UP TIGHTER THAN A RUSTY FLY ON AN OLD PAIR OF LEVI'S.

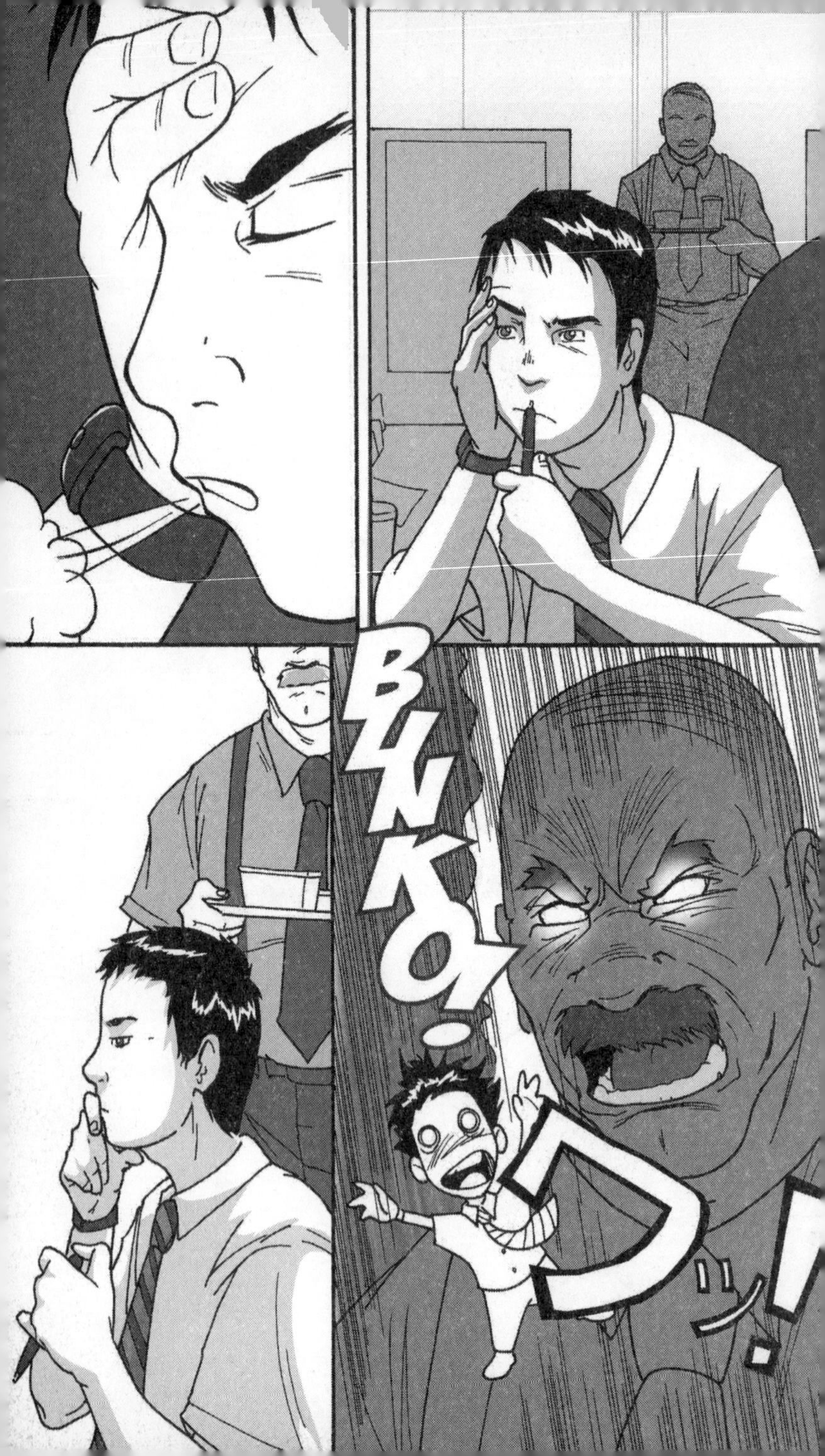

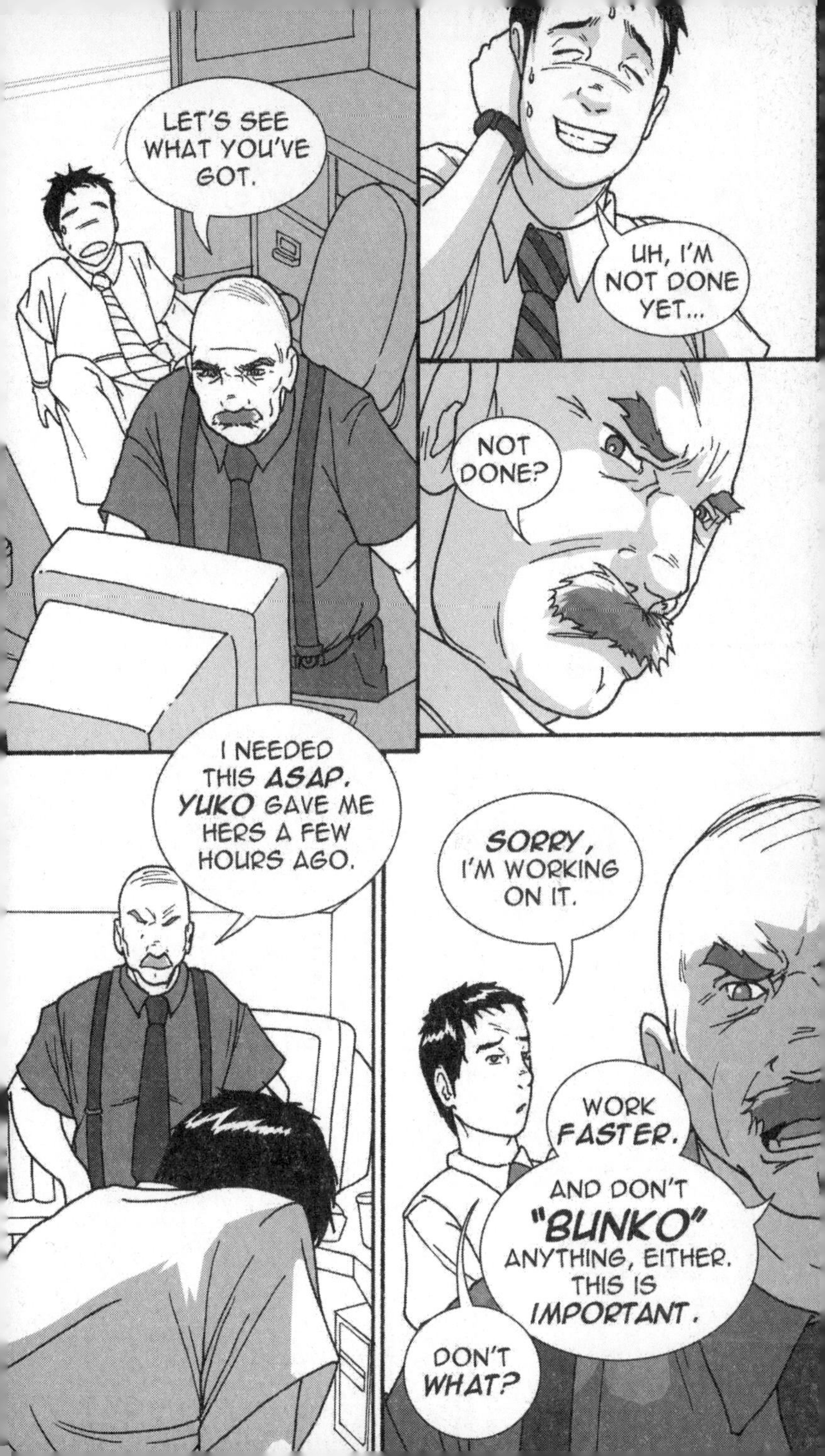
LET'S SEE WHAT YOU'VE GOT.
UH, I'M NOT DONE YET...
NOT DONE?
I NEEDED THIS ASAP. YUKO GAVE ME HERS A FEW HOURS AGO.
SORRY, I'M WORKING ON IT.
WORK FASTER.
AND DON'T "BUNKO" ANYTHING, EITHER. THIS IS IMPORTANT.
DON'T WHAT?

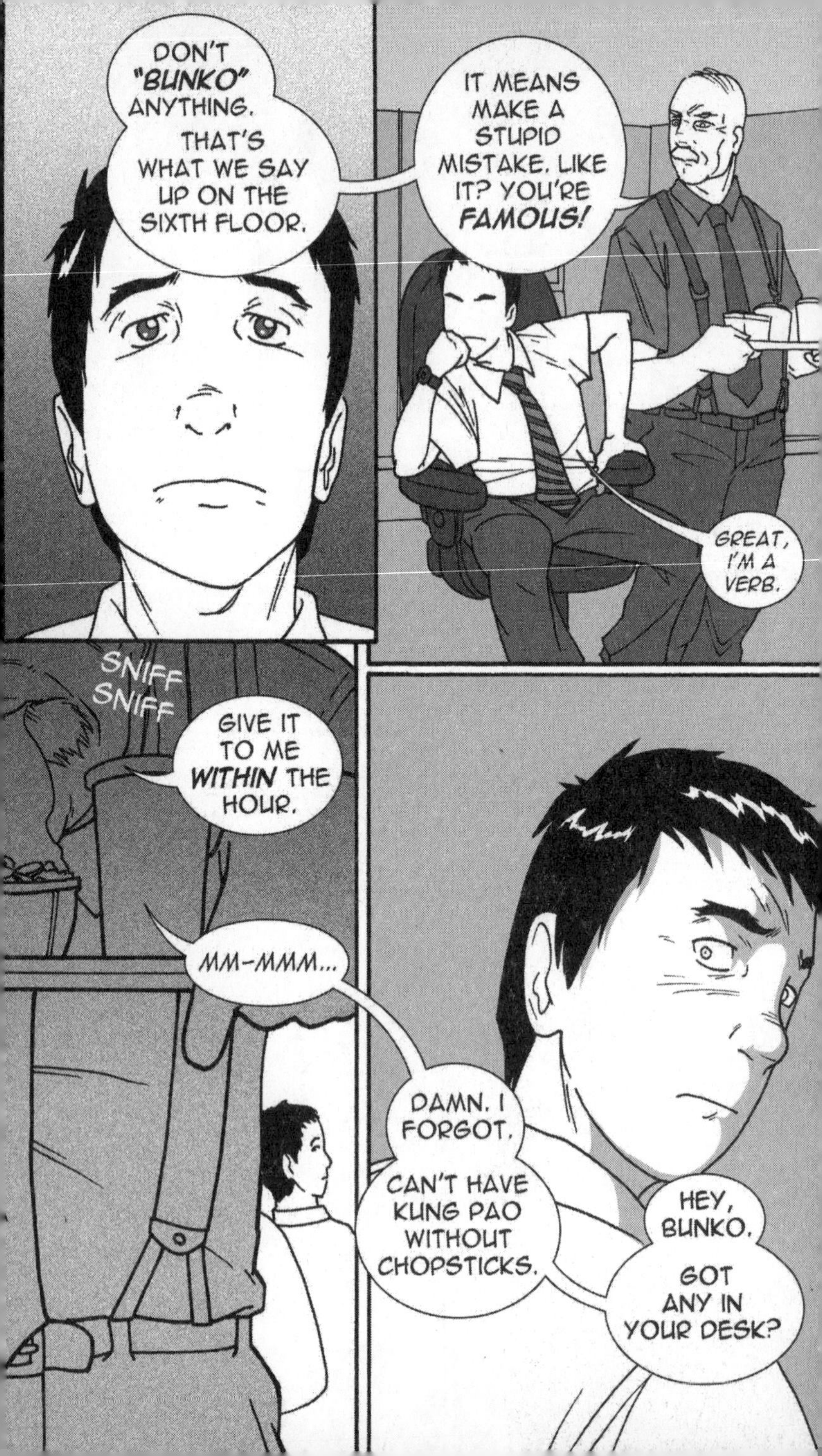
DON'T "BUNKO" ANYTHING.
THAT'S WHAT WE SAY UP ON THE SIXTH FLOOR.
IT MEANS MAKE A STUPID MISTAKE. LIKE IT? YOU'RE FAMOUS!
GREAT, I'M A VERB.
SNIFF SNIFF
GIVE IT TO ME WITHIN THE HOUR.
MM-MMM...
DAMN. I FORGOT.
CAN'T HAVE KUNG PAO WITHOUT CHOPSTICKS.
HEY, BUNKO.
GOT ANY IN YOUR DESK?

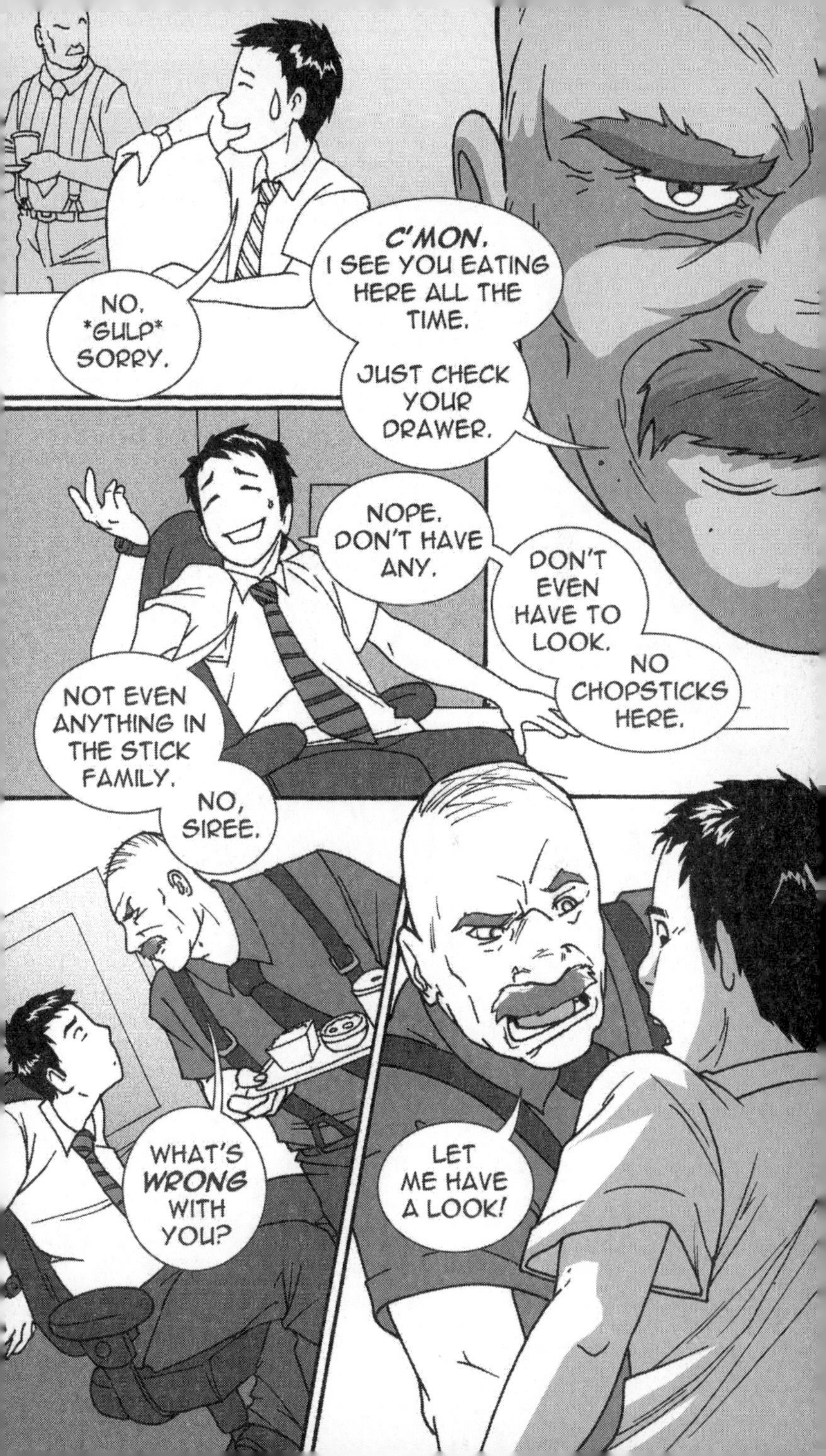

C'MON. I SEE YOU EATING HERE ALL THE TIME.
NO. *GULP* SORRY.
JUST CHECK YOUR DRAWER.
NOPE. DON'T HAVE ANY.
DON'T EVEN HAVE TO LOOK.
NO CHOPSTICKS HERE.
NOT EVEN ANYTHING IN THE STICK FAMILY.
NO, SIREE.
WHAT'S *WRONG* WITH YOU?
LET ME HAVE A LOOK!

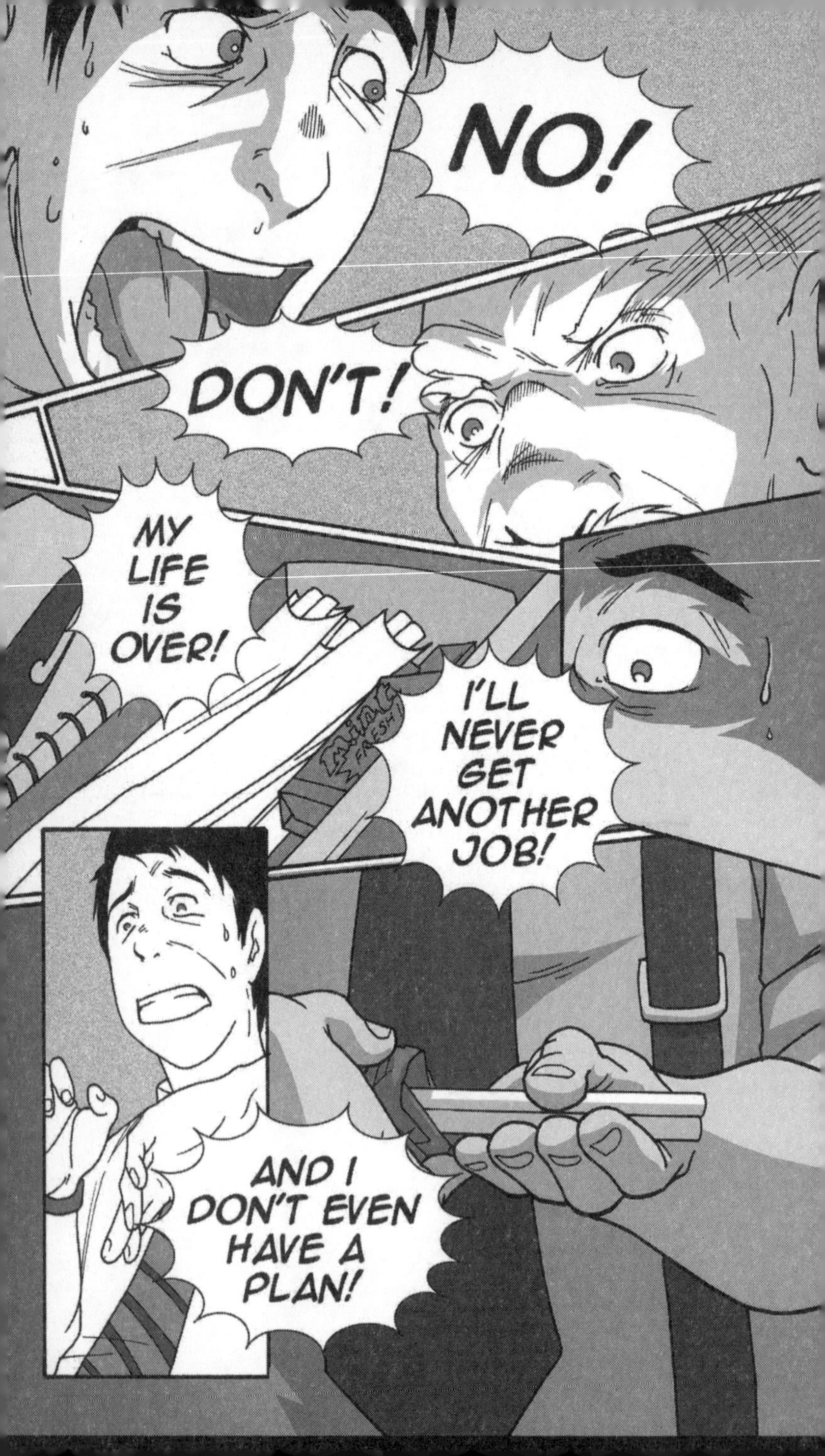
NO!
DON'T!
MY LIFE IS OVER!
I'LL NEVER GET ANOTHER JOB!
AND I DON'T EVEN HAVE A PLAN!

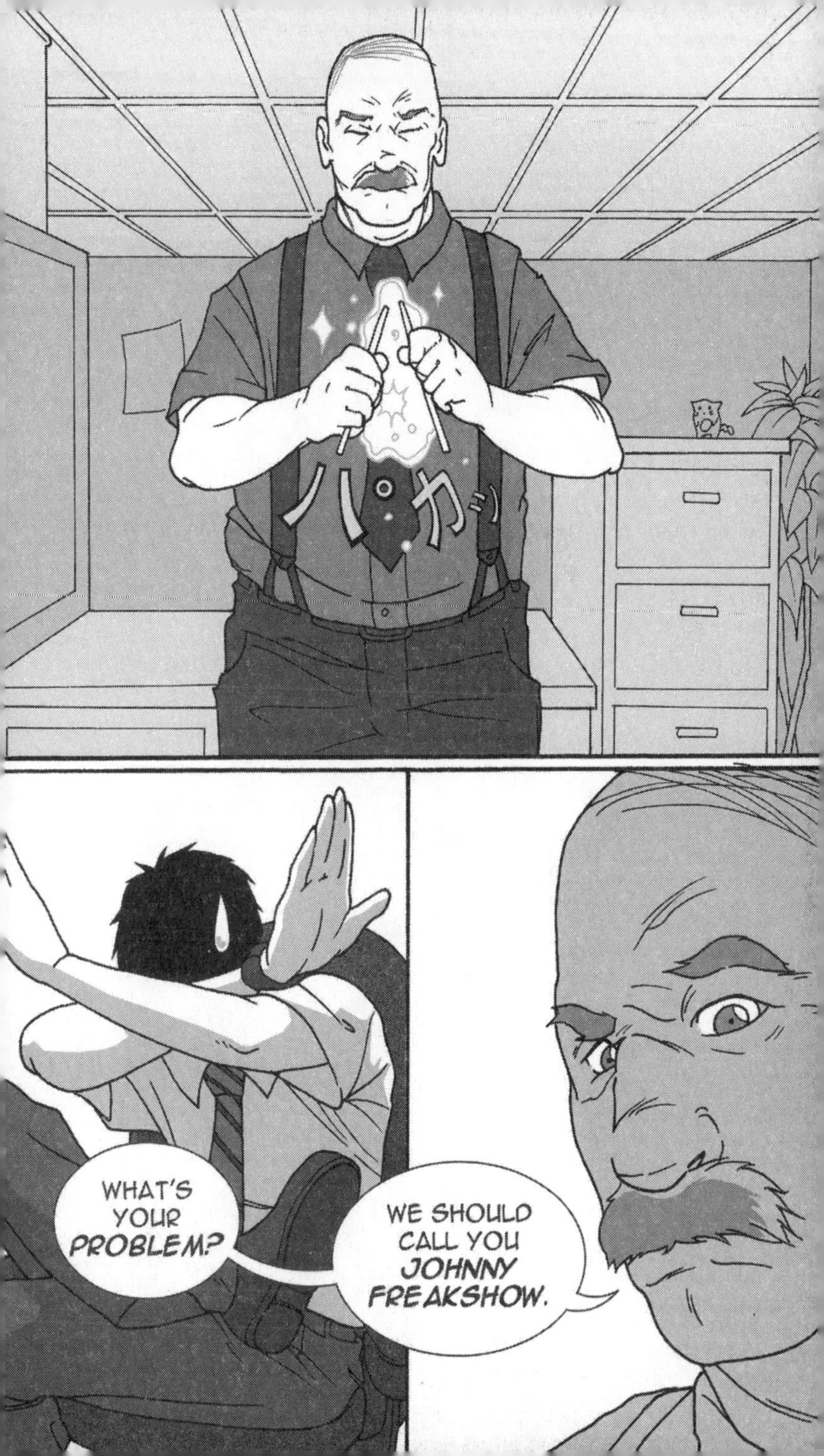
WHAT'S YOUR *PROBLEM?*
WE SHOULD CALL YOU *JOHNNY FREAKSHOW.*

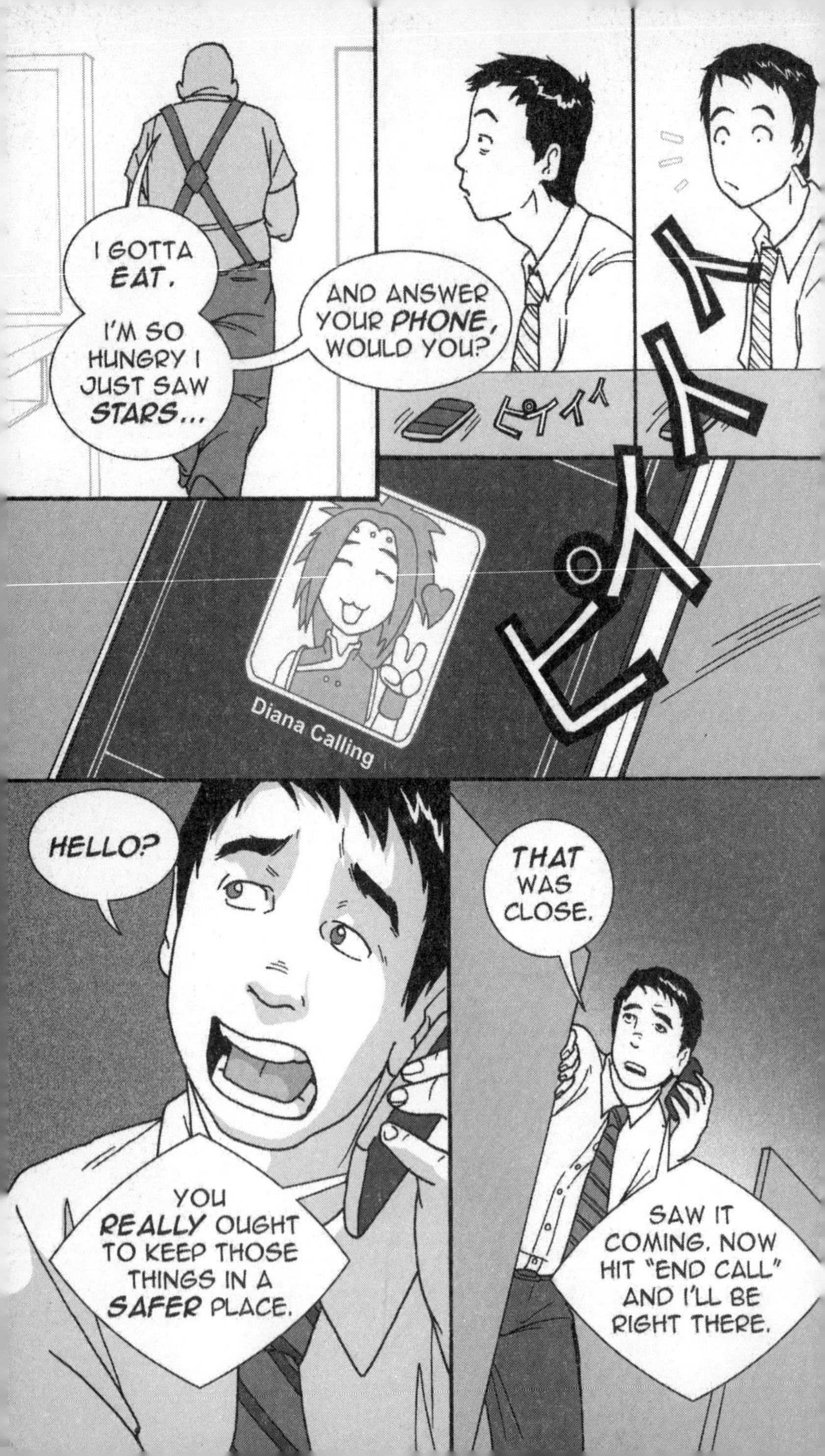
I GOTTA EAT.
I'M SO HUNGRY I JUST SAW STARS...
AND ANSWER YOUR PHONE, WOULD YOU?
ピイイ
ピイイ
Diana Calling
HELLO?
YOU REALLY OUGHT TO KEEP THOSE THINGS IN A SAFER PLACE.
THAT WAS CLOSE.
SAW IT COMING. NOW HIT "END CALL" AND I'LL BE RIGHT THERE.

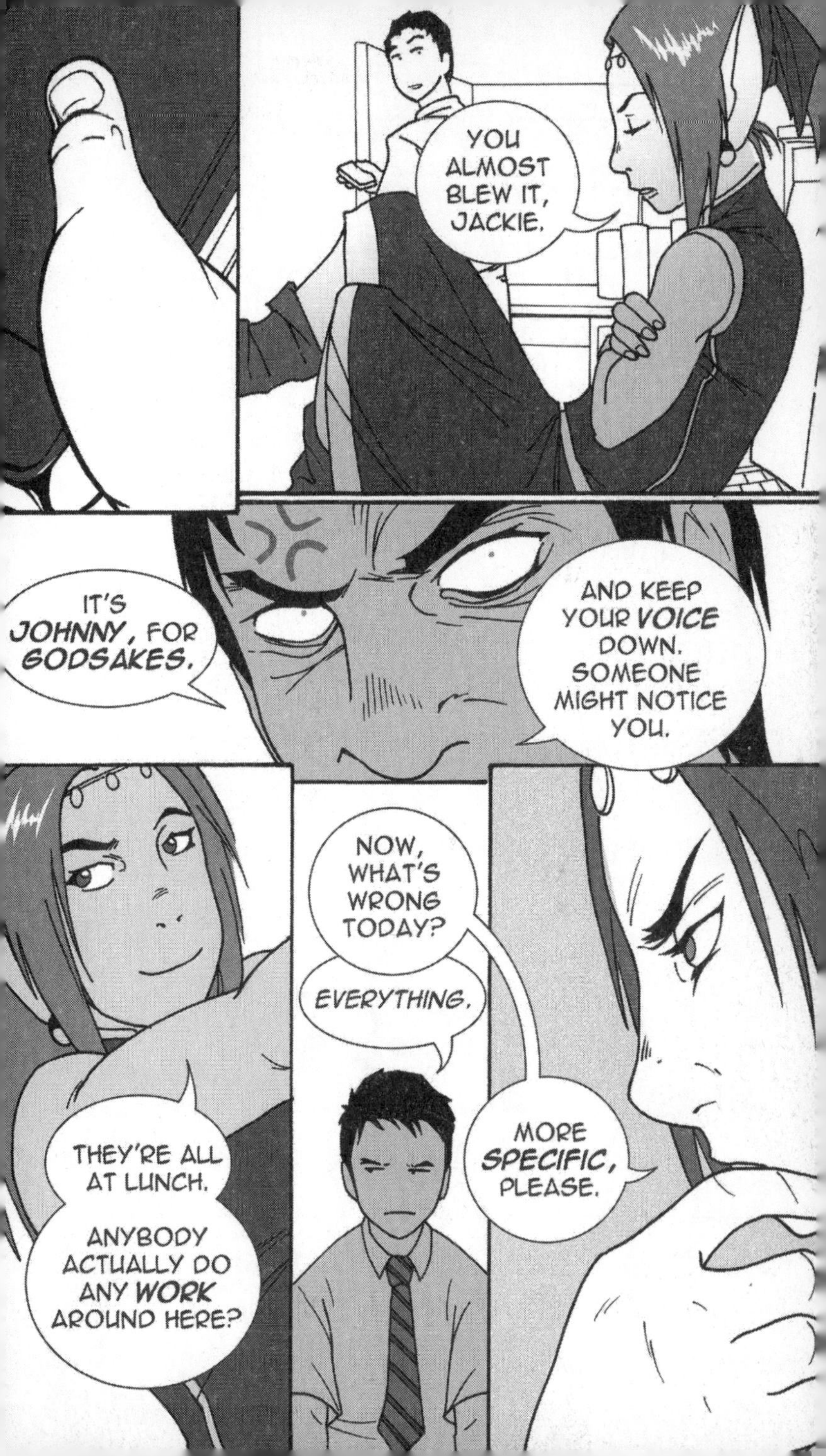
YOU ALMOST BLEW IT, JACKIE.
IT'S JOHNNY, FOR GODSAKES.
AND KEEP YOUR VOICE DOWN. SOMEONE MIGHT NOTICE YOU.
THEY'RE ALL AT LUNCH.
ANYBODY ACTUALLY DO ANY WORK AROUND HERE?
NOW, WHAT'S WRONG TODAY?
EVERYTHING.
MORE SPECIFIC, PLEASE.

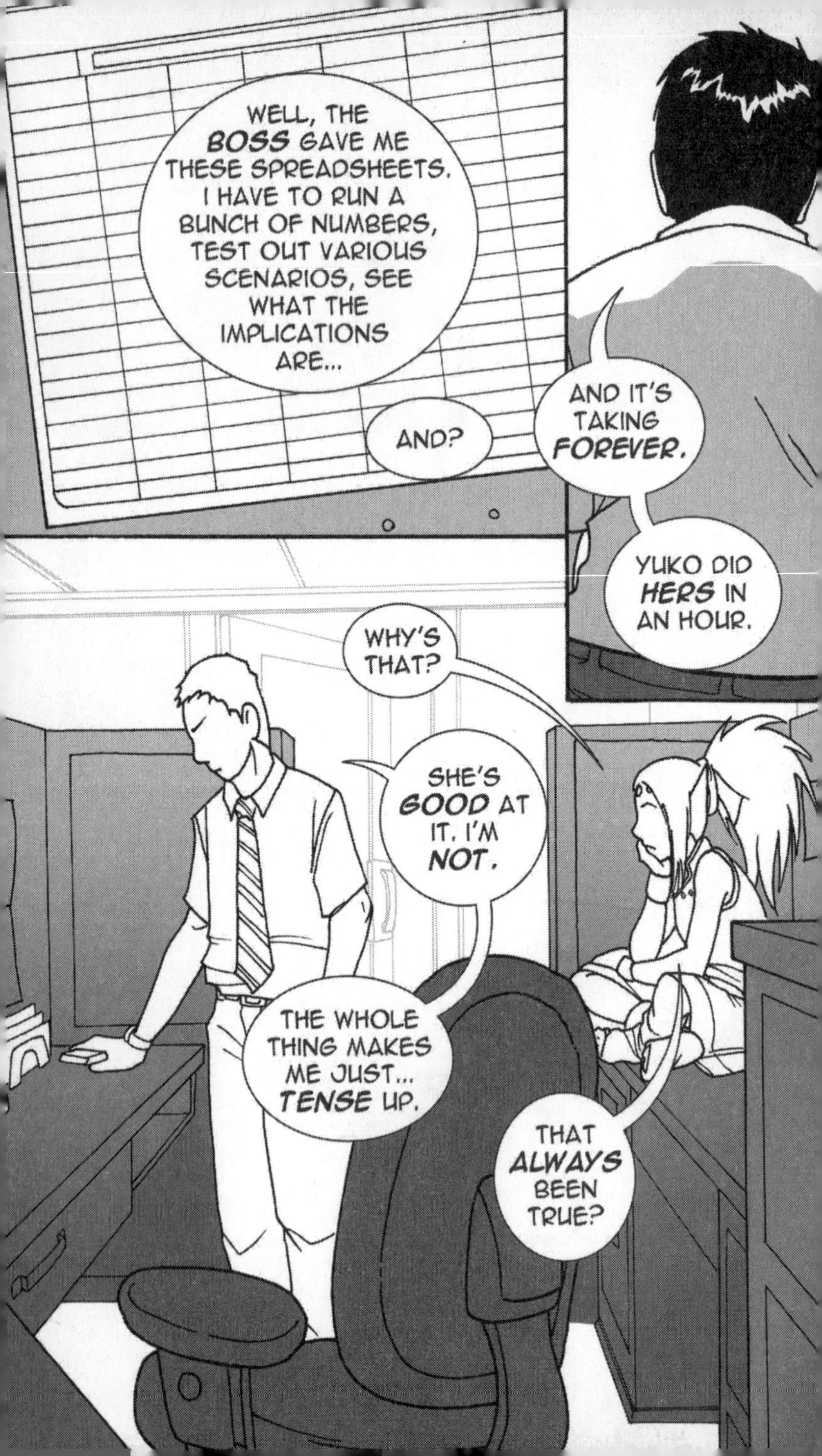
WELL, THE BOSS GAVE ME THESE SPREADSHEETS. I HAVE TO RUN A BUNCH OF NUMBERS, TEST OUT VARIOUS SCENARIOS, SEE WHAT THE IMPLICATIONS ARE...
AND?
AND IT'S TAKING FOREVER.
YUKO DID HERS IN AN HOUR.
WHY'S THAT?
SHE'S GOOD AT IT. I'M NOT.
THE WHOLE THING MAKES ME JUST... TENSE UP.
THAT ALWAYS BEEN TRUE?

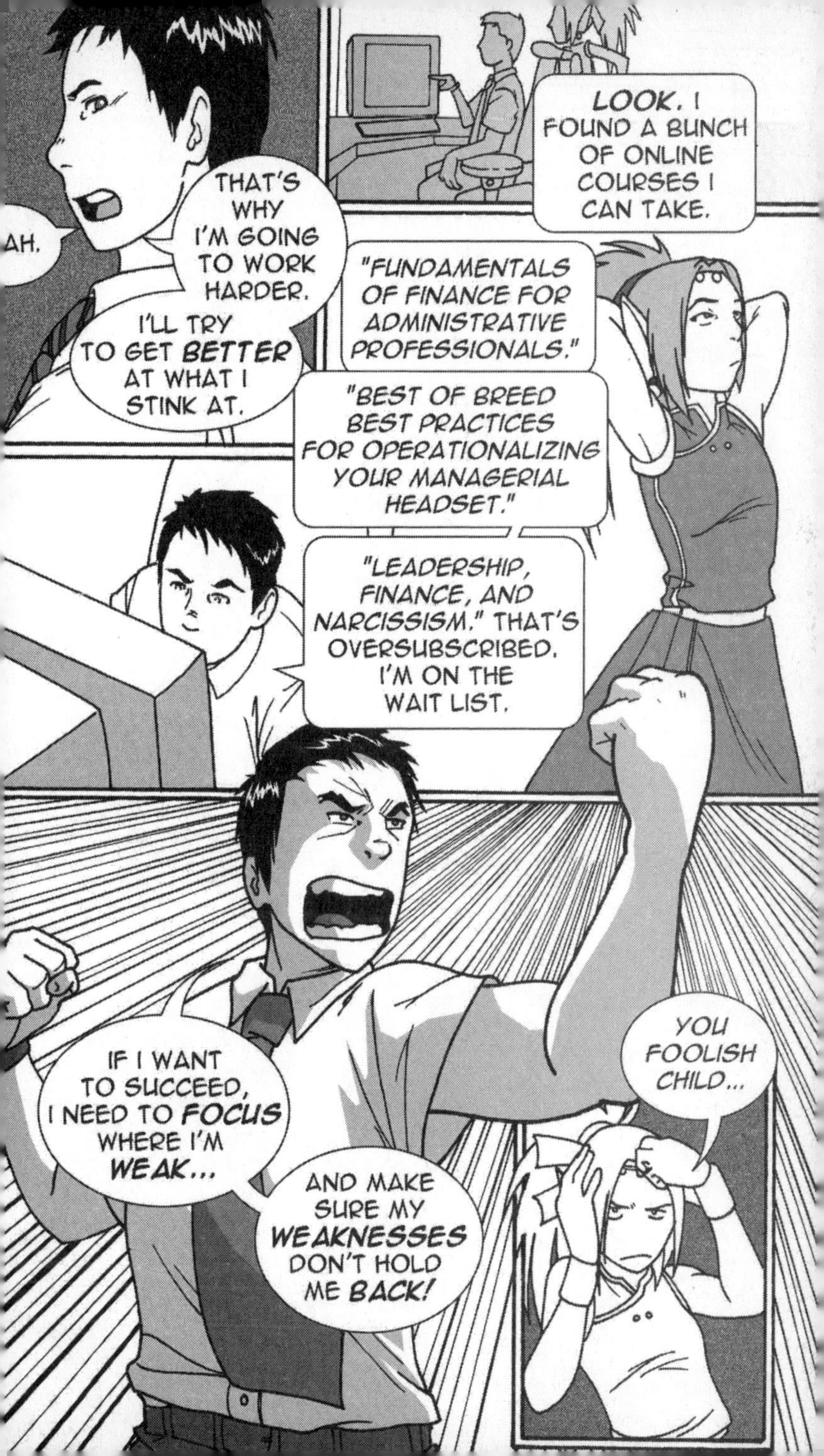
AH.
THAT'S WHY I'M GOING TO WORK HARDER.
I'LL TRY TO GET BETTER AT WHAT I STINK AT.
LOOK. I FOUND A BUNCH OF ONLINE COURSES I CAN TAKE.
"FUNDAMENTALS OF FINANCE FOR ADMINISTRATIVE PROFESSIONALS."
"BEST OF BREED BEST PRACTICES FOR OPERATIONALIZING YOUR MANAGERIAL HEADSET."
"LEADERSHIP, FINANCE, AND NARCISSISM." THAT'S OVERSUBSCRIBED. I'M ON THE WAIT LIST.
IF I WANT TO SUCCEED, I NEED TO FOCUS WHERE I'M WEAK...
AND MAKE SURE MY WEAKNESSES DON'T HOLD ME BACK!
YOU FOOLISH CHILD...

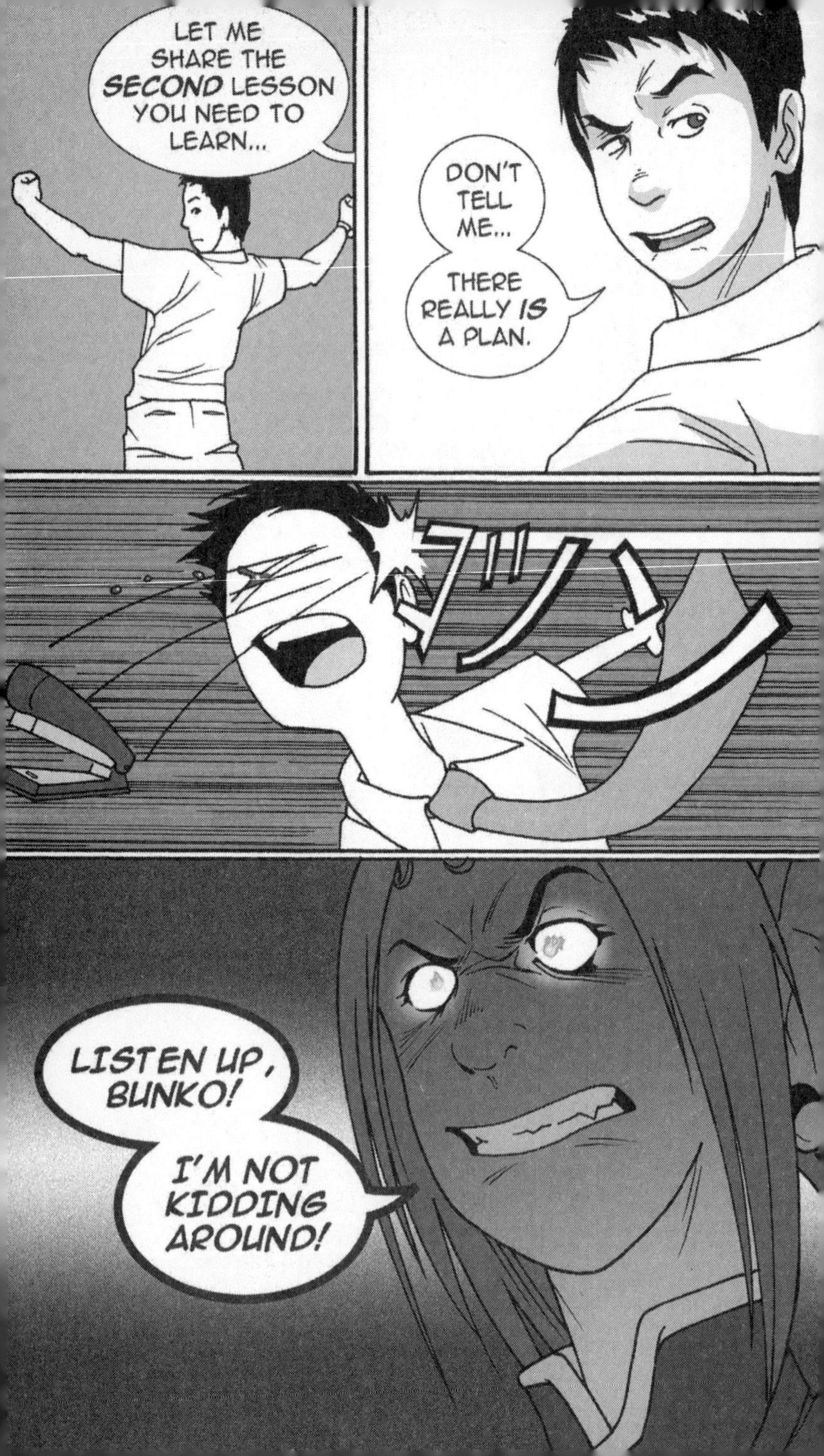
LET ME SHARE THE SECOND LESSON YOU NEED TO LEARN...
DON'T TELL ME...
THERE REALLY IS A PLAN.
LISTEN UP, BUNKO!
I'M NOT KIDDING AROUND!

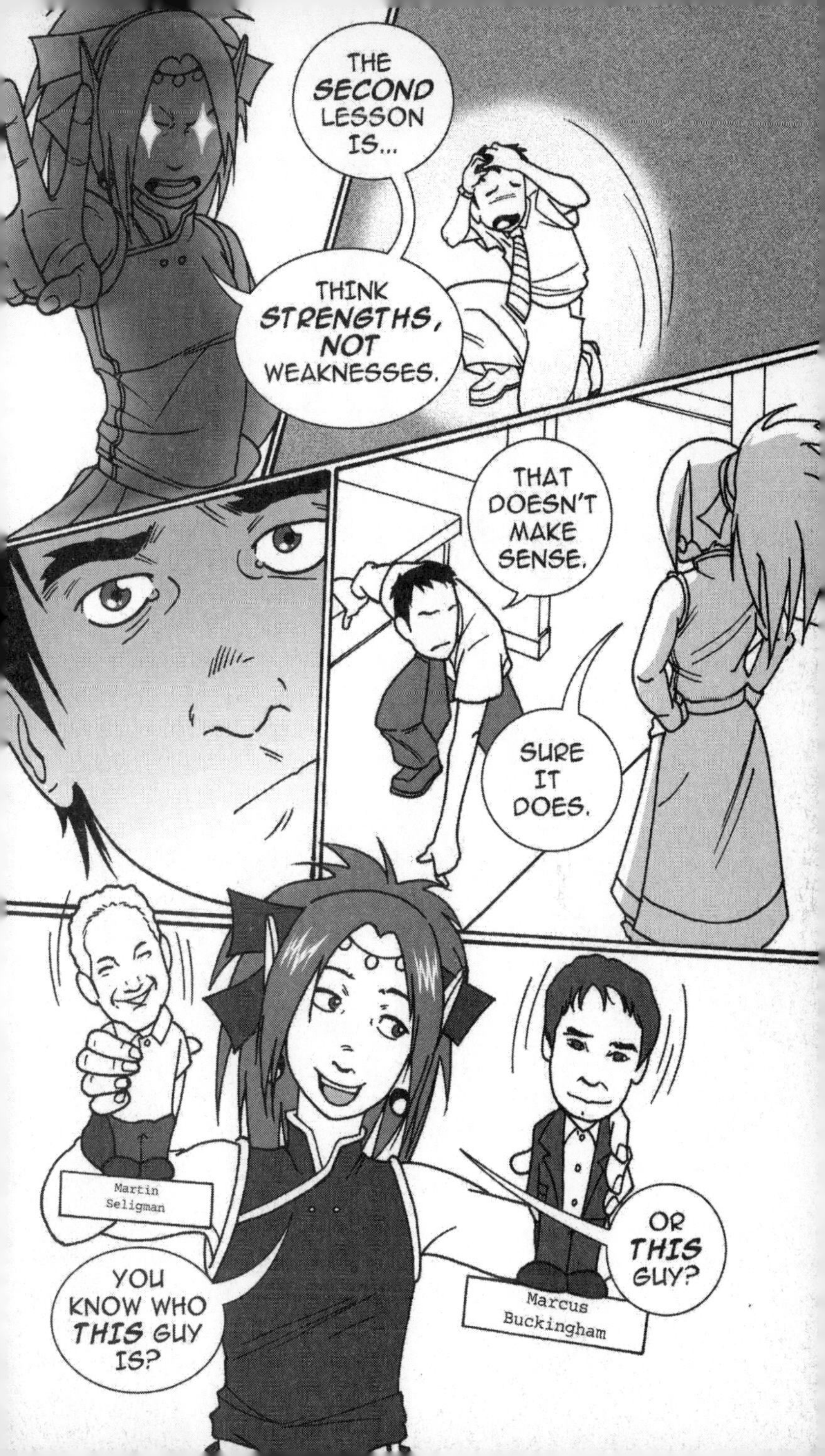

THE SECOND LESSON IS...
THINK STRENGTHS, NOT WEAKNESSES.
THAT DOESN'T MAKE SENSE.
SURE IT DOES.
Martin Seligman
YOU KNOW WHO THIS GUY IS?
OR THIS GUY?
Marcus Buckingham

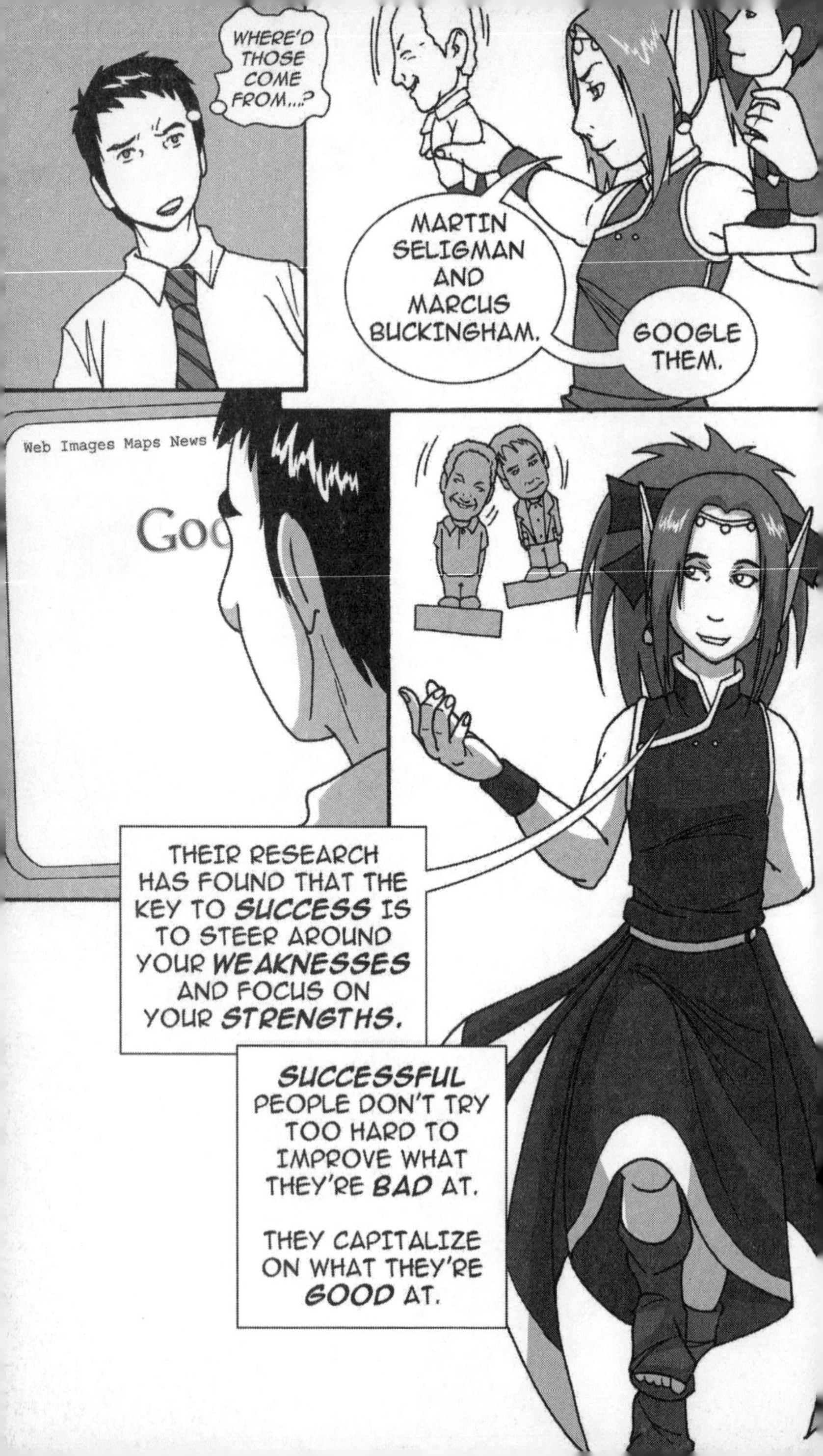
WHERE'D THOSE COME FROM...?
MARTIN SELIGMAN AND MARCUS BUCKINGHAM.
GOOGLE THEM.
Web Images Maps News
Goo
THEIR RESEARCH HAS FOUND THAT THE KEY TO SUCCESS IS TO STEER AROUND YOUR WEAKNESSES AND FOCUS ON YOUR STRENGTHS.
SUCCESSFUL PEOPLE DON'T TRY TOO HARD TO IMPROVE WHAT THEY'RE BAD AT.
THEY CAPITALIZE ON WHAT THEY'RE GOOD AT.

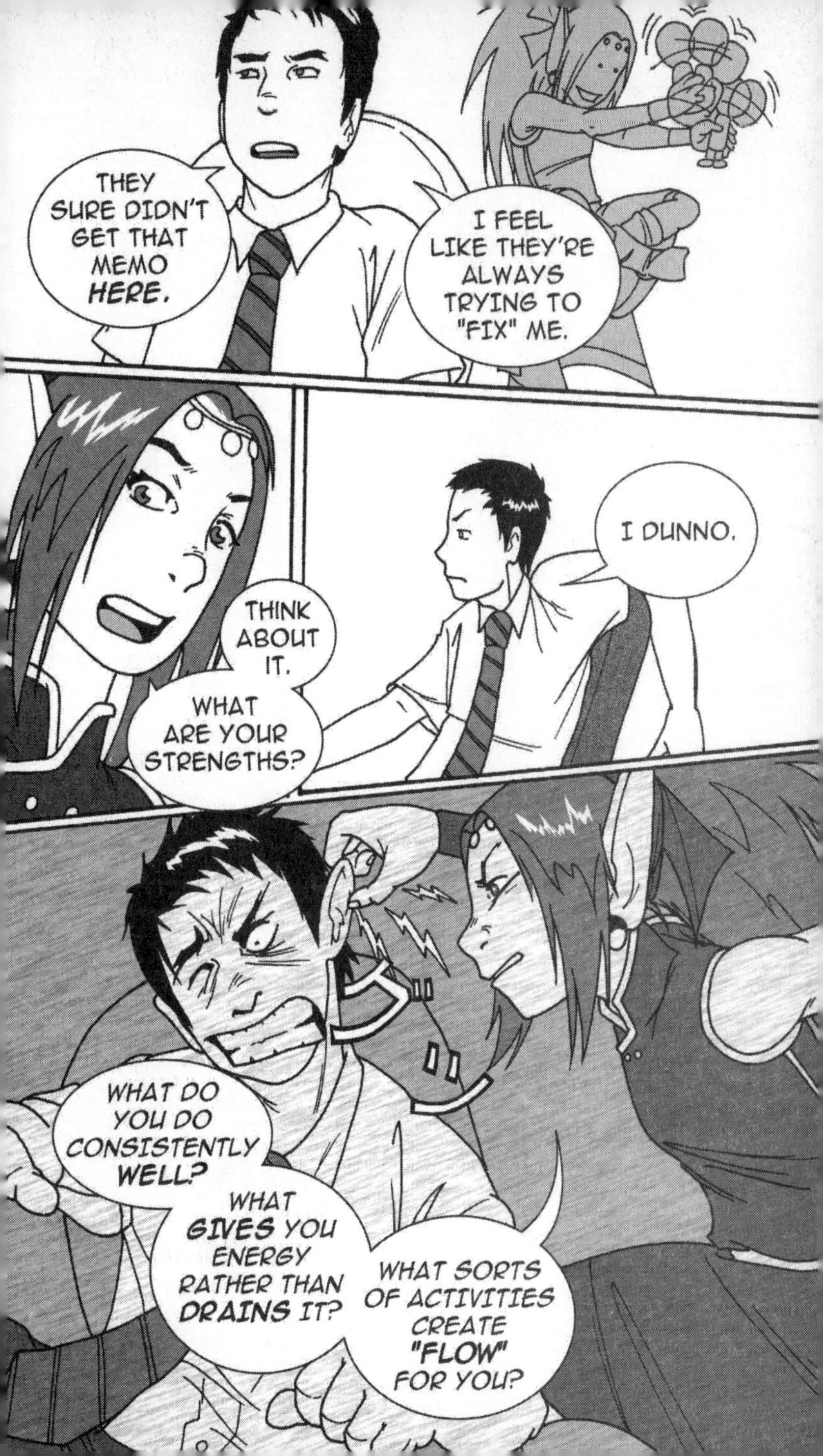

THEY SURE DIDN'T GET THAT MEMO **HERE.**
I FEEL LIKE THEY'RE ALWAYS TRYING TO "FIX" ME.
I DUNNO.
THINK ABOUT IT.
WHAT ARE YOUR STRENGTHS?
WHAT DO YOU DO CONSISTENTLY **WELL?**
WHAT **GIVES** YOU ENERGY RATHER THAN **DRAINS** IT?
WHAT SORTS OF ACTIVITIES CREATE **"FLOW"** FOR YOU?

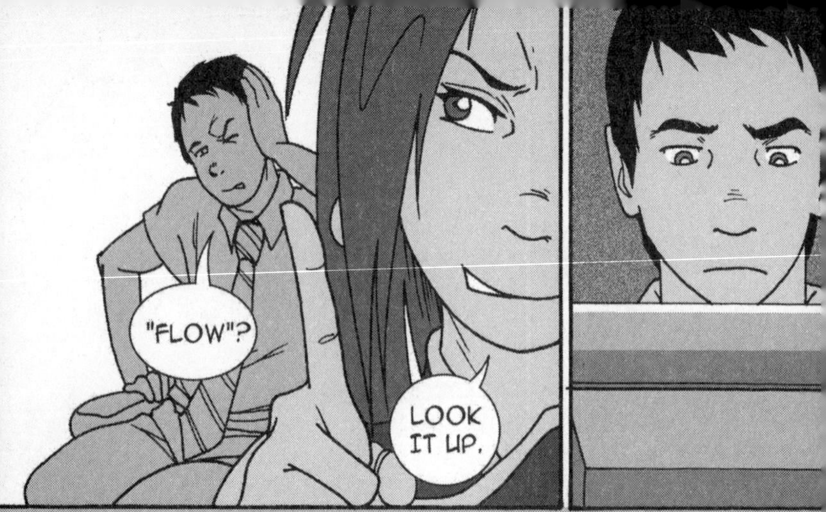
"FLOW"?
LOOK IT UP.

FLOW is the mental state of operation in which the person is fully immers
in what he or she is doing, characterized by a feeling of energized focus
involvement, and success in the process of the activity.

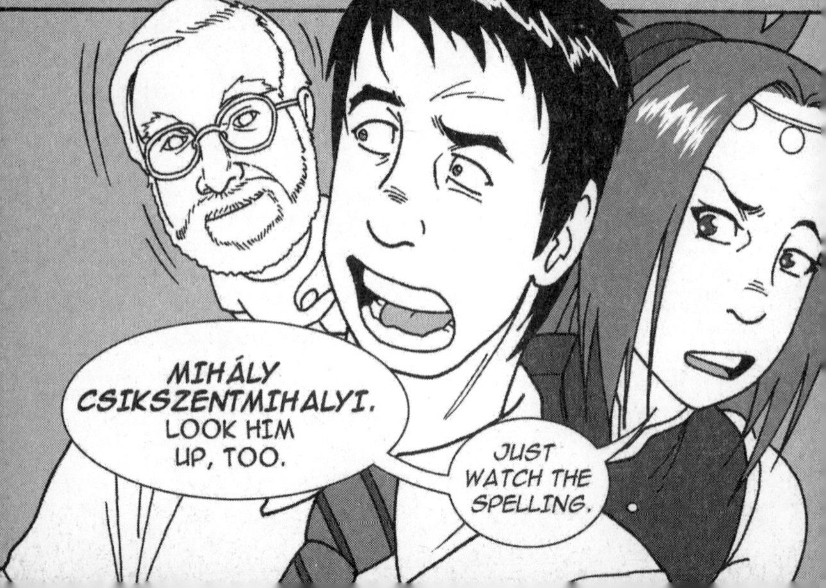
MIHÁLY CSIKSZENTMIHALYI. LOOK HIM UP, TOO.
JUST WATCH THE SPELLING.

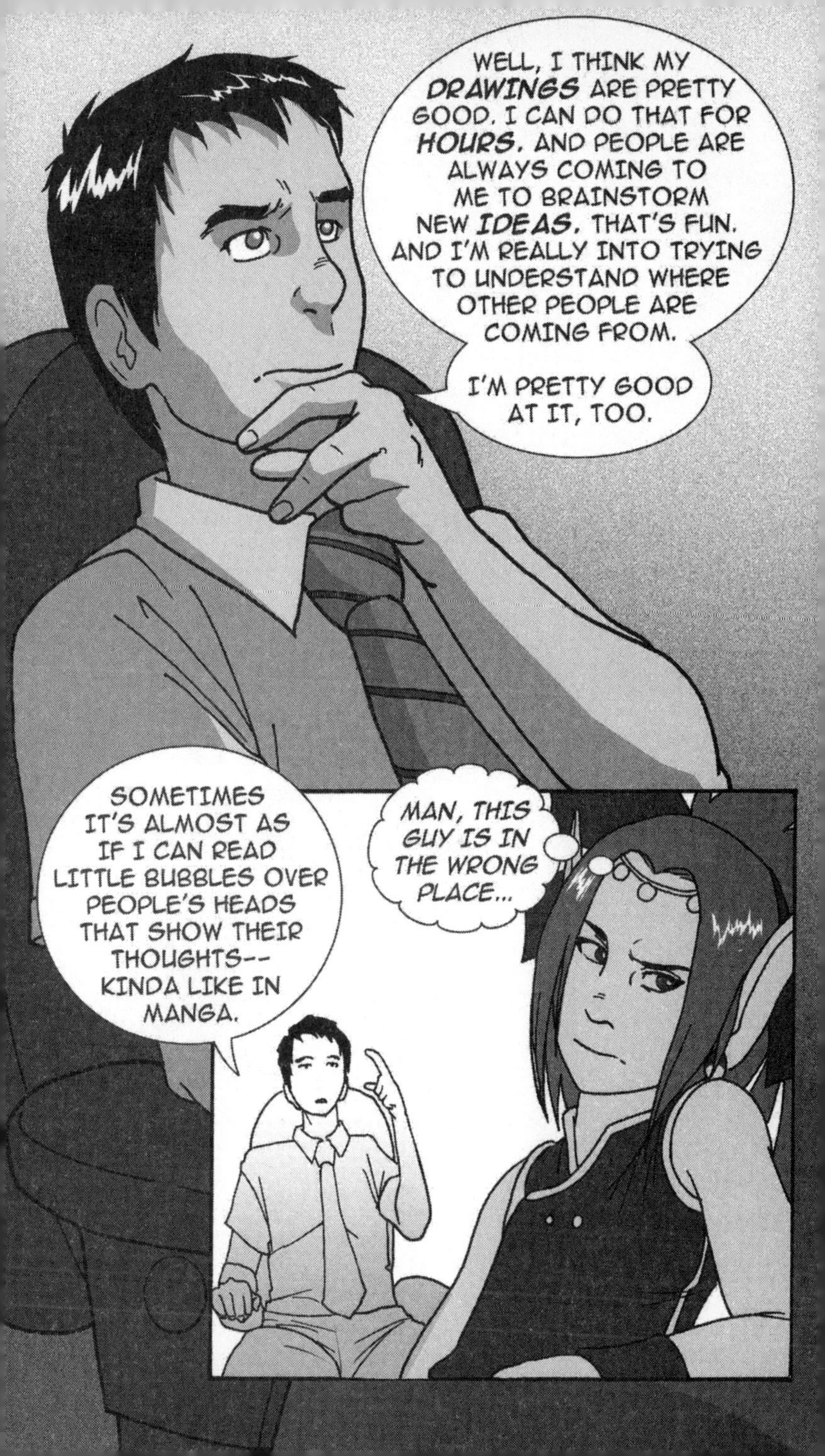

WELL, I THINK MY DRAWINGS ARE PRETTY GOOD. I CAN DO THAT FOR HOURS. AND PEOPLE ARE ALWAYS COMING TO ME TO BRAINSTORM NEW IDEAS. THAT'S FUN. AND I'M REALLY INTO TRYING TO UNDERSTAND WHERE OTHER PEOPLE ARE COMING FROM.
I'M PRETTY GOOD AT IT, TOO.
SOMETIMES IT'S ALMOST AS IF I CAN READ LITTLE BUBBLES OVER PEOPLE'S HEADS THAT SHOW THEIR THOUGHTS-- KINDA LIKE IN MANGA.
MAN, THIS GUY IS IN THE WRONG PLACE...

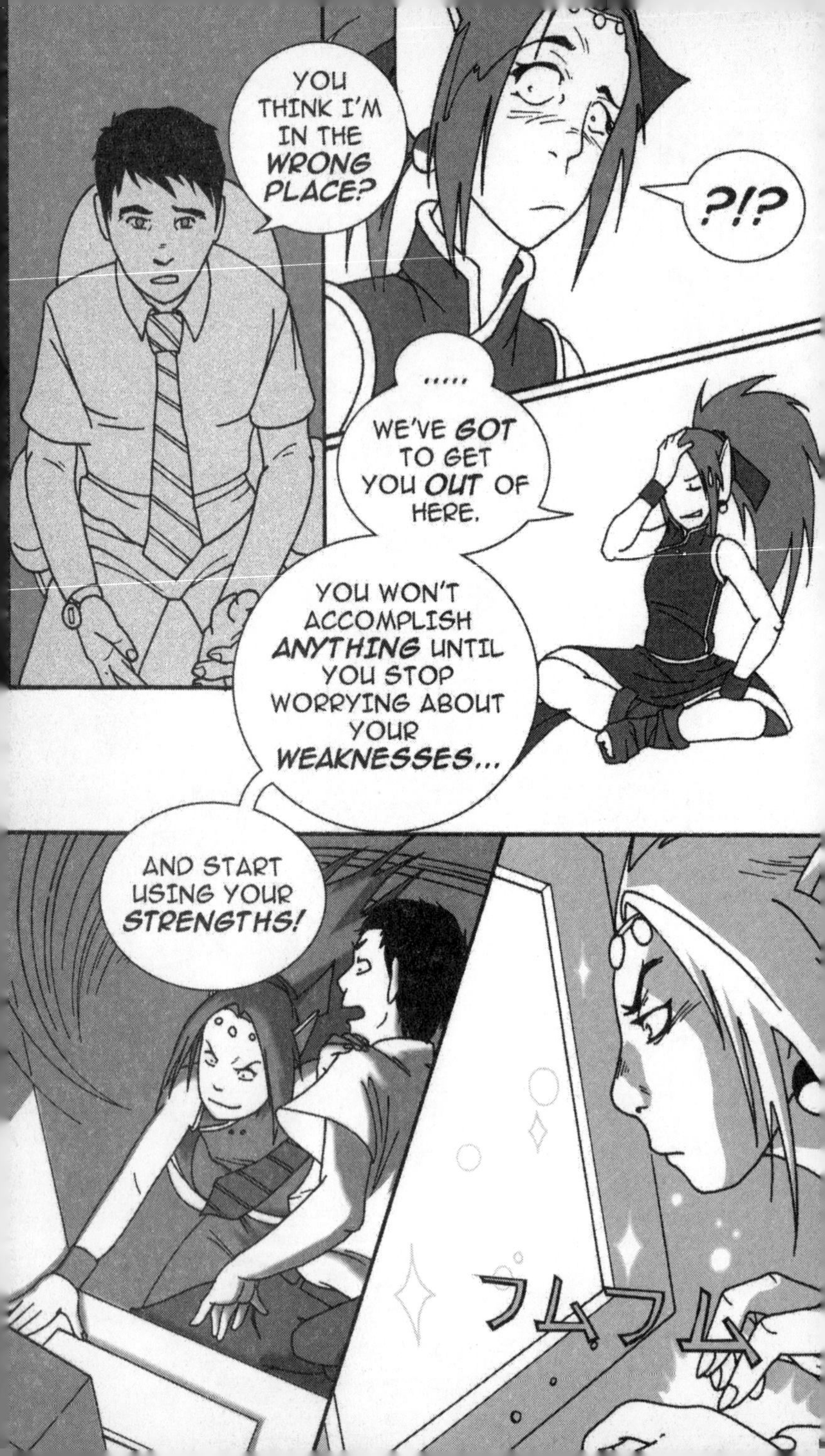
YOU THINK I'M IN THE WRONG PLACE?
?!?
.....
WE'VE GOT TO GET YOU OUT OF HERE.
YOU WON'T ACCOMPLISH ANYTHING UNTIL YOU STOP WORRYING ABOUT YOUR WEAKNESSES...
AND START USING YOUR STRENGTHS!
フムフム

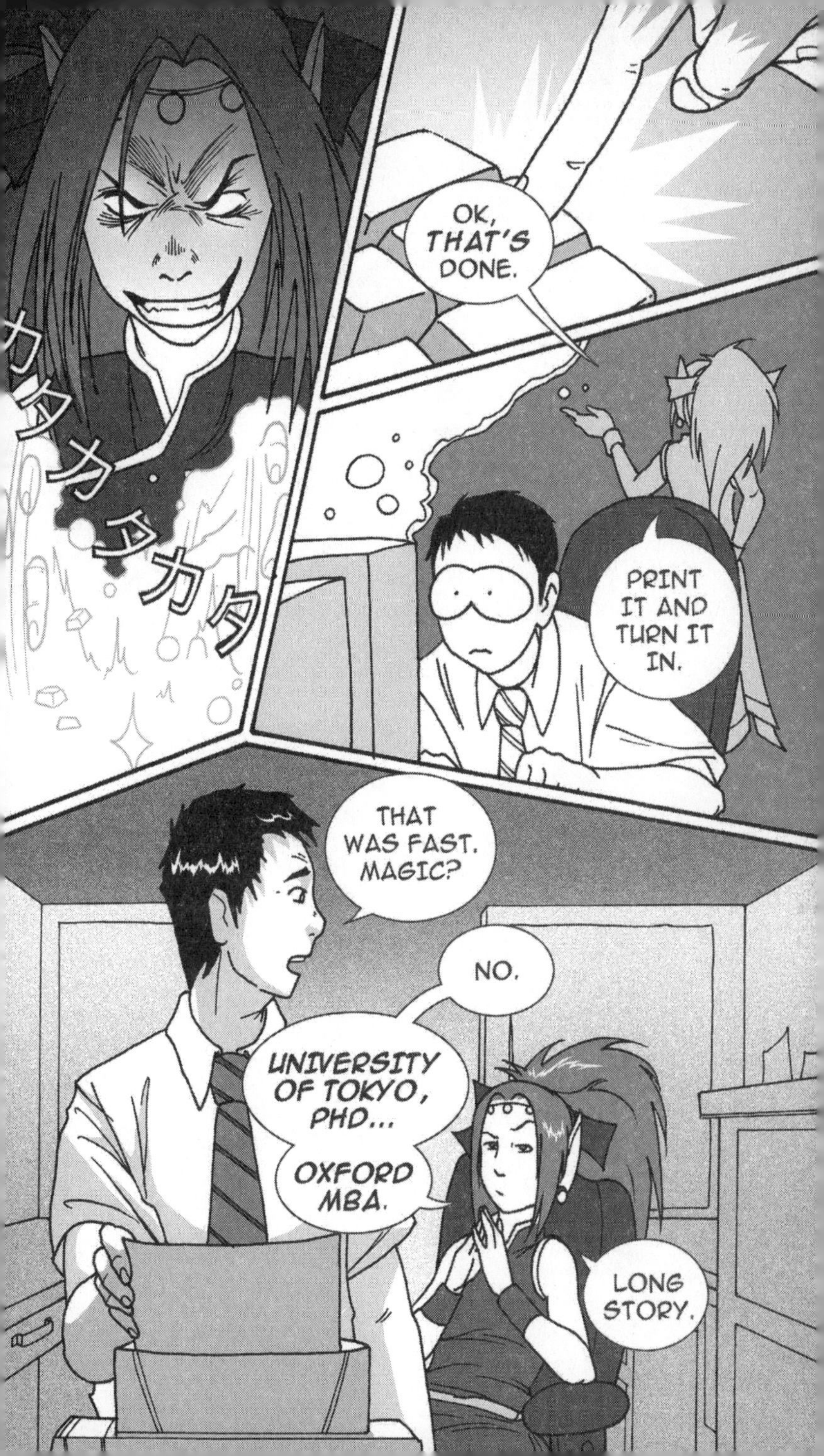
カタカタカタ
OK, THAT'S DONE.
PRINT IT AND TURN IT IN.
THAT WAS FAST. MAGIC?
NO.
UNIVERSITY OF TOKYO, PHD...
OXFORD MBA.
LONG STORY.

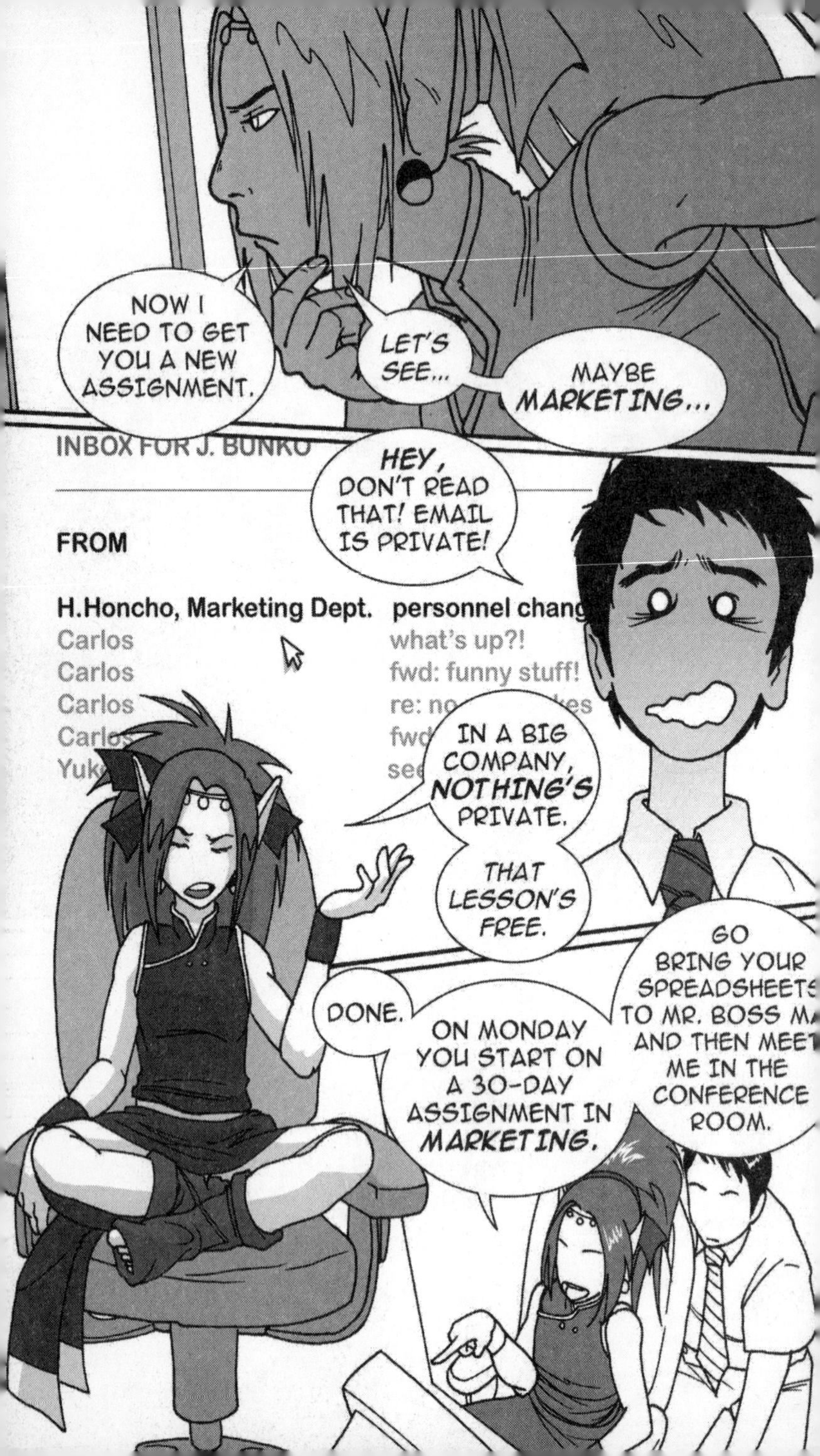
NOW I NEED TO GET YOU A NEW ASSIGNMENT.
LET'S SEE...
MAYBE MARKETING...
INBOX FOR J. BUNKO
FROM
H.Honcho, Marketing Dept.
personnel chang
Carlos
what's up?!
Carlos
fwd: funny stuff!
Carlos
Carlos
HEY, DON'T READ THAT! EMAIL IS PRIVATE!
IN A BIG COMPANY, NOTHING'S PRIVATE.
THAT LESSON'S FREE.
DONE.
ON MONDAY YOU START ON A 30-DAY ASSIGNMENT IN MARKETING.
GO BRING YOUR SPREADSHEETS TO MR. BOSS MA AND THEN MEET ME IN THE CONFERENCE ROOM.

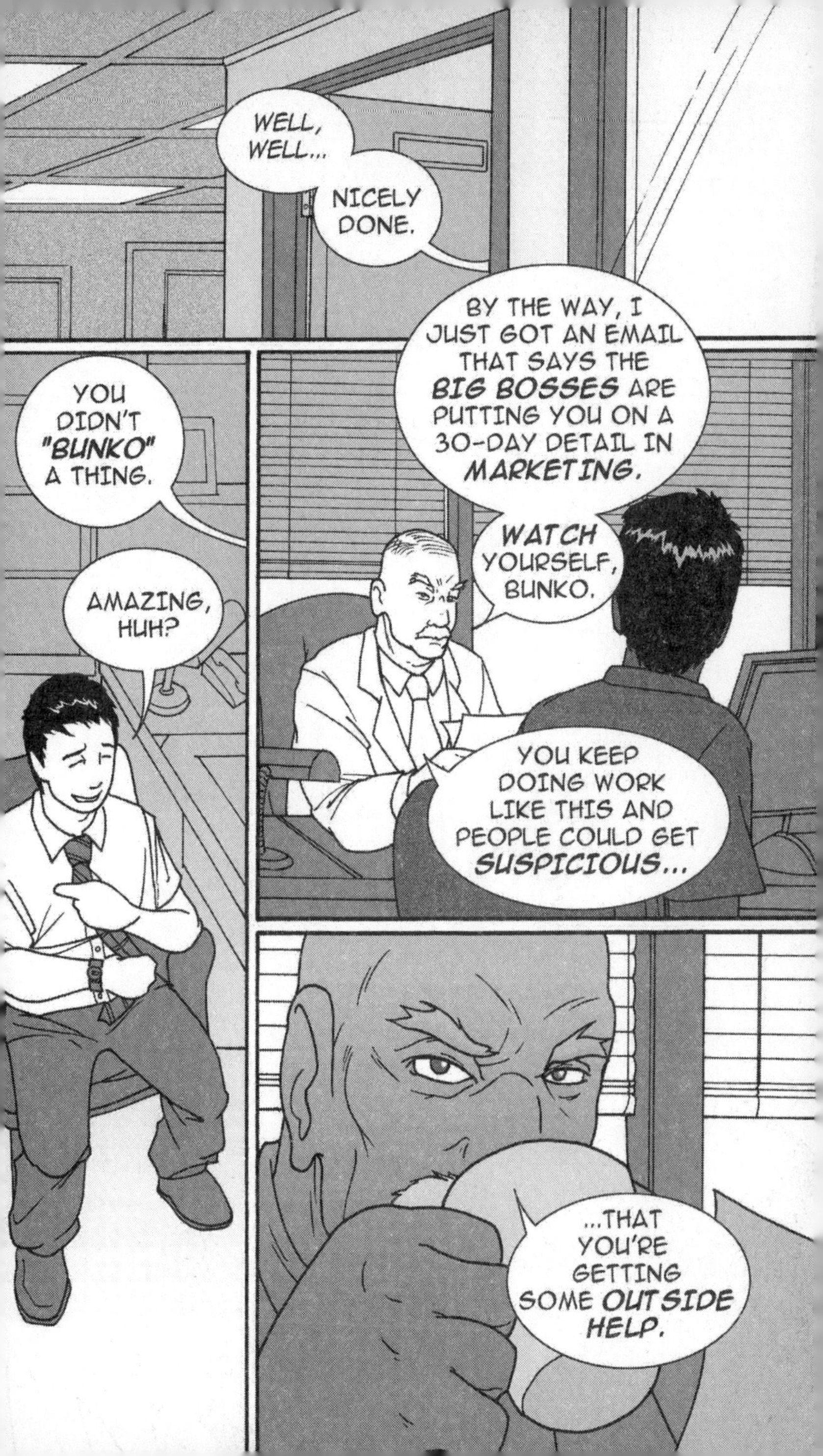
WELL, WELL...
NICELY DONE.
YOU DIDN'T "BUNKO" A THING.
AMAZING, HUH?
BY THE WAY, I JUST GOT AN EMAIL THAT SAYS THE BIG BOSSES ARE PUTTING YOU ON A 30-DAY DETAIL IN MARKETING.
WATCH YOURSELF, BUNKO.
YOU KEEP DOING WORK LIKE THIS AND PEOPLE COULD GET SUSPICIOUS...
...THAT YOU'RE GETTING SOME OUTSIDE HELP.

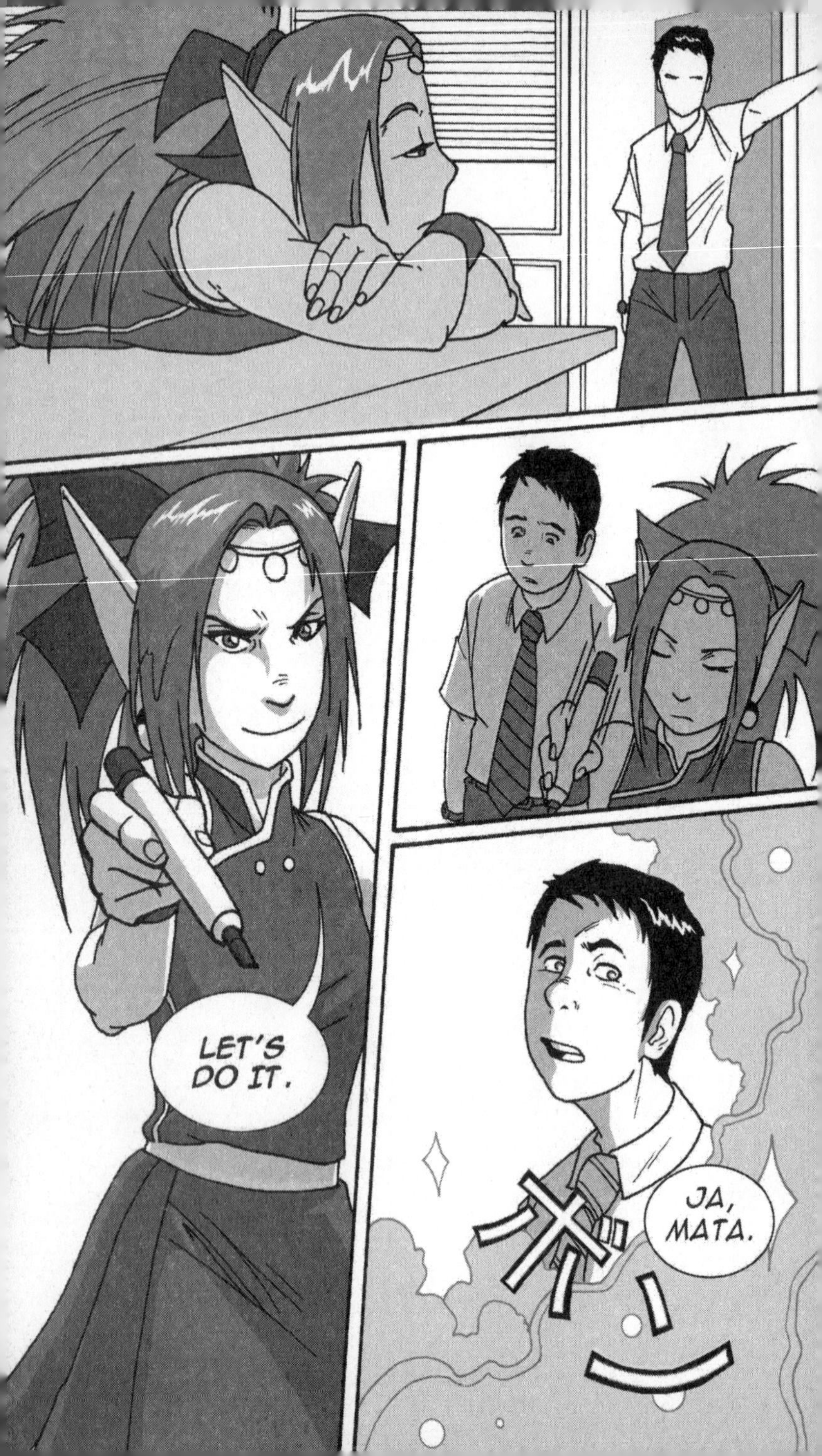
LET'S DO IT.
JA, MATA.

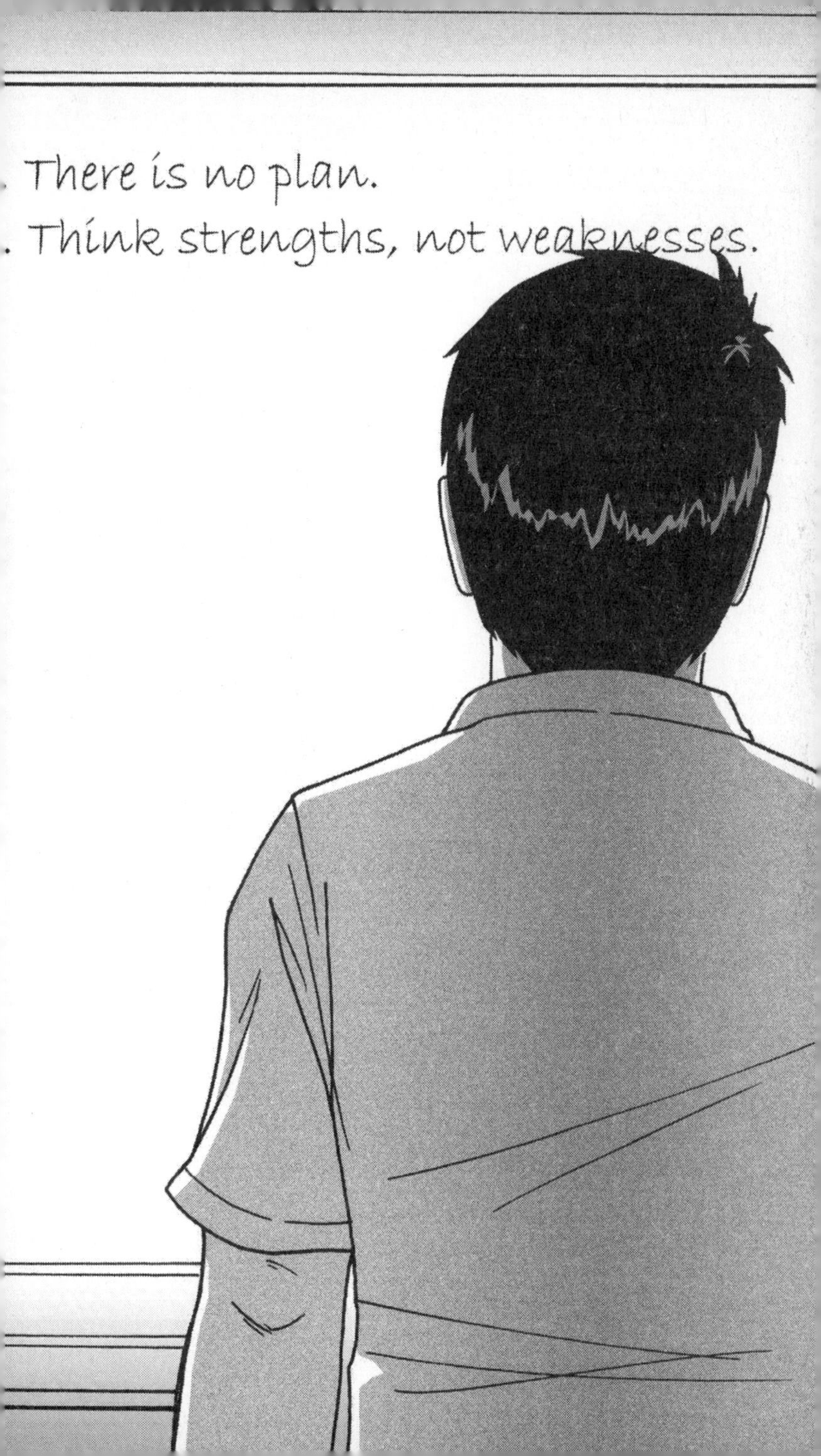
There is no plan.
Think strengths, not weaknesses.

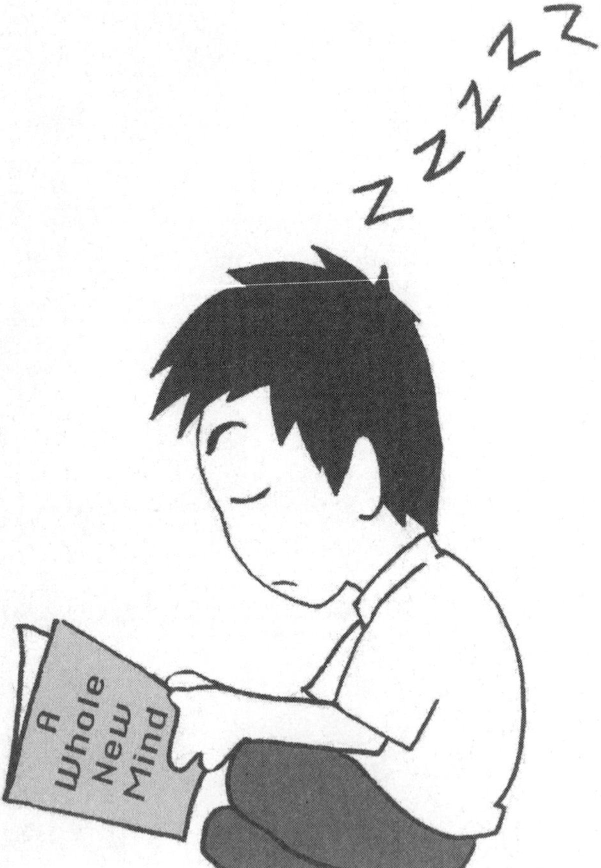

ZZZZZZ
A Whole New Mind

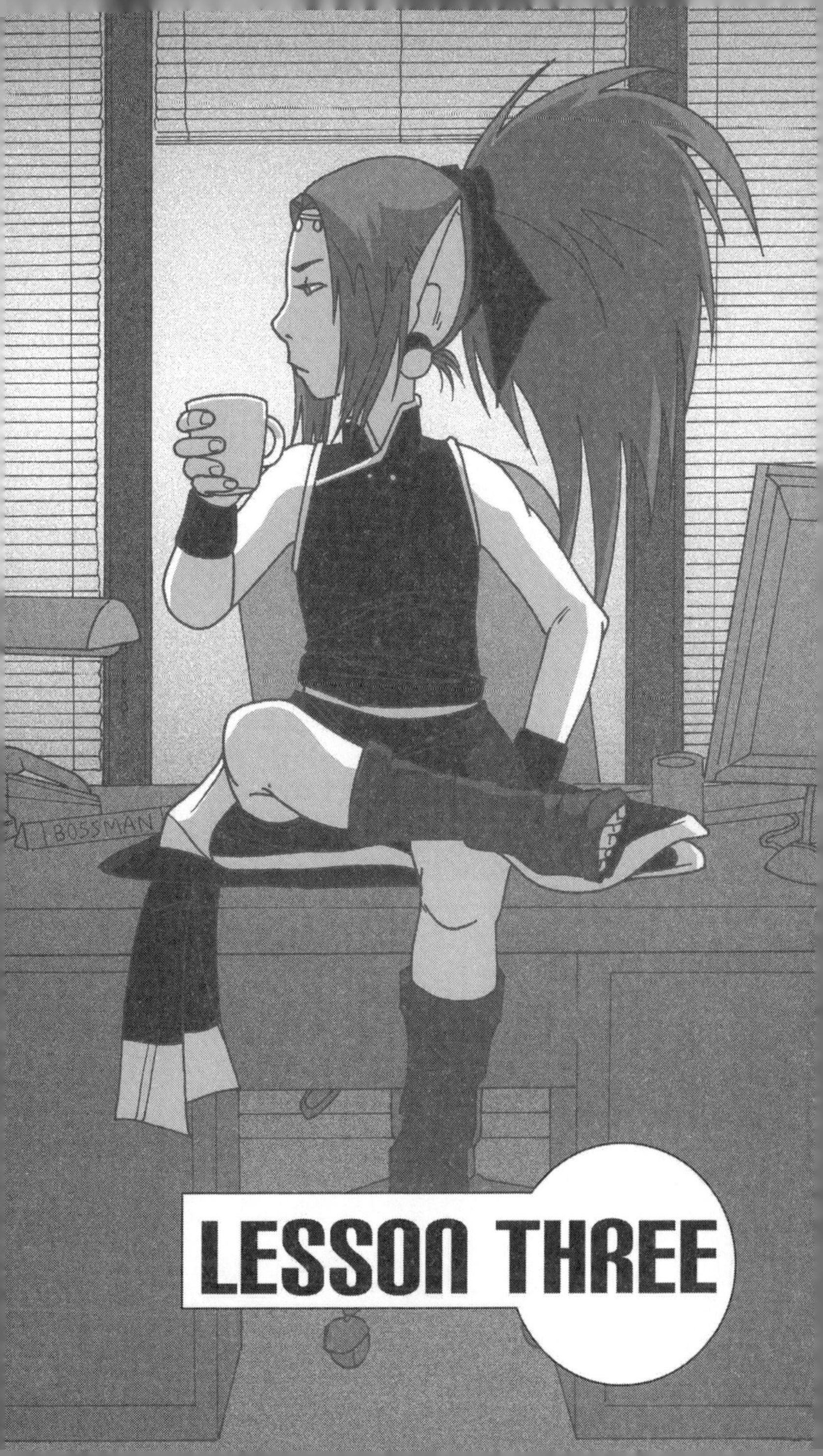
BOSSMAN
LESSON THREE

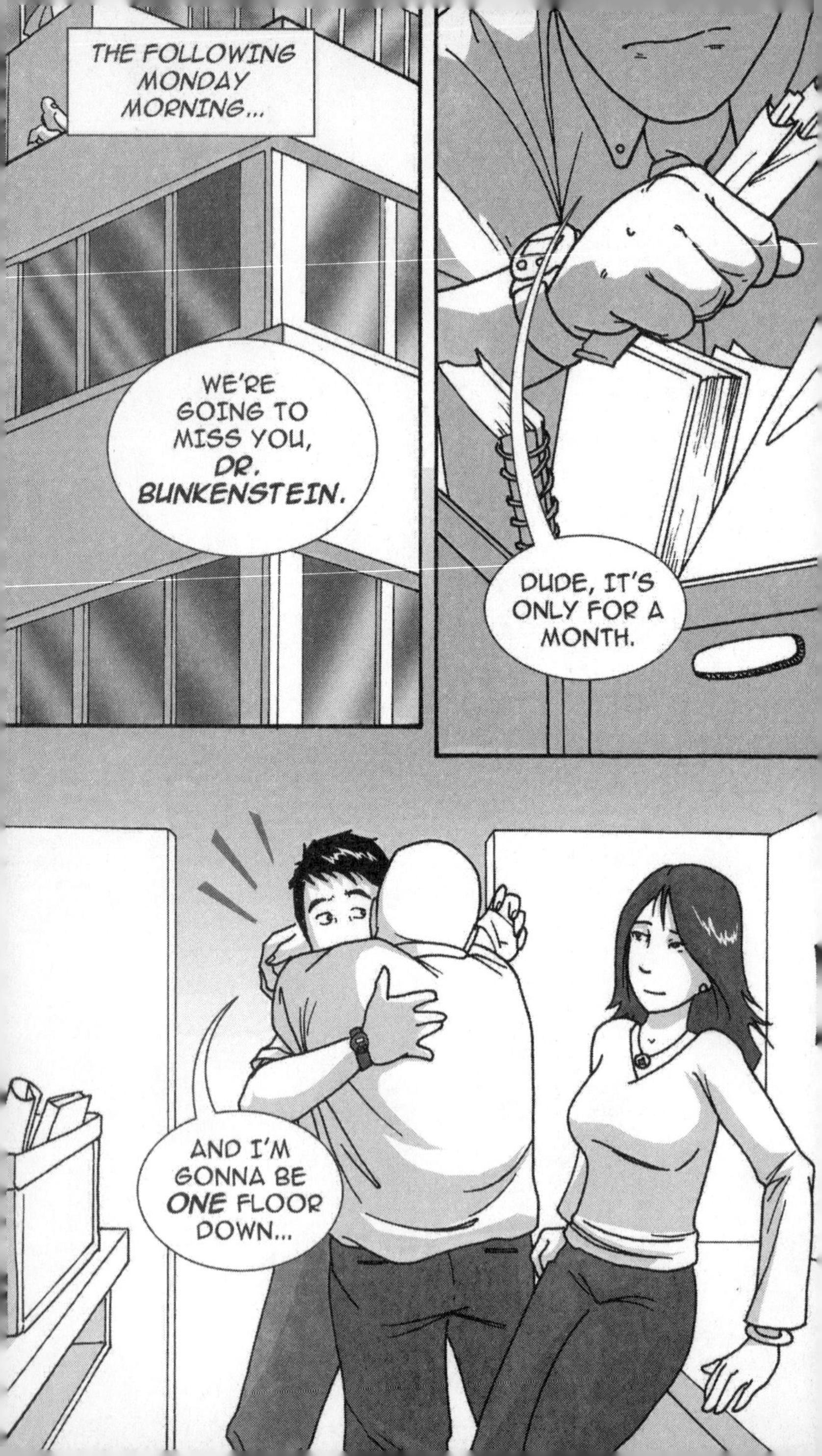
THE FOLLOWING MONDAY MORNING...
WE'RE GOING TO MISS YOU, DR. BUNKENSTEIN.
DUDE, IT'S ONLY FOR A MONTH.
AND I'M GONNA BE ONE FLOOR DOWN...

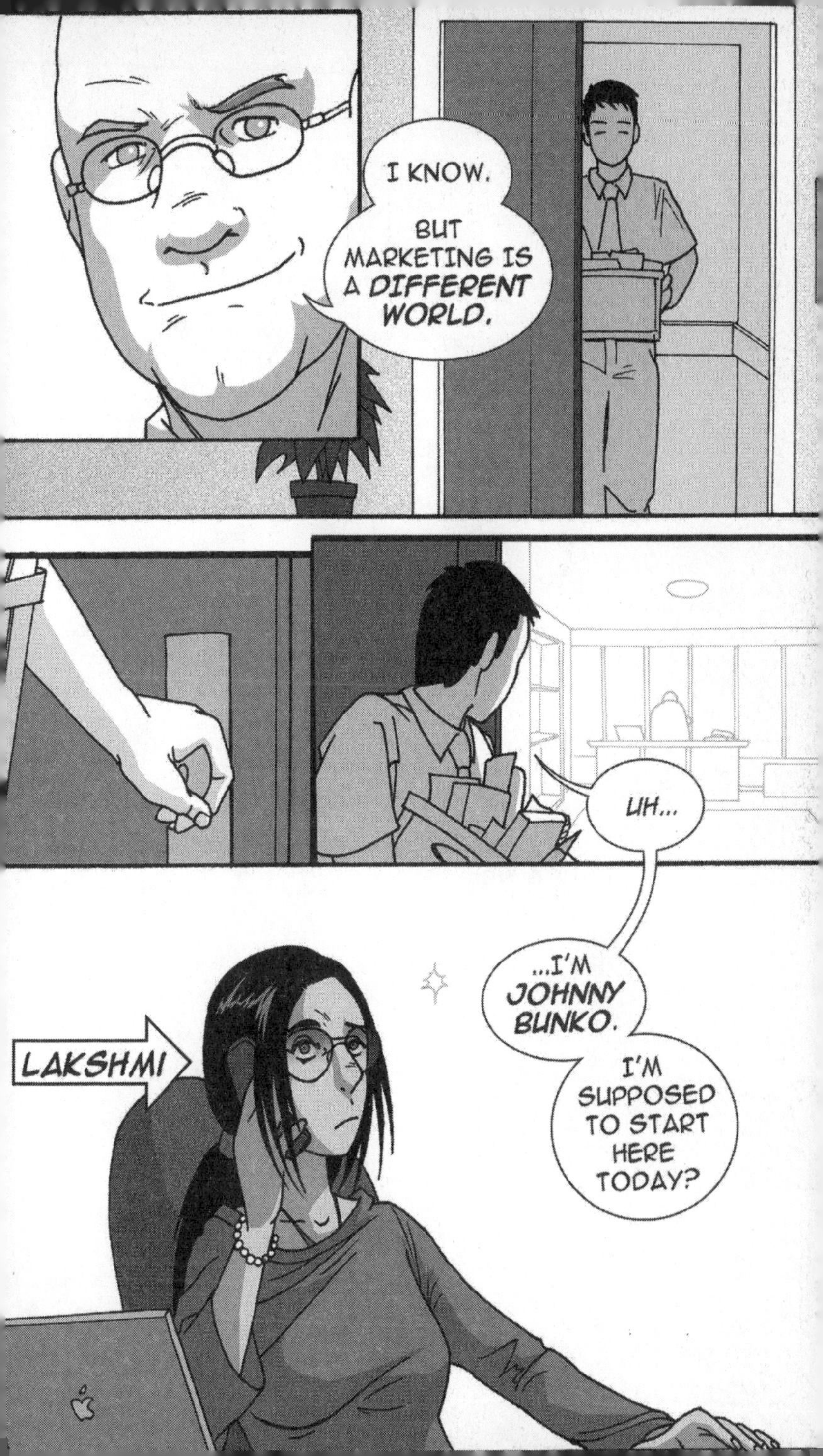
I KNOW.
BUT MARKETING IS A DIFFERENT WORLD.
UH...
...I'M JOHNNY BUNKO.
I'M SUPPOSED TO START HERE TODAY?
LAKSHMI

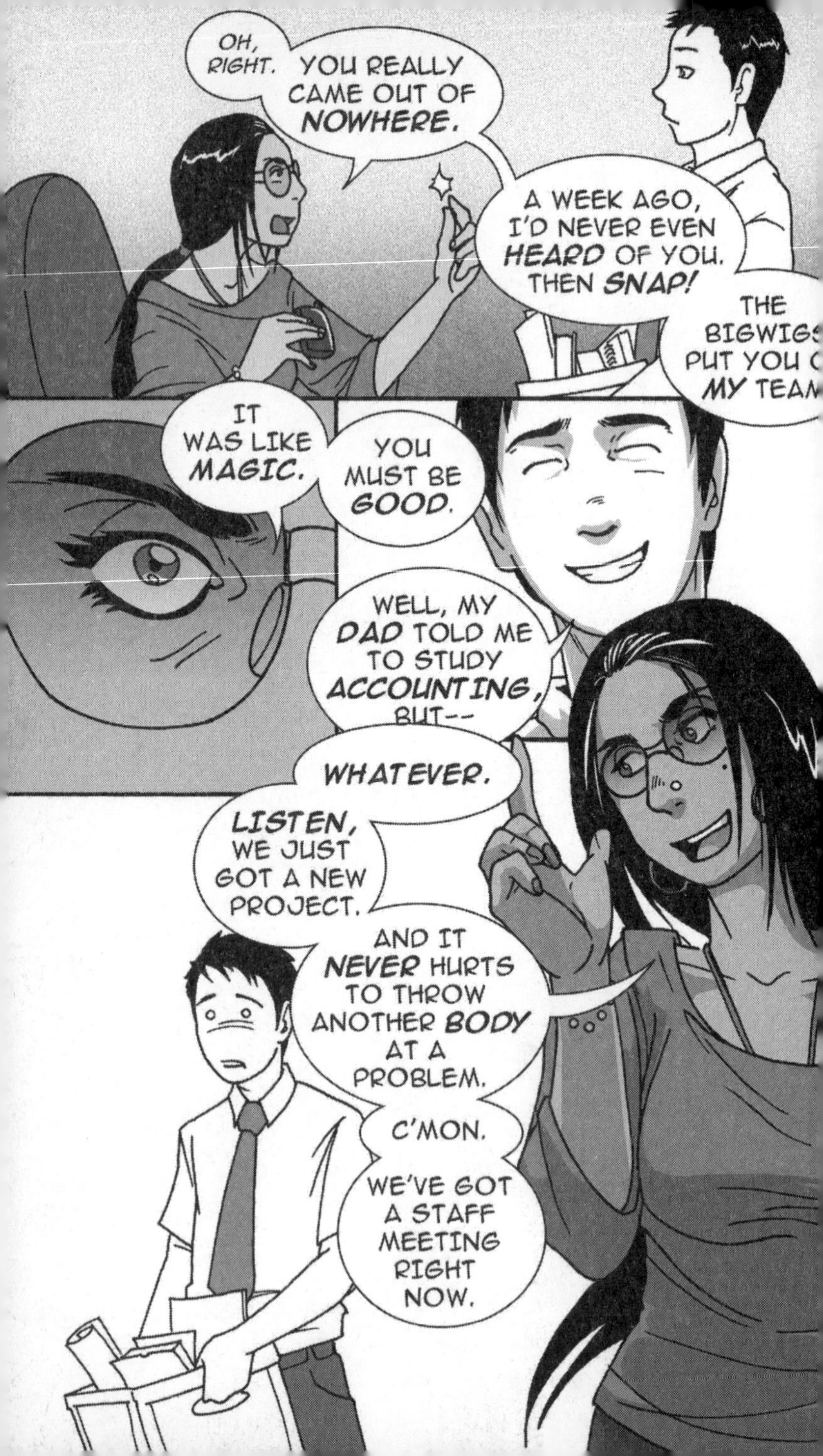
OH, RIGHT.
YOU REALLY CAME OUT OF NOWHERE.
A WEEK AGO, I'D NEVER EVEN HEARD OF YOU. THEN SNAP!
IT WAS LIKE MAGIC.
YOU MUST BE GOOD.
WELL, MY DAD TOLD ME TO STUDY ACCOUNTING, BUT--
WHATEVER.
LISTEN, WE JUST GOT A NEW PROJECT.
AND IT NEVER HURTS TO THROW ANOTHER BODY AT A PROBLEM.
C'MON.
WE'VE GOT A STAFF MEETING RIGHT NOW.

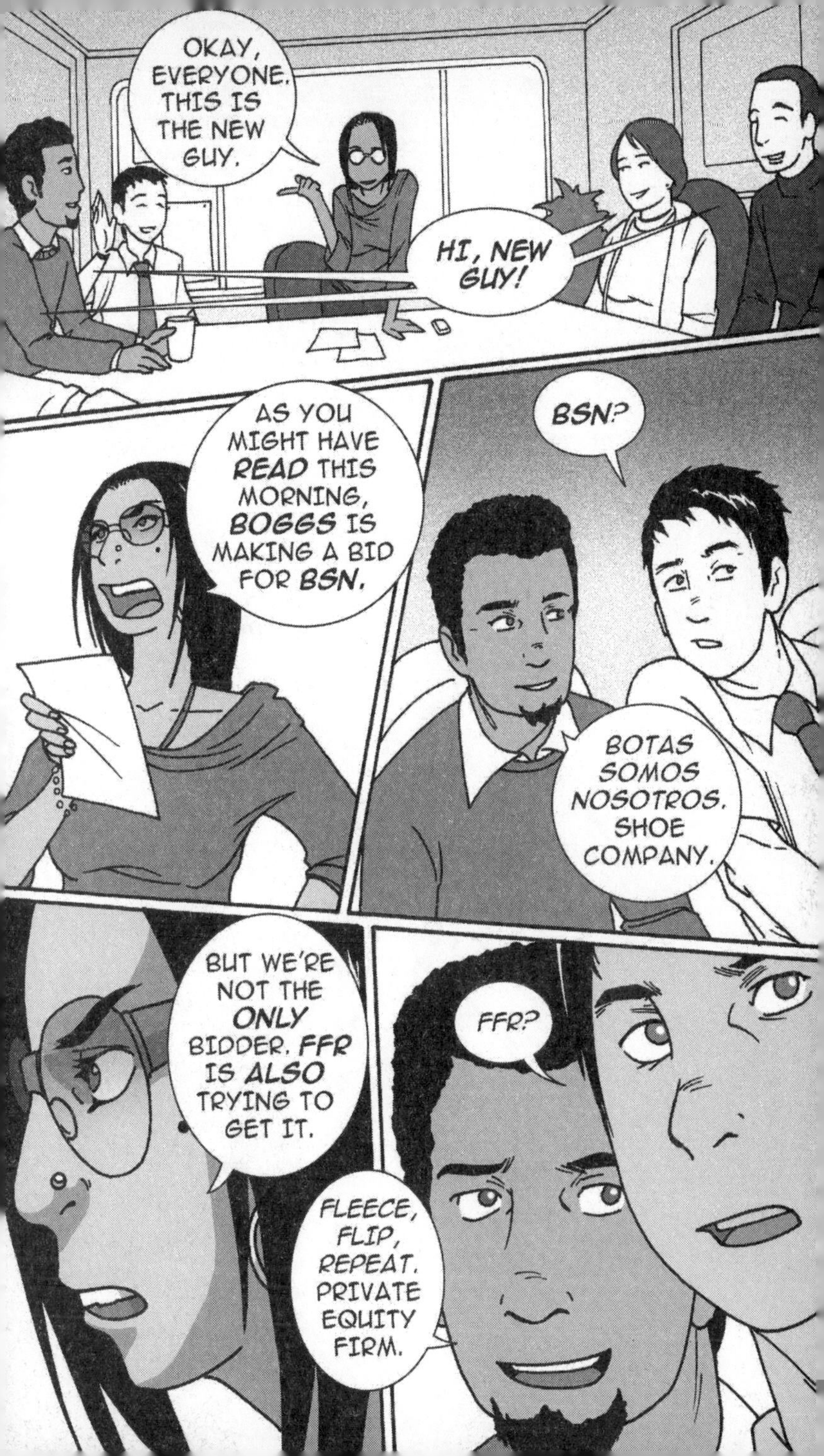
OKAY, EVERYONE. THIS IS THE NEW GUY.
HI, NEW GUY!
AS YOU MIGHT HAVE READ THIS MORNING, BOGGS IS MAKING A BID FOR BSN.
BSN?
BOTAS SOMOS NOSOTROS. SHOE COMPANY.
BUT WE'RE NOT THE ONLY BIDDER. FFR IS ALSO TRYING TO GET IT.
FFR?
FLEECE, FLIP, REPEAT. PRIVATE EQUITY FIRM.

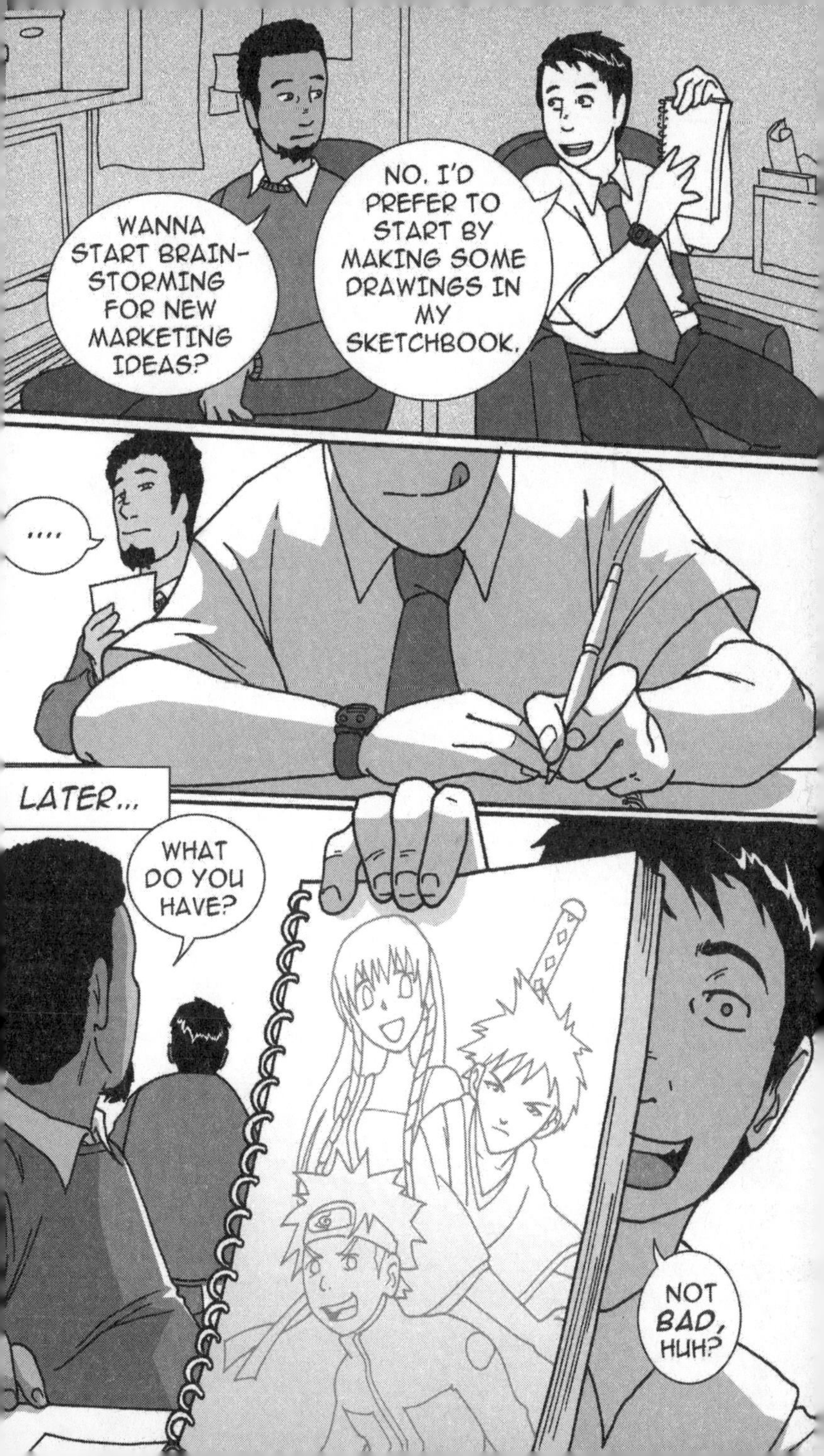
WANNA START BRAIN-STORMING FOR NEW MARKETING IDEAS?
NO. I'D PREFER TO START BY MAKING SOME DRAWINGS IN MY SKETCHBOOK.
....
LATER...
WHAT DO YOU HAVE?
NOT BAD, HUH?

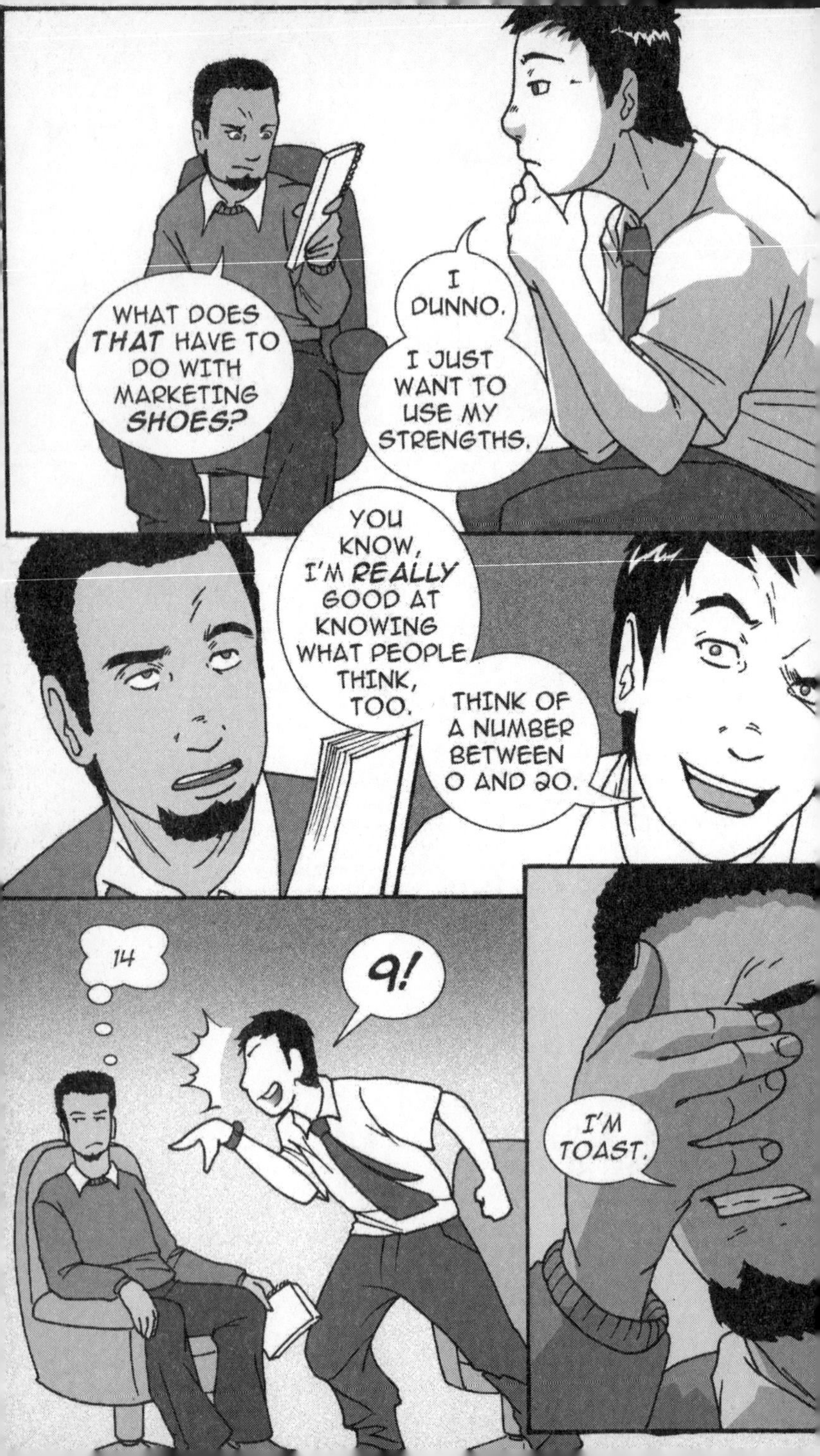
WHAT DOES THAT HAVE TO DO WITH MARKETING SHOES?
I DUNNO.
I JUST WANT TO USE MY STRENGTHS.
YOU KNOW, I'M REALLY GOOD AT KNOWING WHAT PEOPLE THINK, TOO.
THINK OF A NUMBER BETWEEN 0 AND 20.
14
9!
I'M TOAST.

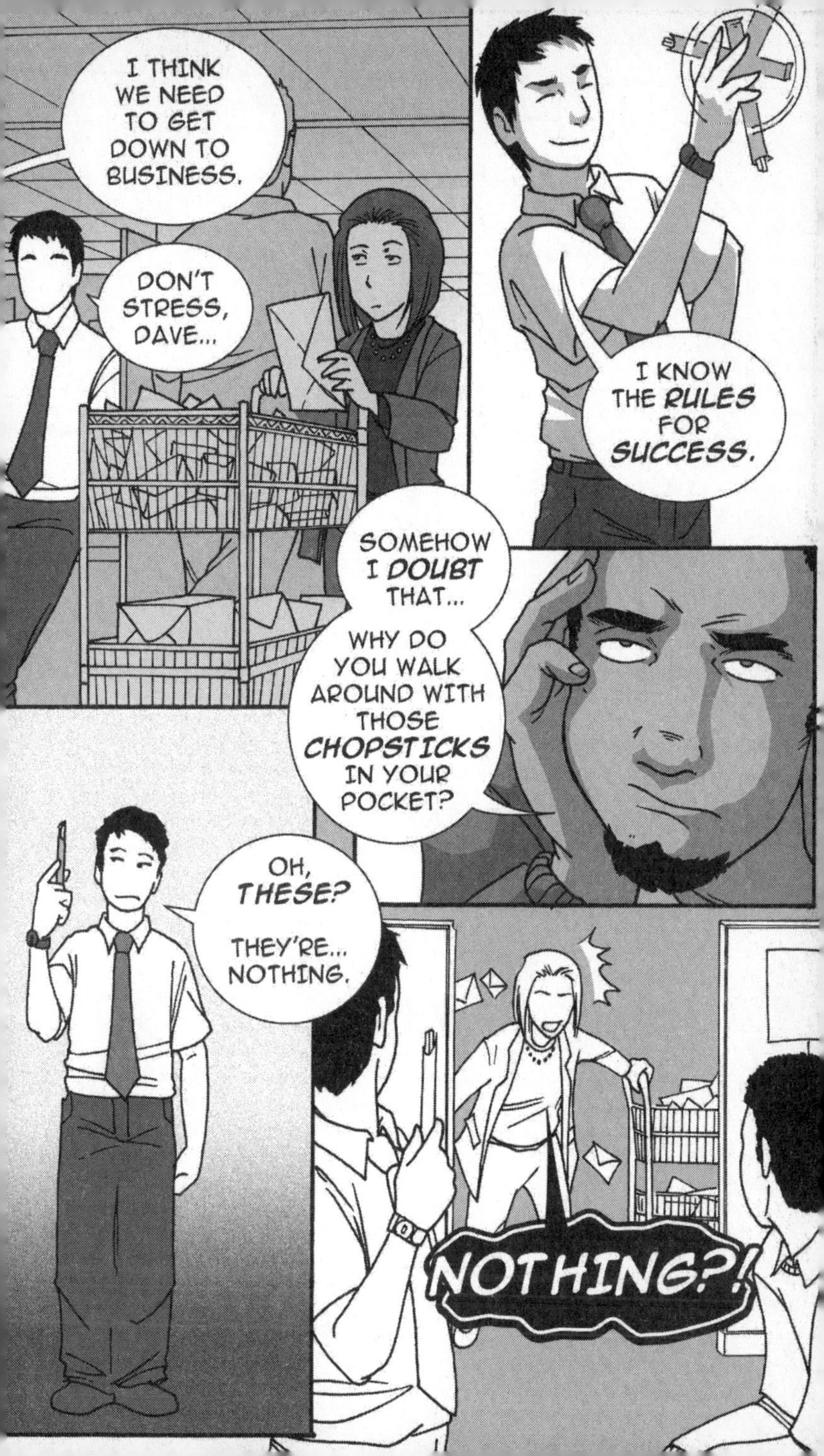
I THINK WE NEED TO GET DOWN TO BUSINESS.
DON'T STRESS, DAVE...
I KNOW THE RULES FOR SUCCESS.
SOMEHOW I DOUBT THAT...
WHY DO YOU WALK AROUND WITH THOSE CHOPSTICKS IN YOUR POCKET?
OH, THESE?
THEY'RE... NOTHING.
NOTHING?!

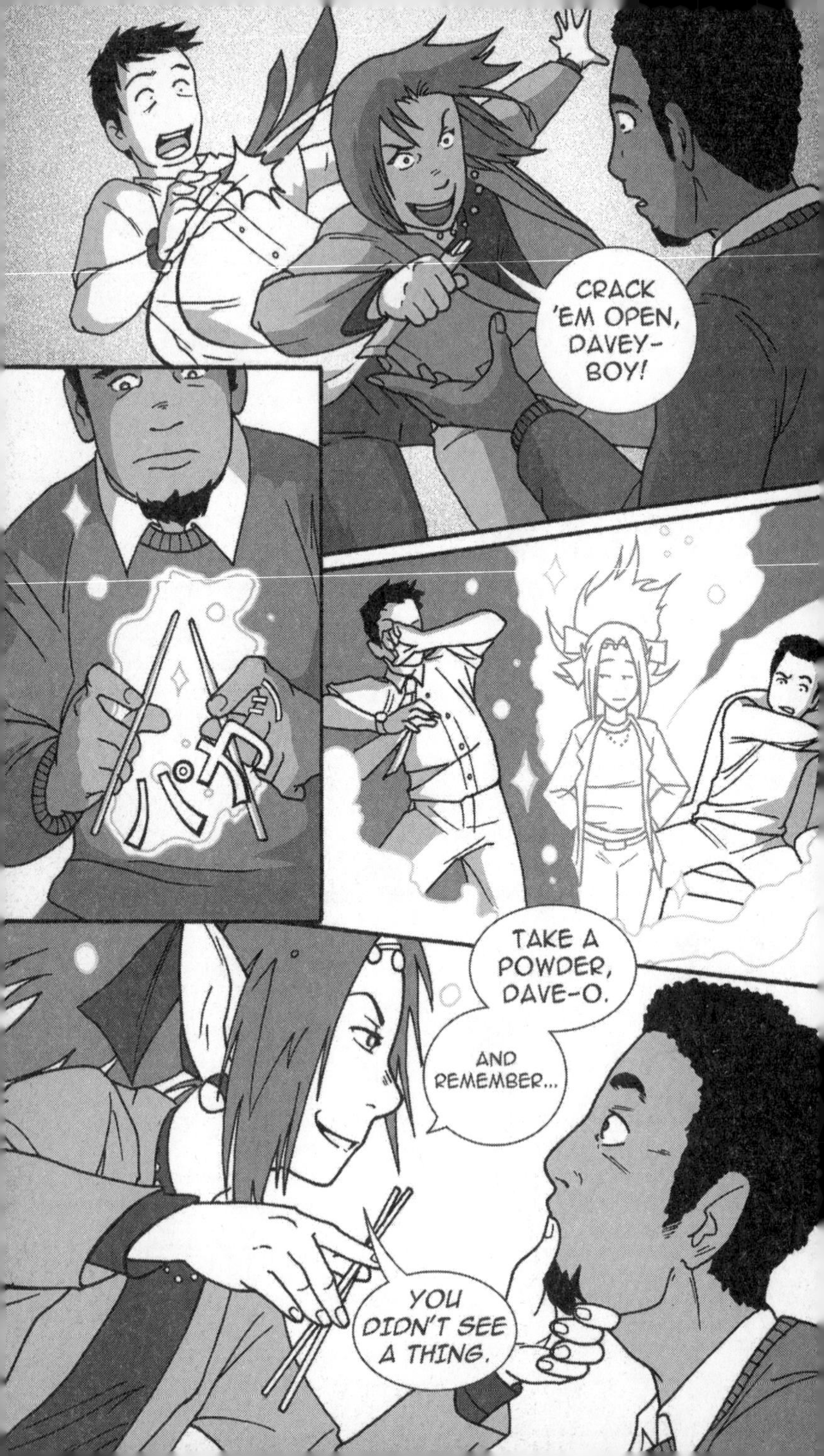
CRACK 'EM OPEN, DAVEY-BOY!
TAKE A POWDER, DAVE-O.
AND REMEMBER...
YOU DIDN'T SEE A THING.

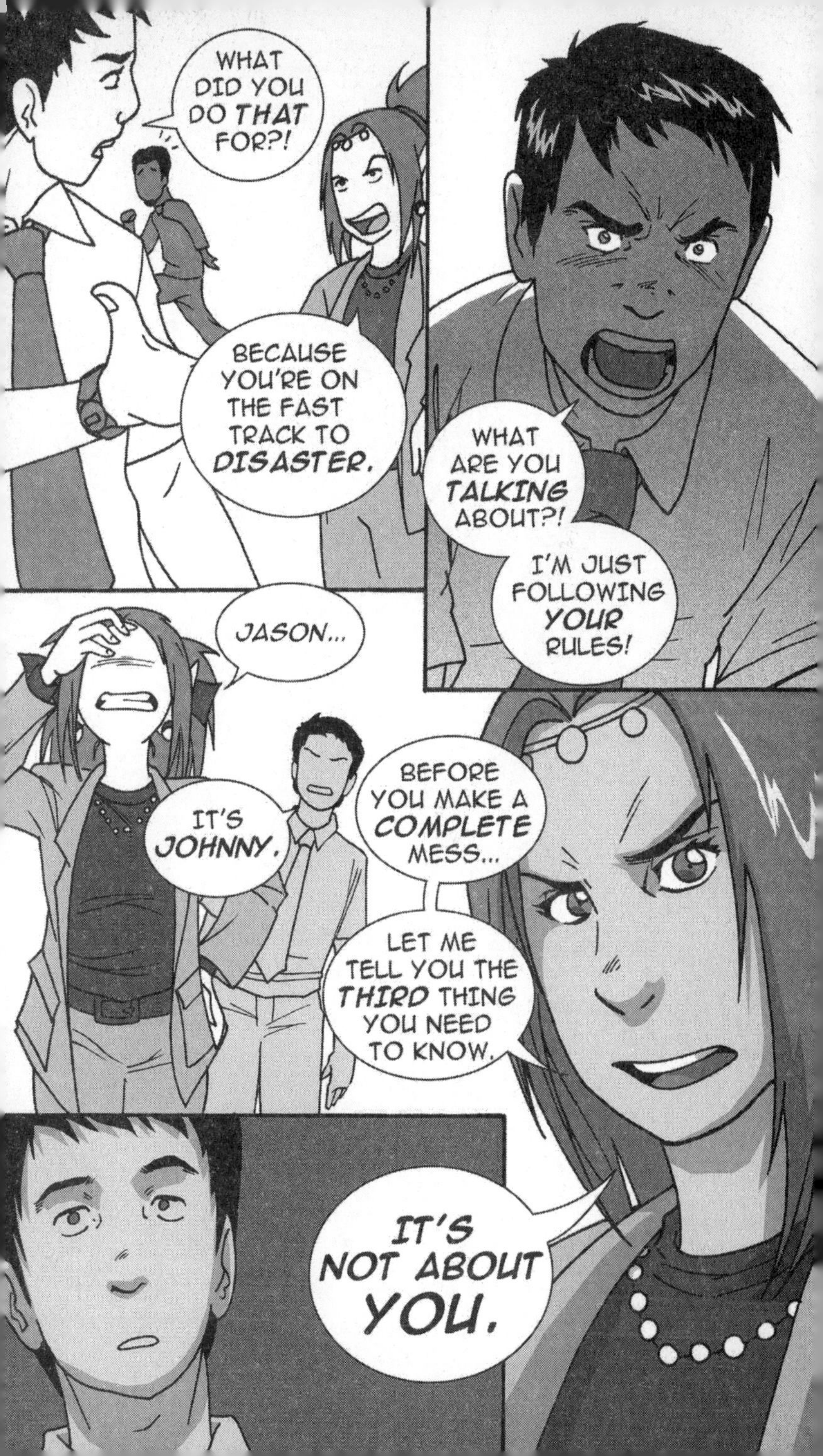
WHAT DID YOU DO THAT FOR?!
BECAUSE YOU'RE ON THE FAST TRACK TO DISASTER.
WHAT ARE YOU TALKING ABOUT?!
I'M JUST FOLLOWING YOUR RULES!
JASON...
IT'S JOHNNY.
BEFORE YOU MAKE A COMPLETE MESS...
LET ME TELL YOU THE THIRD THING YOU NEED TO KNOW.
IT'S NOT ABOUT YOU.

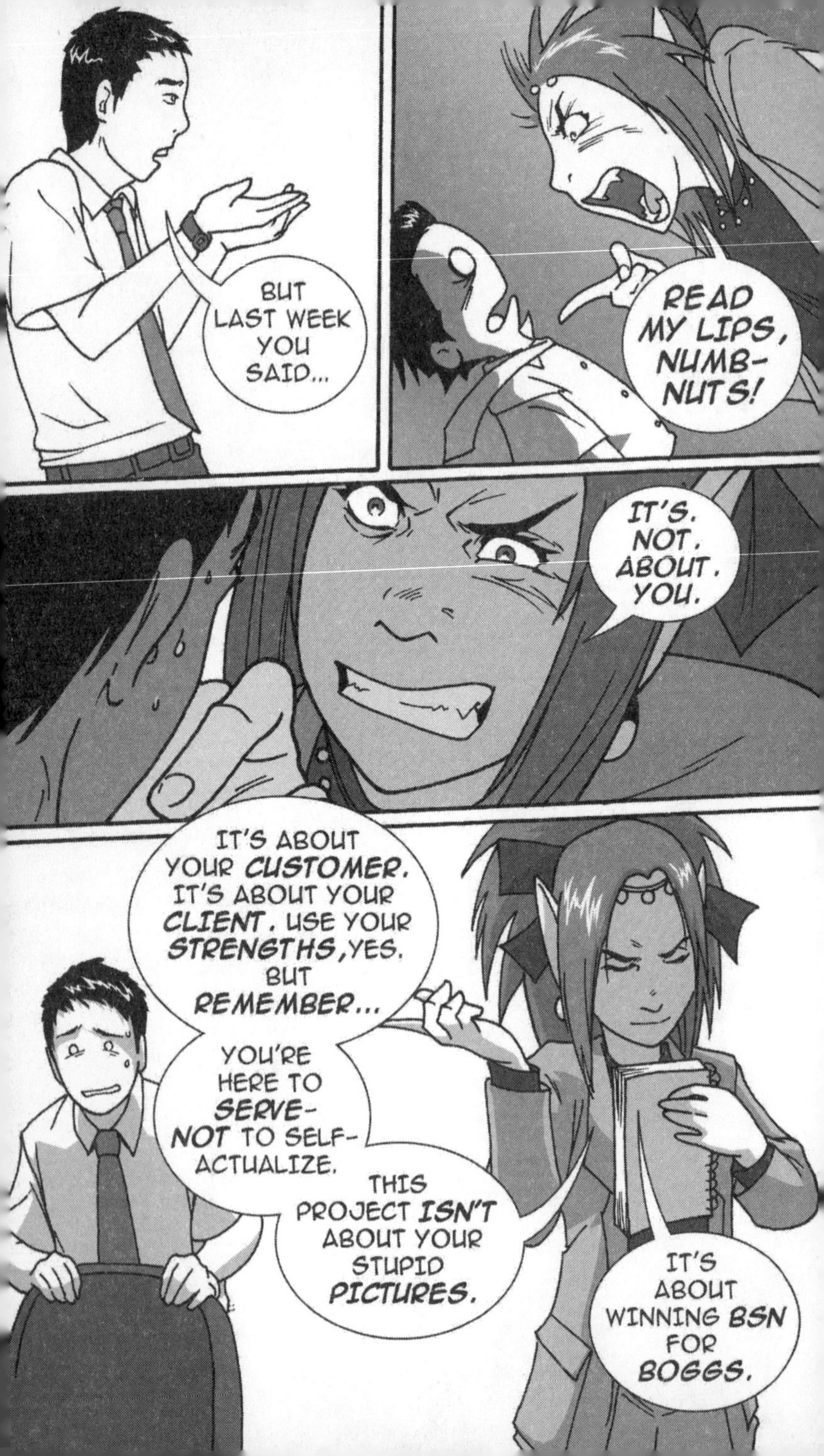
BUT LAST WEEK YOU SAID...
READ MY LIPS, NUMB-NUTS!
IT'S. NOT. ABOUT. YOU.
IT'S ABOUT YOUR **CUSTOMER**. IT'S ABOUT YOUR **CLIENT**. USE YOUR **STRENGTHS**, YES. BUT **REMEMBER...**
YOU'RE HERE TO **SERVE**- **NOT** TO SELF-ACTUALIZE.
THIS PROJECT **ISN'T** ABOUT YOUR STUPID **PICTURES**.
IT'S ABOUT WINNING **BSN** FOR **BOGGS**.

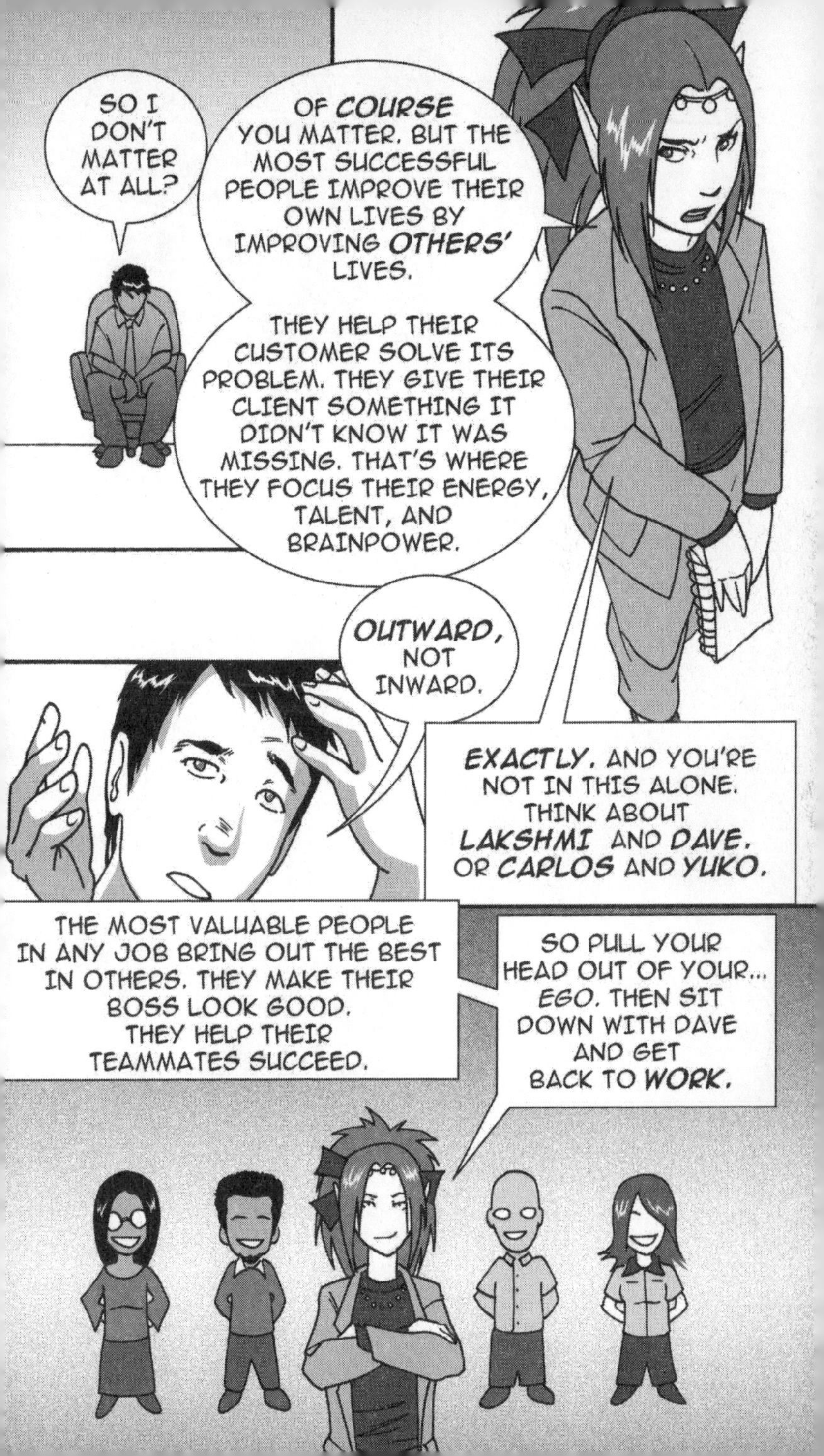
SO I DON'T MATTER AT ALL?
OF COURSE YOU MATTER. BUT THE MOST SUCCESSFUL PEOPLE IMPROVE THEIR OWN LIVES BY IMPROVING OTHERS' LIVES.
THEY HELP THEIR CUSTOMER SOLVE ITS PROBLEM. THEY GIVE THEIR CLIENT SOMETHING IT DIDN'T KNOW IT WAS MISSING. THAT'S WHERE THEY FOCUS THEIR ENERGY, TALENT, AND BRAINPOWER.
OUTWARD, NOT INWARD.
EXACTLY. AND YOU'RE NOT IN THIS ALONE. THINK ABOUT LAKSHMI AND DAVE. OR CARLOS AND YUKO.
THE MOST VALUABLE PEOPLE IN ANY JOB BRING OUT THE BEST IN OTHERS. THEY MAKE THEIR BOSS LOOK GOOD. THEY HELP THEIR TEAMMATES SUCCEED.
SO PULL YOUR HEAD OUT OF YOUR... EGO. THEN SIT DOWN WITH DAVE AND GET BACK TO WORK.

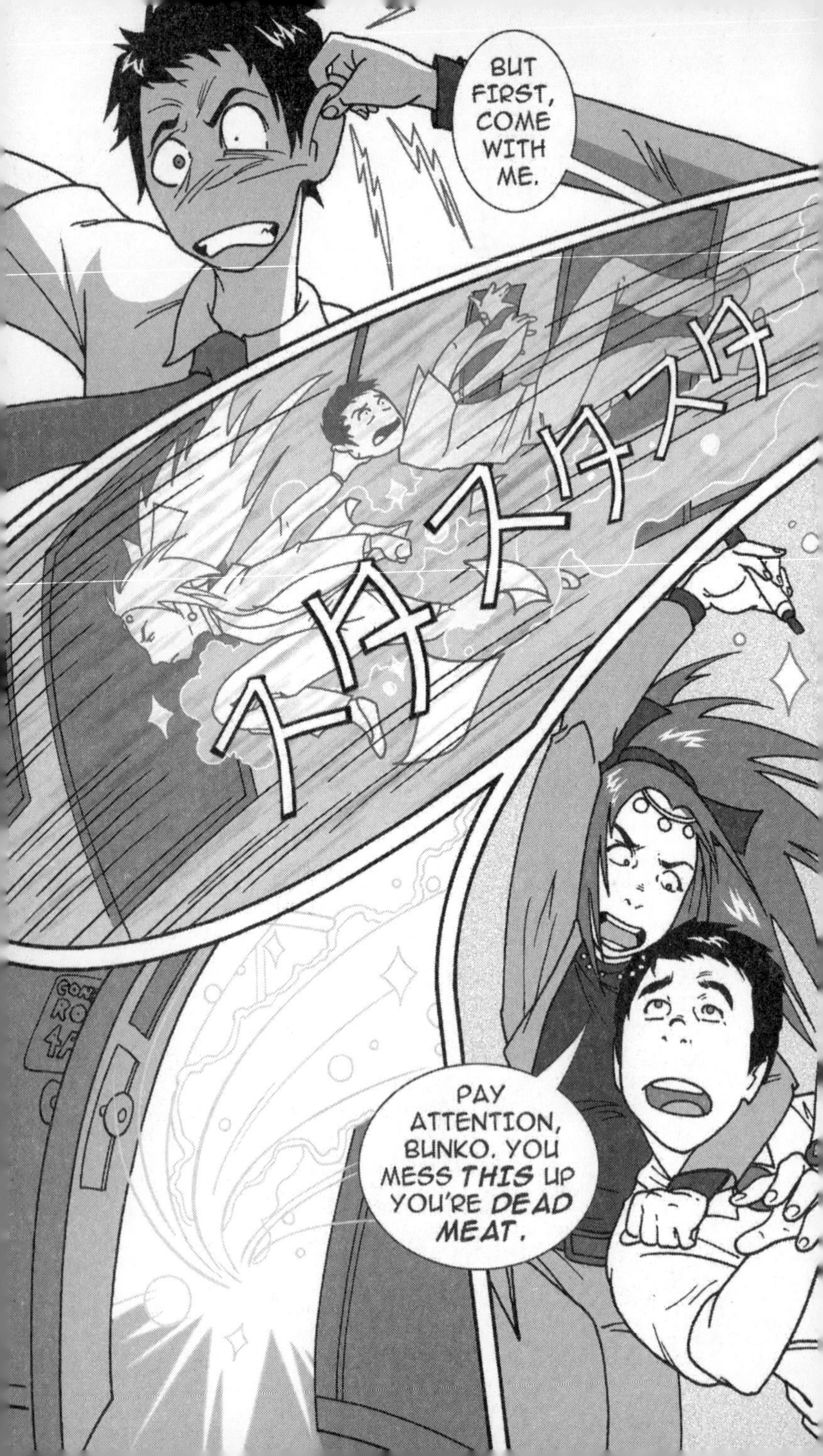
BUT FIRST, COME WITH ME.
PAY ATTENTION, BUNKO. YOU MESS THIS UP YOU'RE DEAD MEAT.

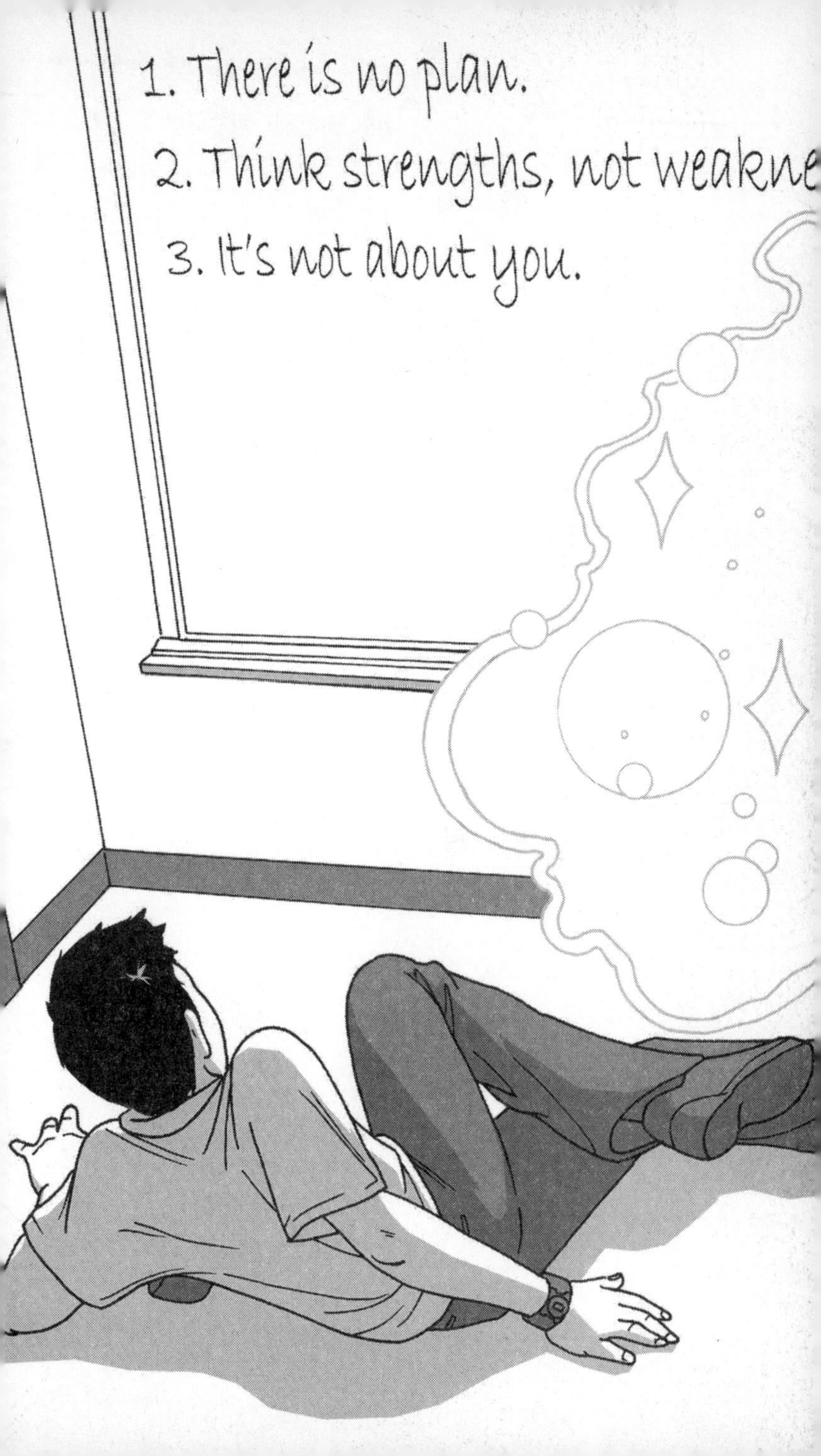
1. There is no plan.
2. Think strengths, not weakne
3. It's not about you.

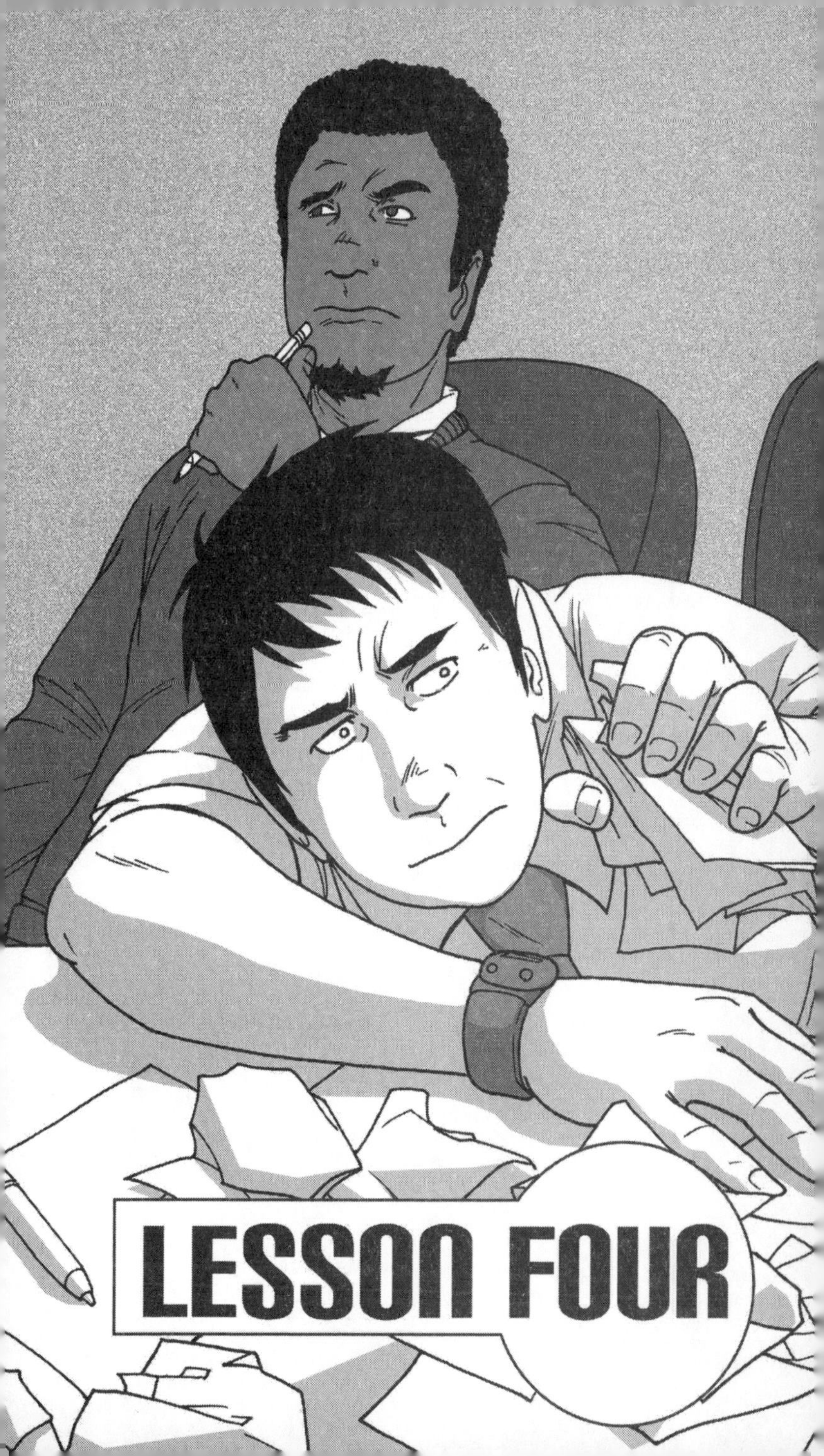

LESSON FOUR

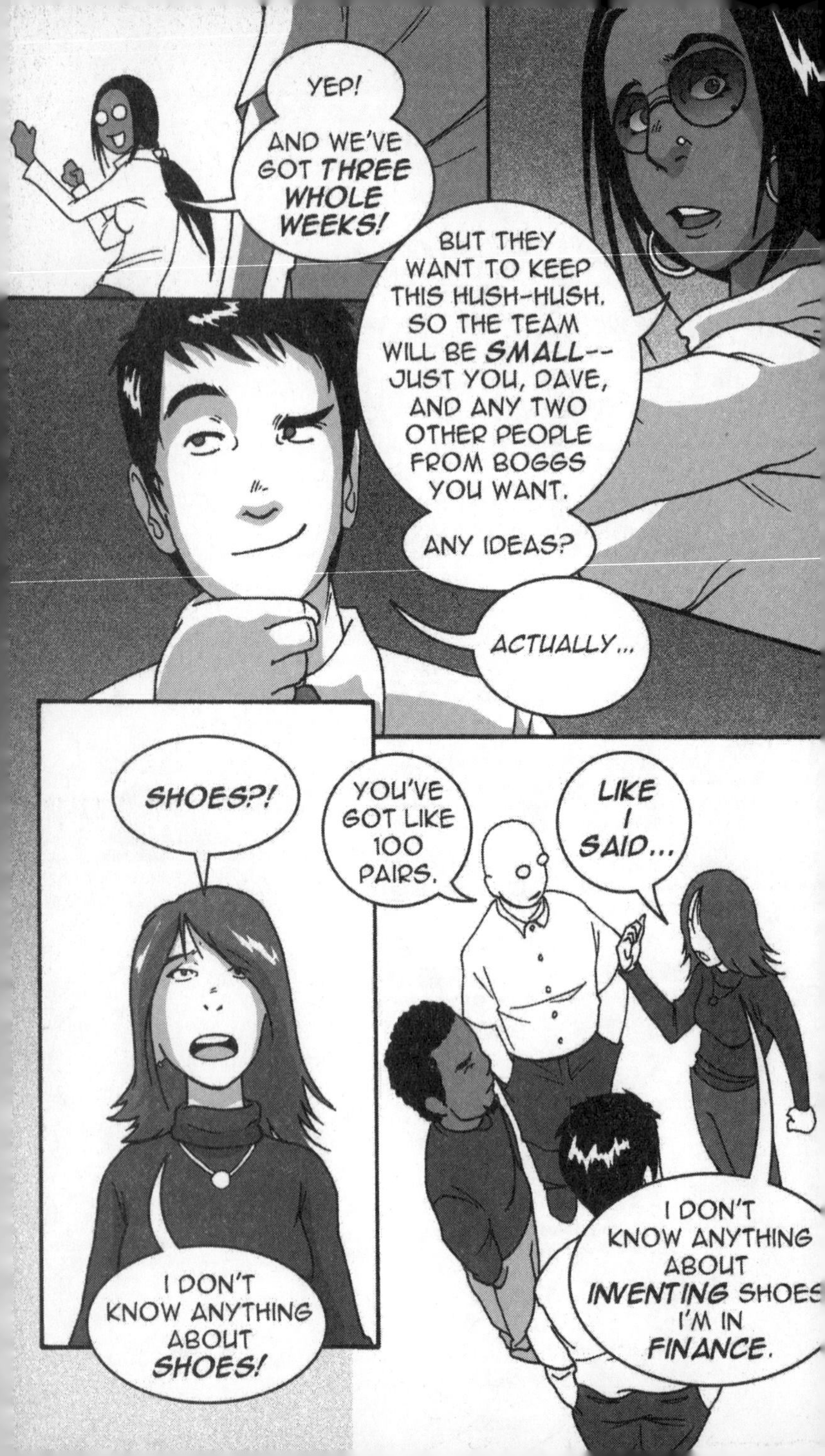

YEP!
AND WE'VE GOT THREE WHOLE WEEKS!
BUT THEY WANT TO KEEP THIS HUSH-HUSH. SO THE TEAM WILL BE SMALL-- JUST YOU, DAVE, AND ANY TWO OTHER PEOPLE FROM BOGGS YOU WANT.
ANY IDEAS?
ACTUALLY...
SHOES?!
I DON'T KNOW ANYTHING ABOUT SHOES!
YOU'VE GOT LIKE 100 PAIRS.
LIKE I SAID...
I DON'T KNOW ANYTHING ABOUT INVENTING SHOES. I'M IN FINANCE.

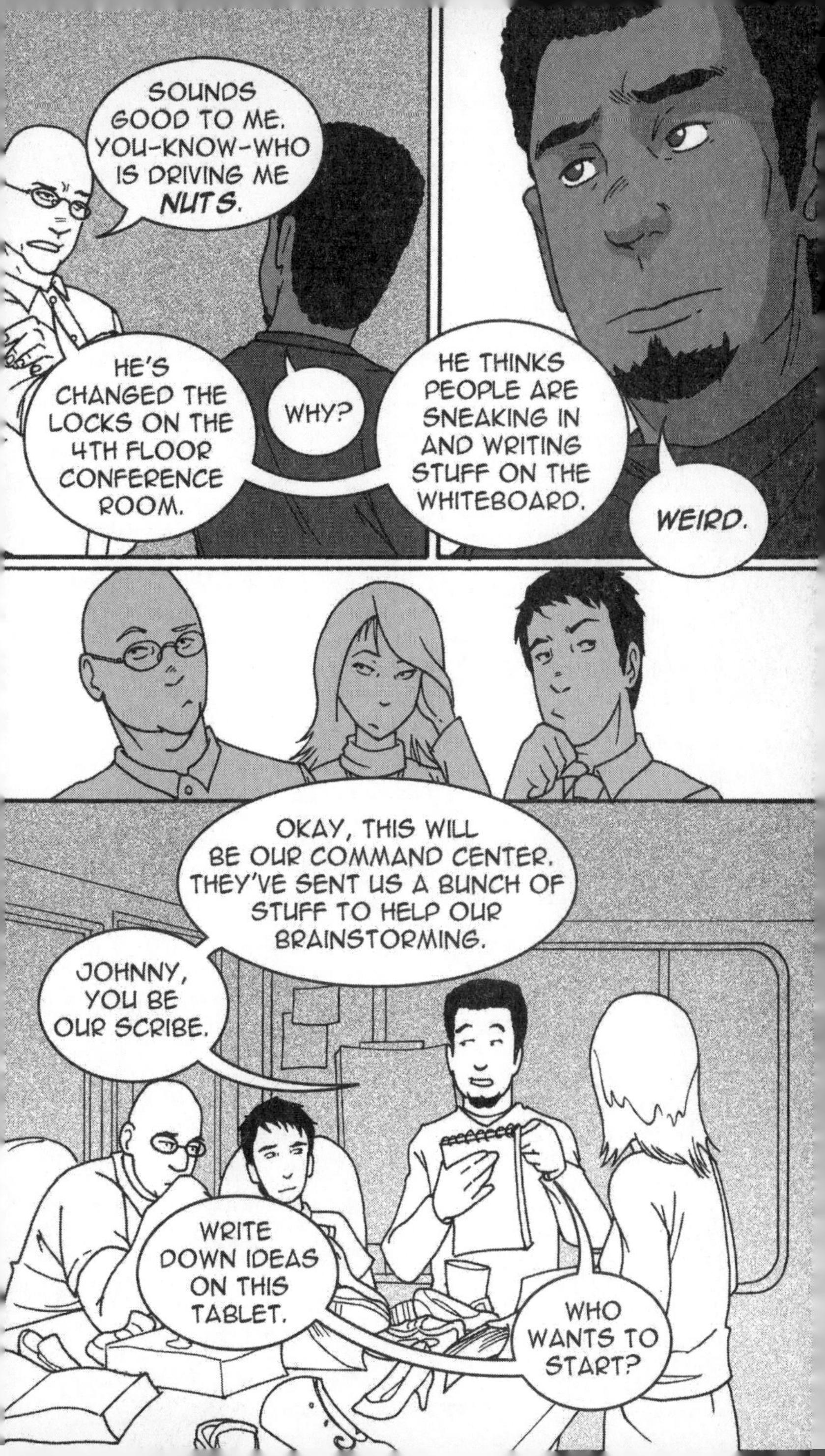
SOUNDS GOOD TO ME. YOU-KNOW-WHO IS DRIVING ME *NUTS*.
HE'S CHANGED THE LOCKS ON THE 4TH FLOOR CONFERENCE ROOM.
WHY?
HE THINKS PEOPLE ARE SNEAKING IN AND WRITING STUFF ON THE WHITEBOARD.
WEIRD.
OKAY, THIS WILL BE OUR COMMAND CENTER. THEY'VE SENT US A BUNCH OF STUFF TO HELP OUR BRAINSTORMING.
JOHNNY, YOU BE OUR SCRIBE.
WRITE DOWN IDEAS ON THIS TABLET.
WHO WANTS TO START?

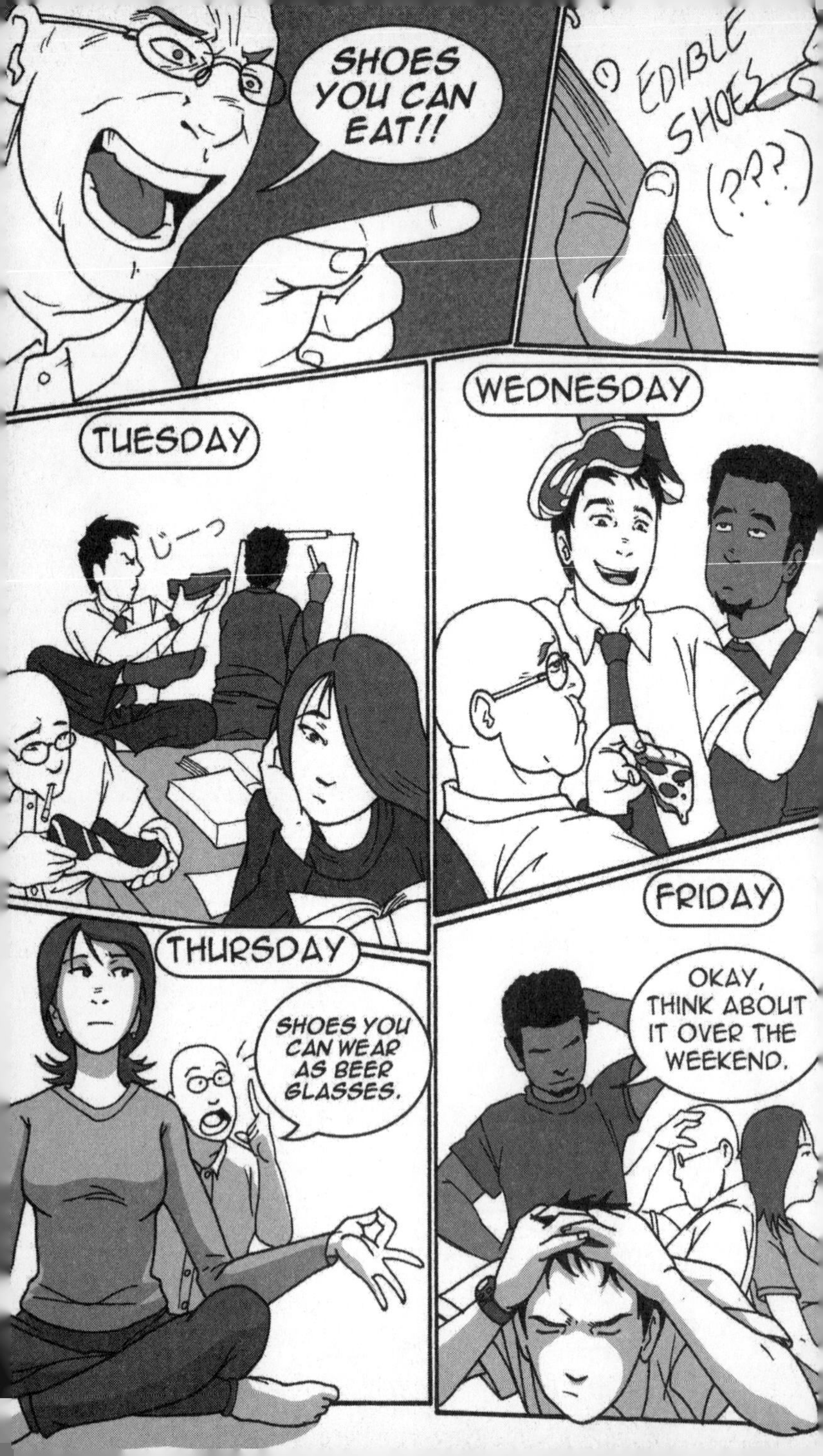
SHOES YOU CAN EAT!!
① EDIBLE SHOES (???)
TUESDAY
じーっ
WEDNESDAY
THURSDAY
SHOES YOU CAN WEAR AS BEER GLASSES.
FRIDAY
OKAY, THINK ABOUT IT OVER THE WEEKEND.

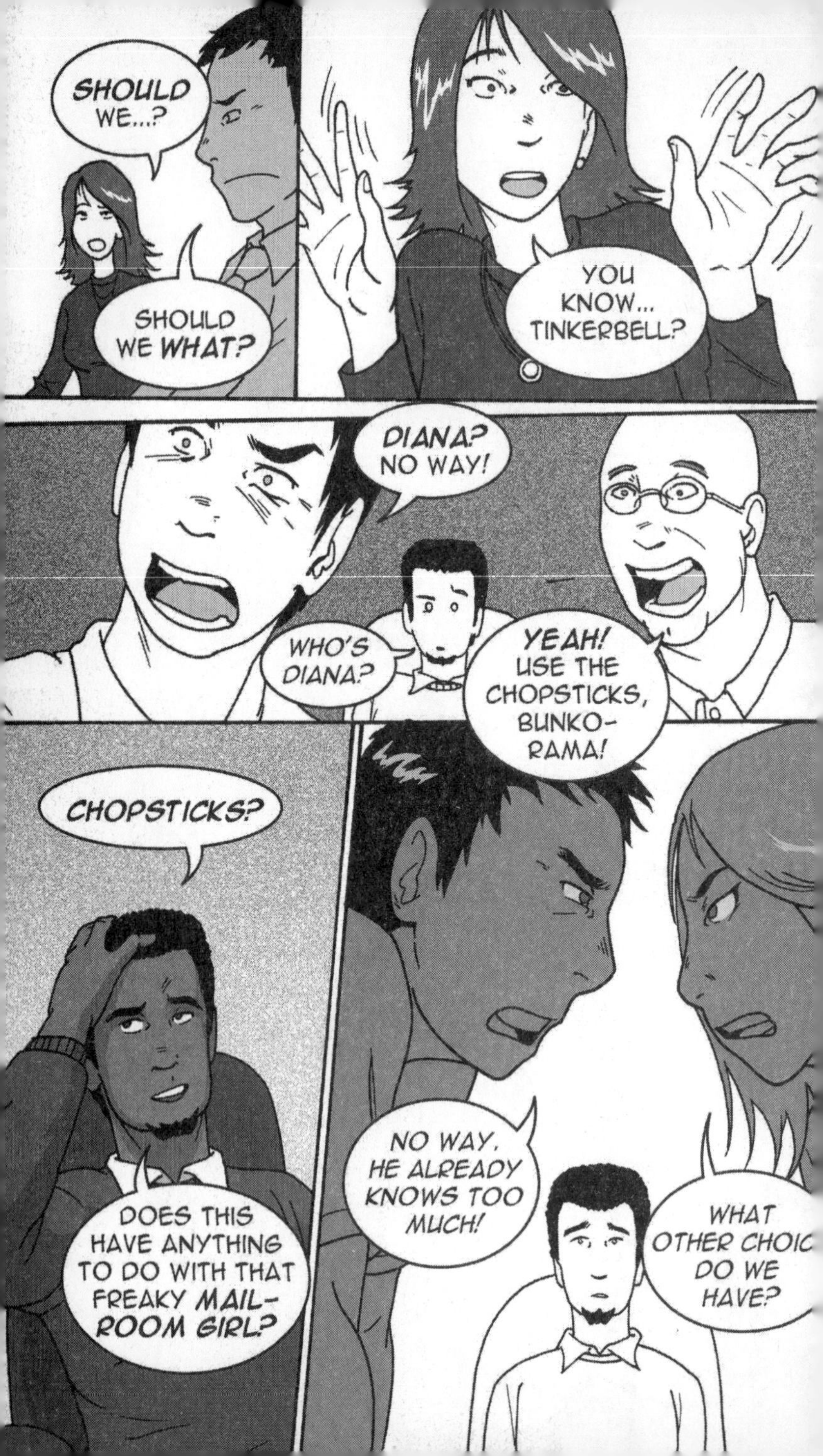
SHOULD WE...?
SHOULD WE WHAT?
YOU KNOW... TINKERBELL?
DIANA? NO WAY!
WHO'S DIANA?
YEAH! USE THE CHOPSTICKS, BUNKO-RAMA!
CHOPSTICKS?
DOES THIS HAVE ANYTHING TO DO WITH THAT FREAKY MAIL-ROOM GIRL?
NO WAY. HE ALREADY KNOWS TOO MUCH!
WHAT OTHER CHOIC DO WE HAVE?

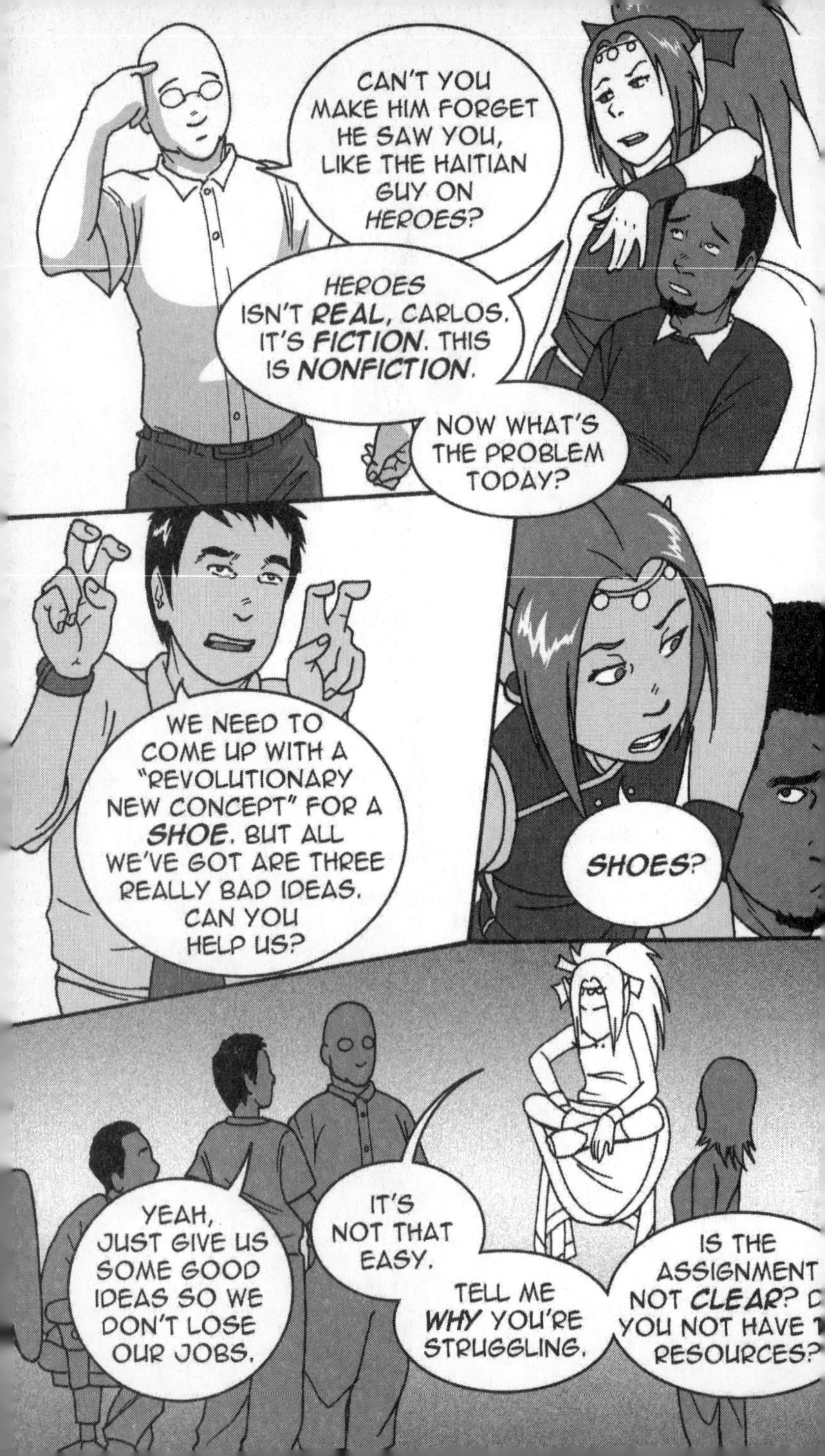
CAN'T YOU MAKE HIM FORGET HE SAW YOU, LIKE THE HAITIAN GUY ON *HEROES*?
HEROES ISN'T **REAL**, CARLOS. IT'S **FICTION**. THIS IS **NONFICTION**.
NOW WHAT'S THE PROBLEM TODAY?
WE NEED TO COME UP WITH A "REVOLUTIONARY NEW CONCEPT" FOR A **SHOE**. BUT ALL WE'VE GOT ARE THREE REALLY BAD IDEAS. CAN YOU HELP US?
SHOES?
YEAH, JUST GIVE US SOME GOOD IDEAS SO WE DON'T LOSE OUR JOBS.
IT'S NOT THAT EASY.
TELL ME **WHY** YOU'RE STRUGGLING.

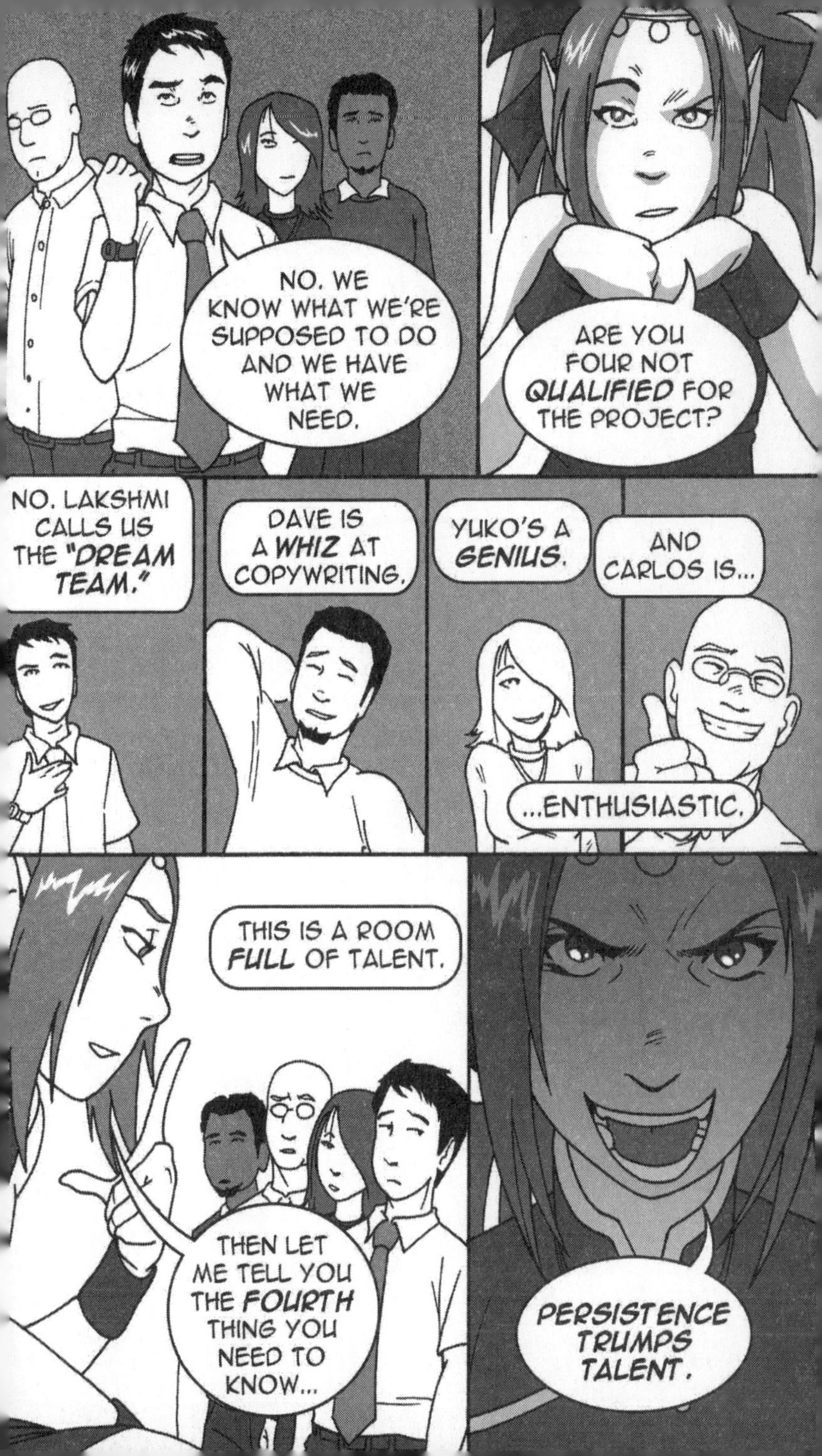
NO. WE KNOW WHAT WE'RE SUPPOSED TO DO AND WE HAVE WHAT WE NEED.
ARE YOU FOUR NOT QUALIFIED FOR THE PROJECT?
NO. LAKSHMI CALLS US THE "DREAM TEAM."
DAVE IS A WHIZ AT COPYWRITING.
YUKO'S A GENIUS.
AND CARLOS IS...
...ENTHUSIASTIC.
THIS IS A ROOM FULL OF TALENT.
THEN LET ME TELL YOU THE FOURTH THING YOU NEED TO KNOW...
PERSISTENCE TRUMPS TALENT.

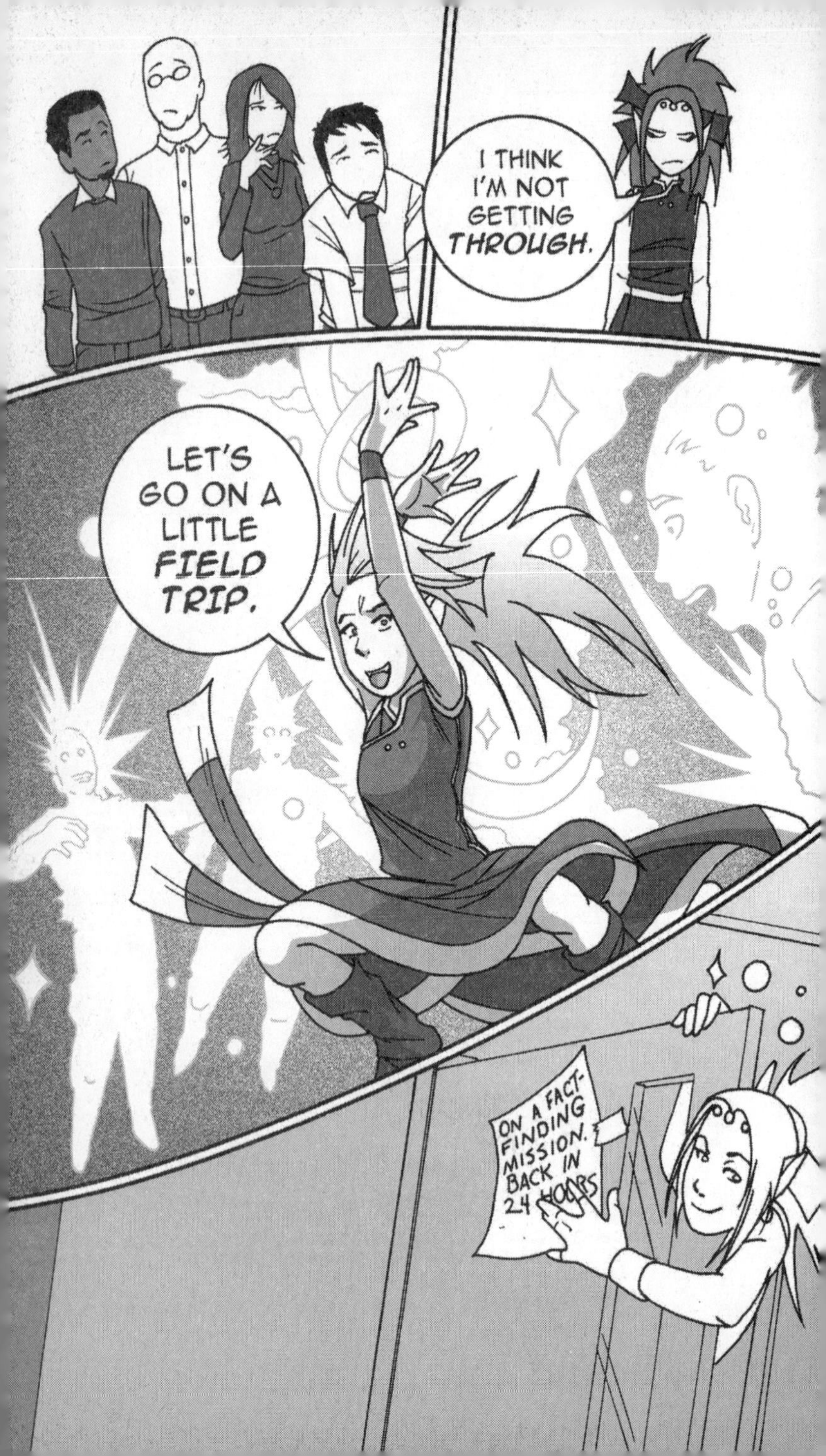
I THINK I'M NOT GETTING THROUGH.
LET'S GO ON A LITTLE FIELD TRIP.
ON A FACT-FINDING MISSION. BACK IN 24 HOURS

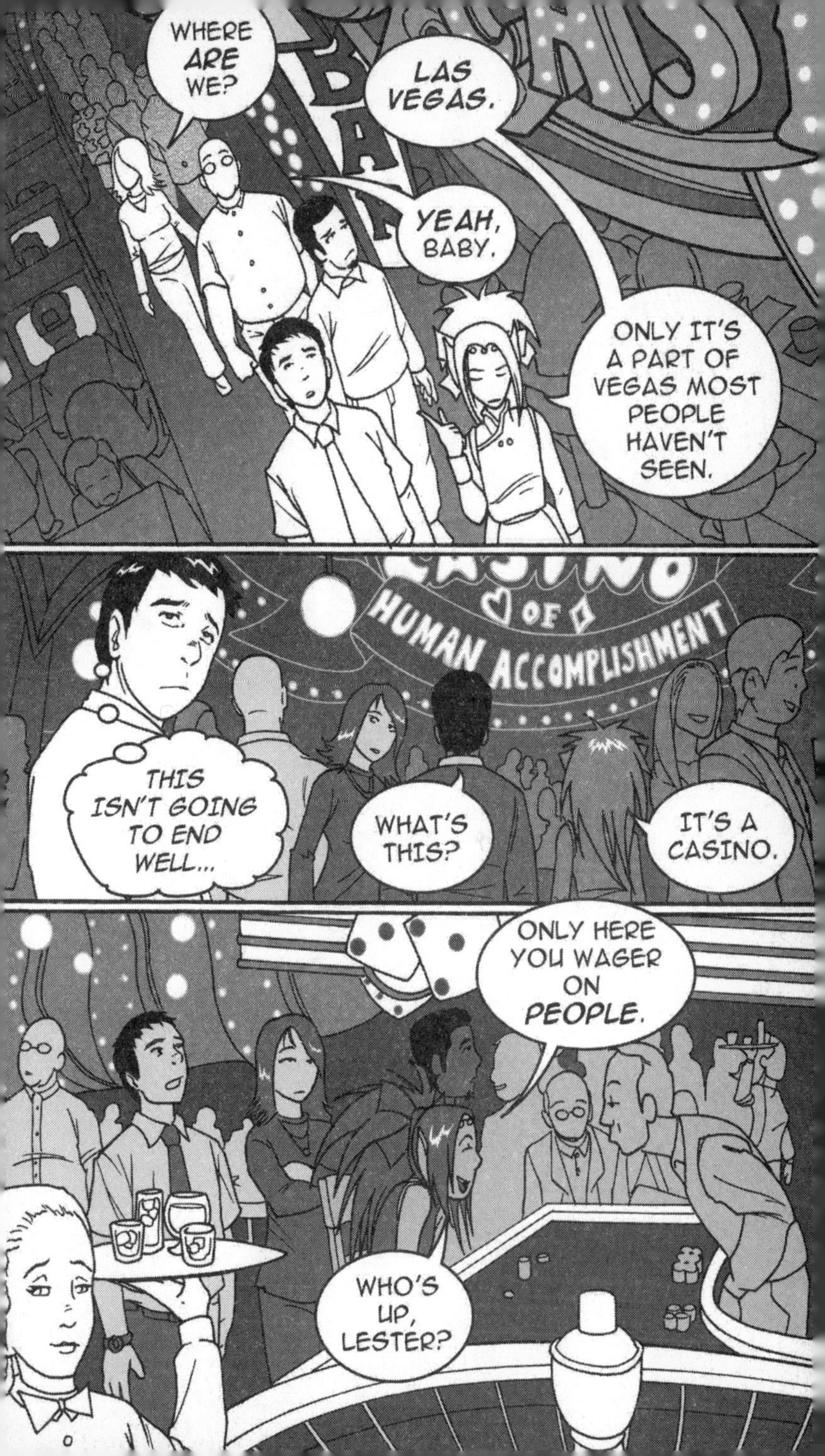
WHERE ARE WE?
LAS VEGAS.
YEAH, BABY.
ONLY IT'S A PART OF VEGAS MOST PEOPLE HAVEN'T SEEN.
CASINO OF HUMAN ACCOMPLISHMENT
THIS ISN'T GOING TO END WELL...
WHAT'S THIS?
IT'S A CASINO.
ONLY HERE YOU WAGER ON PEOPLE.
WHO'S UP, LESTER?

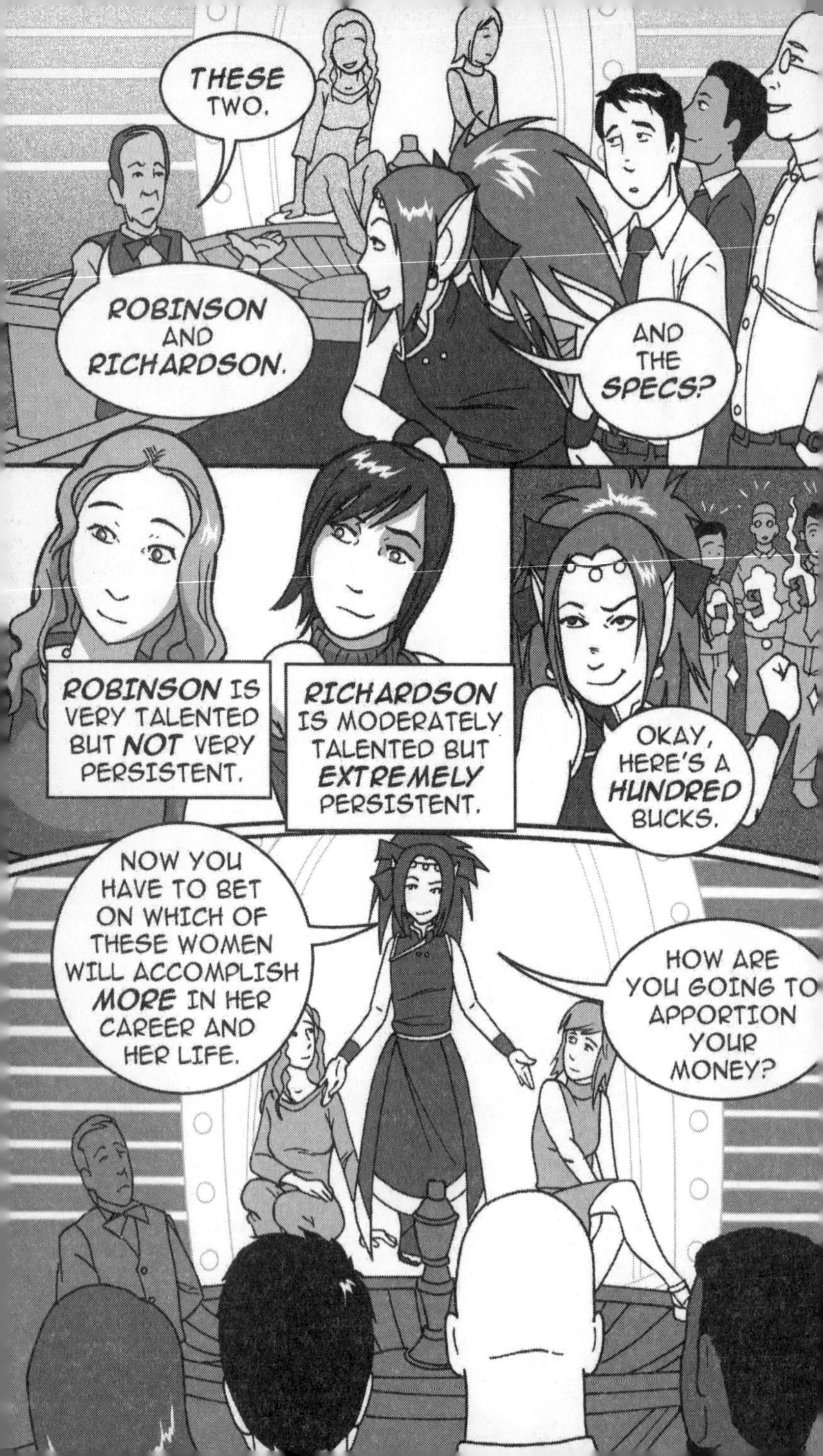

THESE TWO.
ROBINSON AND RICHARDSON.
AND THE SPECS?
ROBINSON IS VERY TALENTED BUT NOT VERY PERSISTENT.
RICHARDSON IS MODERATELY TALENTED BUT EXTREMELY PERSISTENT.
OKAY, HERE'S A HUNDRED BUCKS.
NOW YOU HAVE TO BET ON WHICH OF THESE WOMEN WILL ACCOMPLISH MORE IN HER CAREER AND HER LIFE.
HOW ARE YOU GOING TO APPORTION YOUR MONEY?

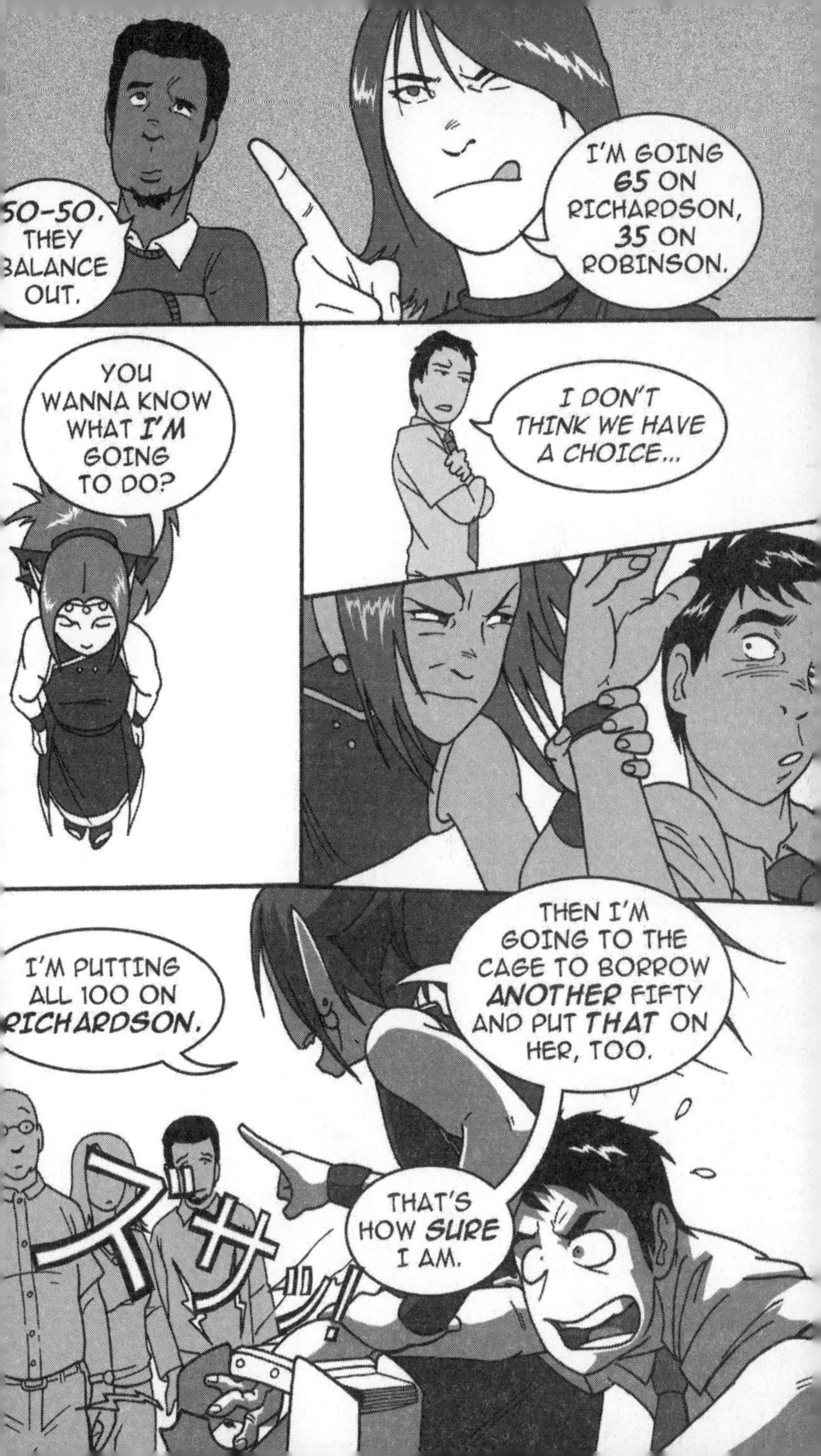
50-50. THEY BALANCE OUT.
I'M GOING 65 ON RICHARDSON, 35 ON ROBINSON.
YOU WANNA KNOW WHAT I'M GOING TO DO?
I DON'T THINK WE HAVE A CHOICE...
I'M PUTTING ALL 100 ON RICHARDSON.
THEN I'M GOING TO THE CAGE TO BORROW ANOTHER FIFTY AND PUT THAT ON HER, TOO.
THAT'S HOW SURE I AM.

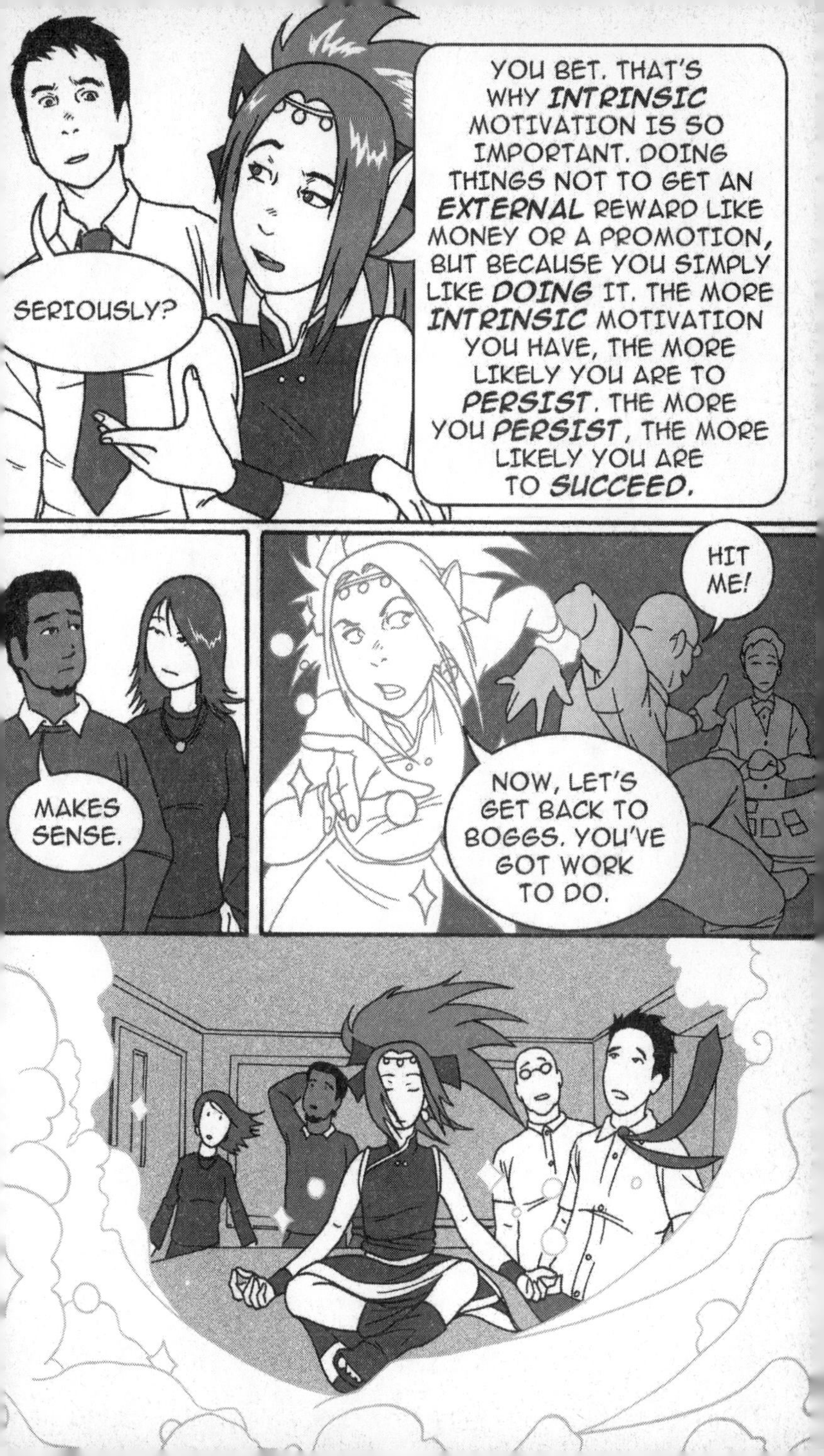
YOU BET. THAT'S WHY INTRINSIC MOTIVATION IS SO IMPORTANT. DOING THINGS NOT TO GET AN EXTERNAL REWARD LIKE MONEY OR A PROMOTION, BUT BECAUSE YOU SIMPLY LIKE DOING IT. THE MORE INTRINSIC MOTIVATION YOU HAVE, THE MORE LIKELY YOU ARE TO PERSIST. THE MORE YOU PERSIST, THE MORE LIKELY YOU ARE TO SUCCEED.
SERIOUSLY?
MAKES SENSE.
HIT ME!
NOW, LET'S GET BACK TO BOGGS. YOU'VE GOT WORK TO DO.

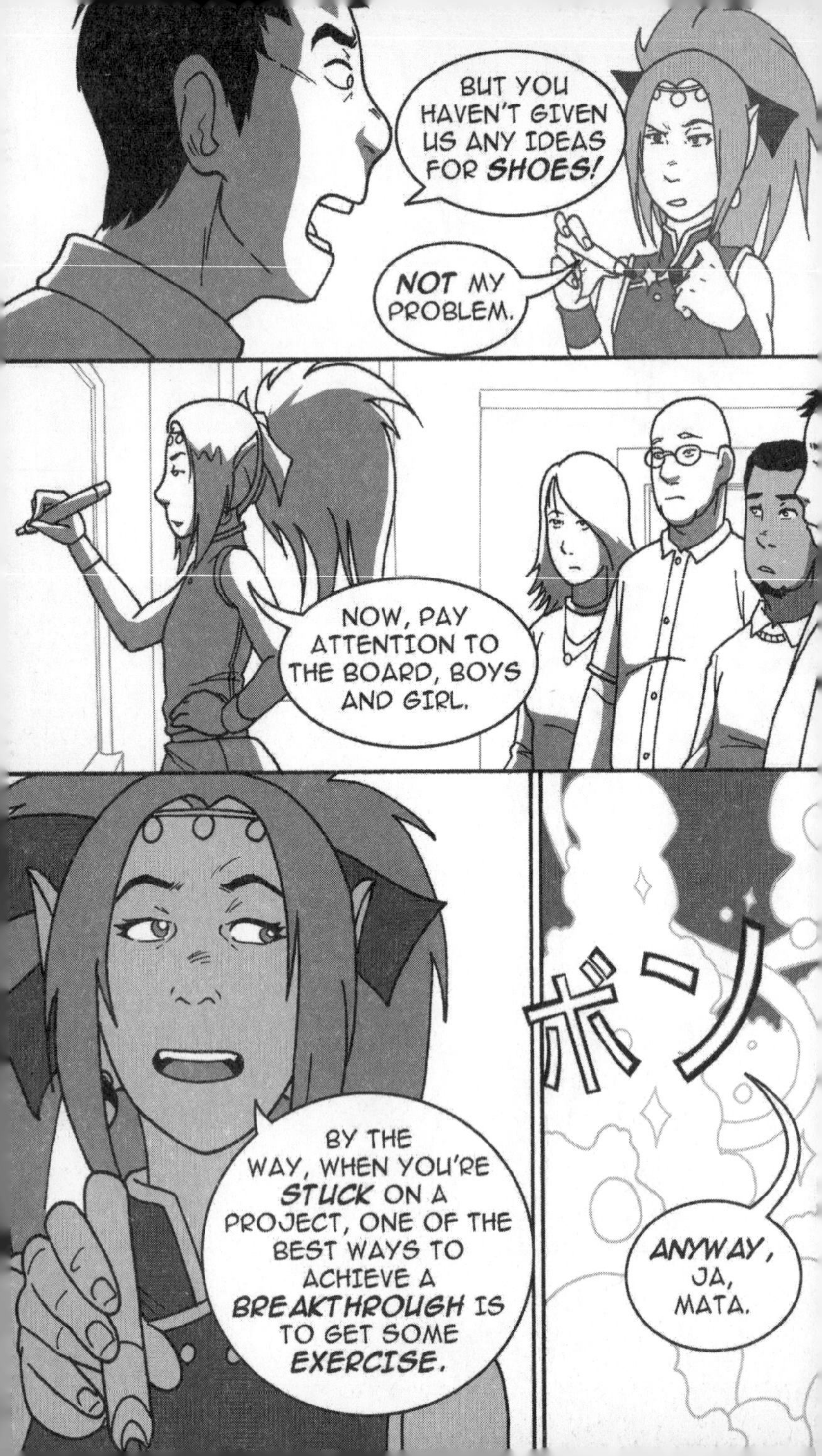
BUT YOU HAVEN'T GIVEN US ANY IDEAS FOR SHOES!
NOT MY PROBLEM.
NOW, PAY ATTENTION TO THE BOARD, BOYS AND GIRL.
BY THE WAY, WHEN YOU'RE STUCK ON A PROJECT, ONE OF THE BEST WAYS TO ACHIEVE A BREAKTHROUGH IS TO GET SOME EXERCISE.
ボーン
ANYWAY, JA, MATA.

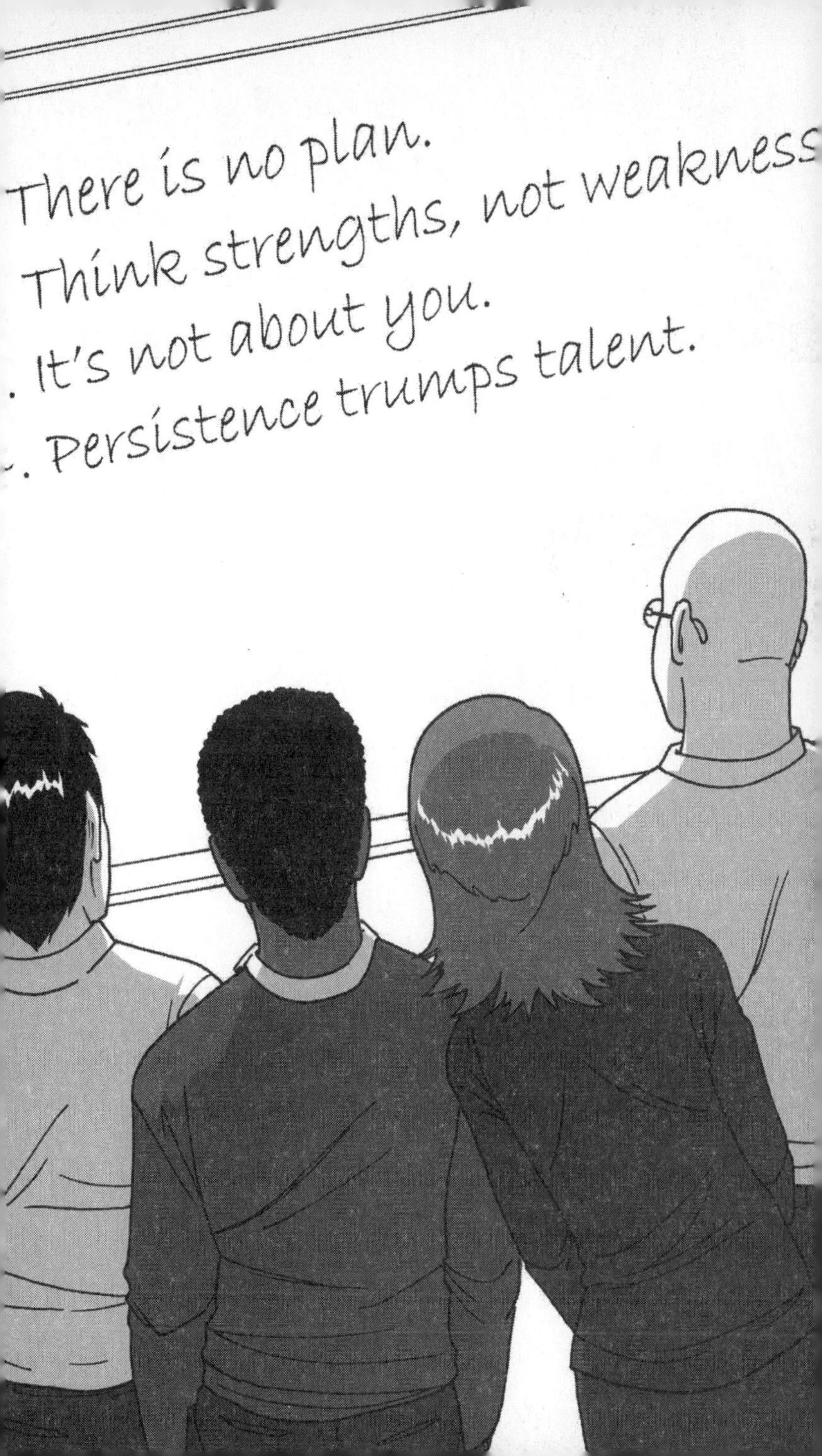
There is no plan.
Think strengths, not weakness
. It's not about you.
. Persistence trumps talent.

LESSON FIVE

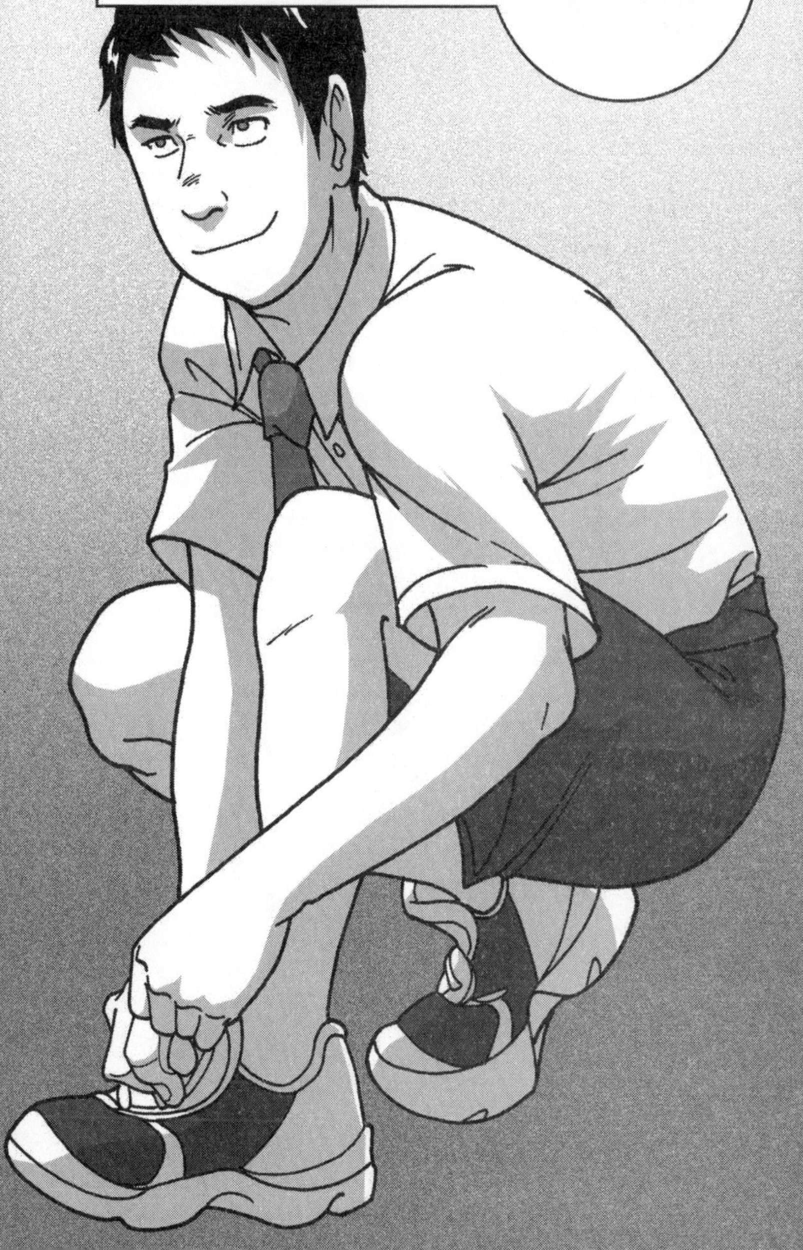

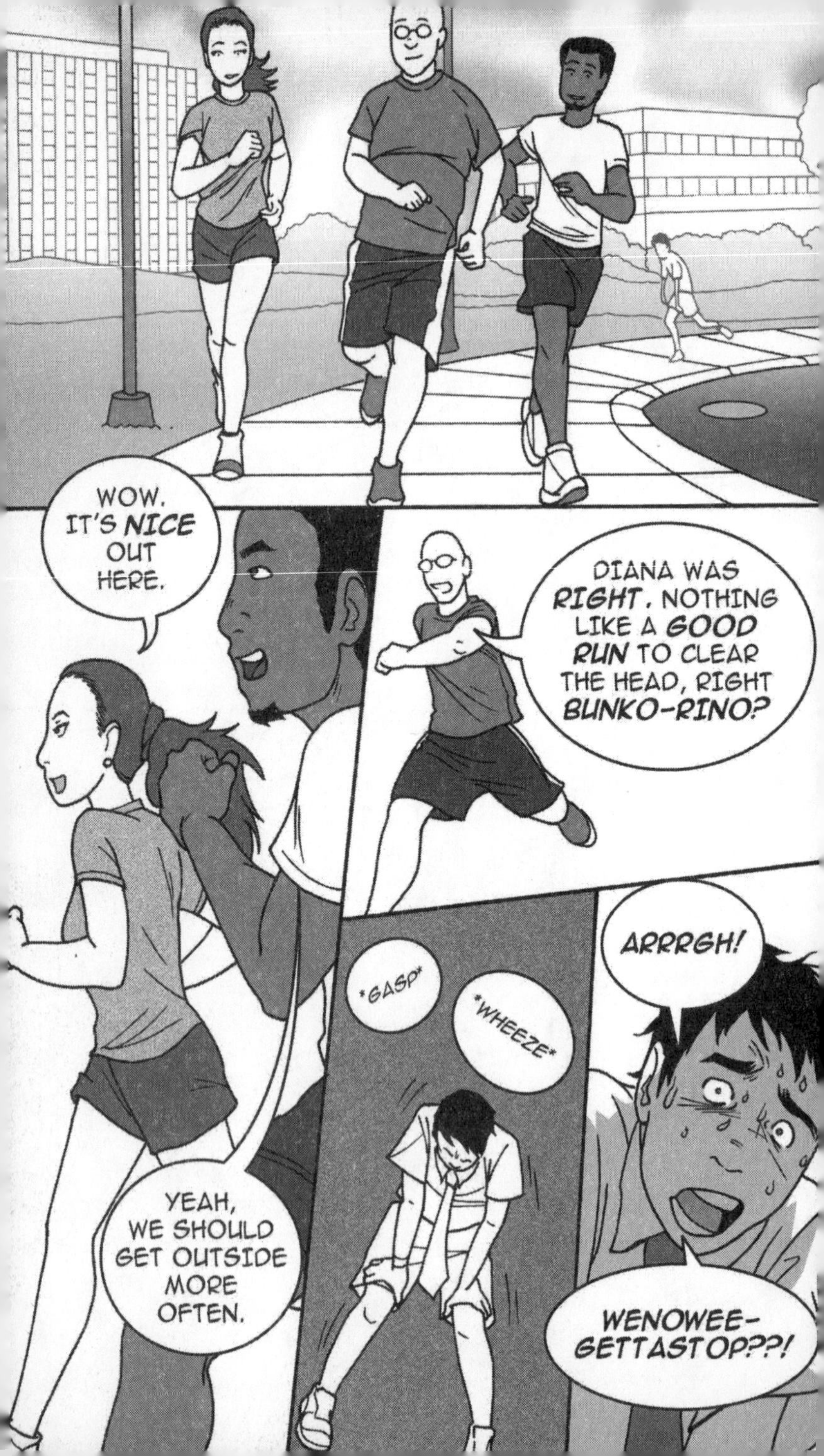
WOW. IT'S NICE OUT HERE.
DIANA WAS RIGHT. NOTHING LIKE A GOOD RUN TO CLEAR THE HEAD, RIGHT BUNKO-RINO?
YEAH, WE SHOULD GET OUTSIDE MORE OFTEN.
GASP
WHEEZE
ARRRGH!
WENOWEE-GETTASTOP??!

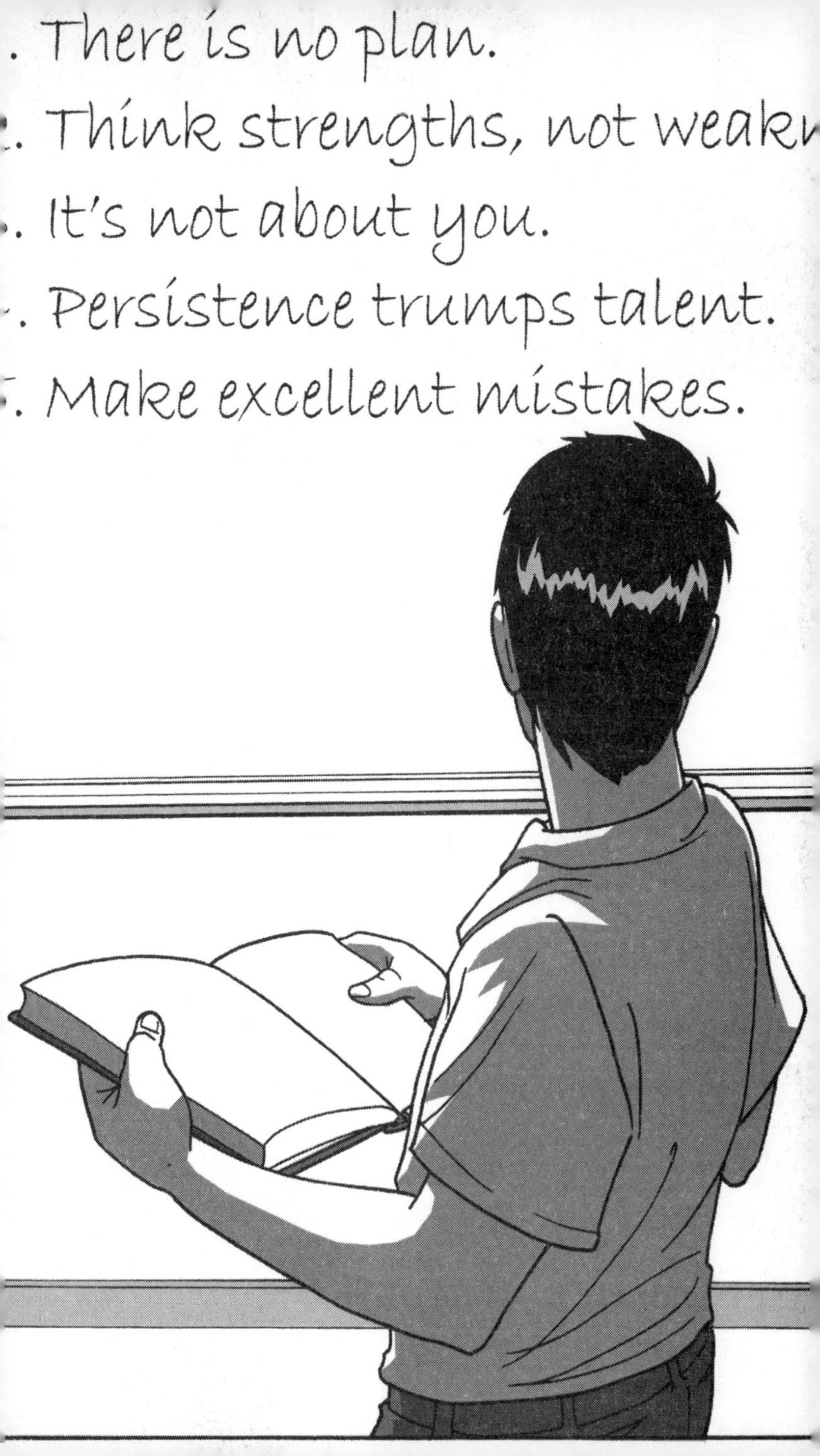
. There is no plan.
. Think strengths, not weak
. It's not about you.
. Persistence trumps talent.
. Make excellent mistakes.

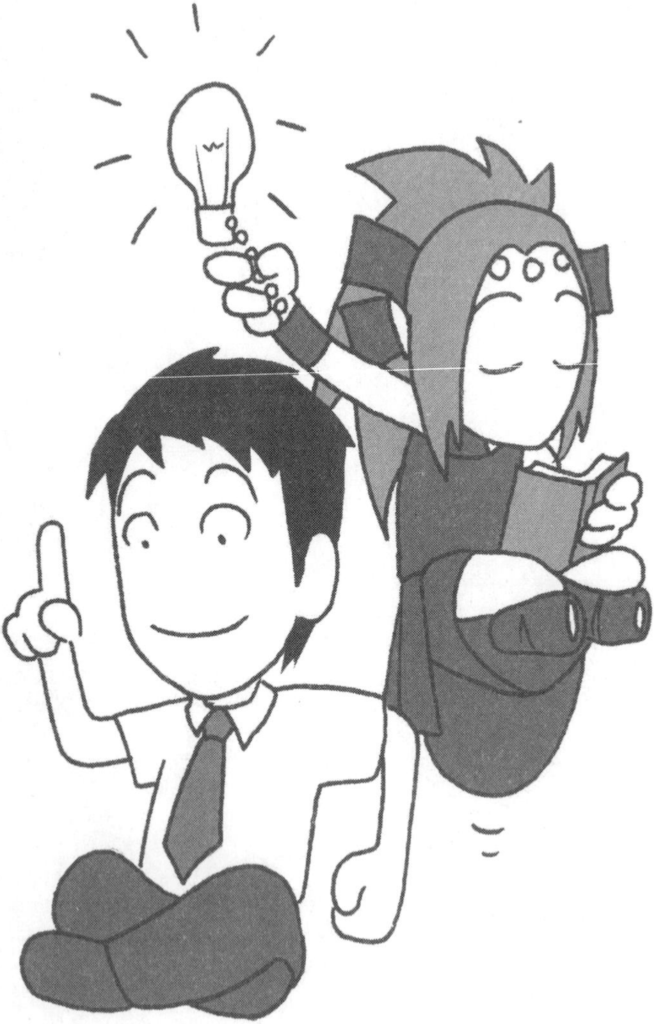

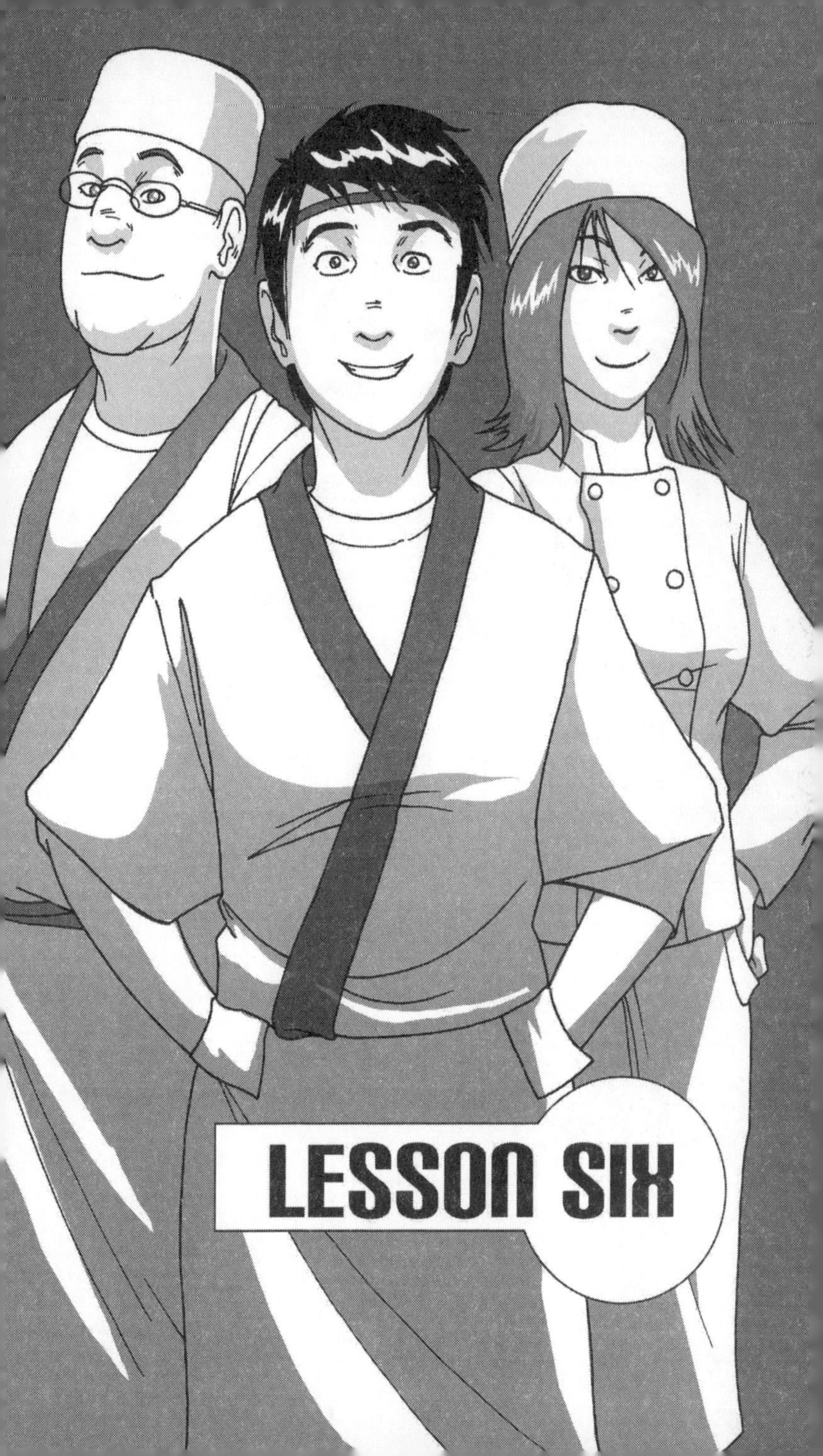
LESSON SIX

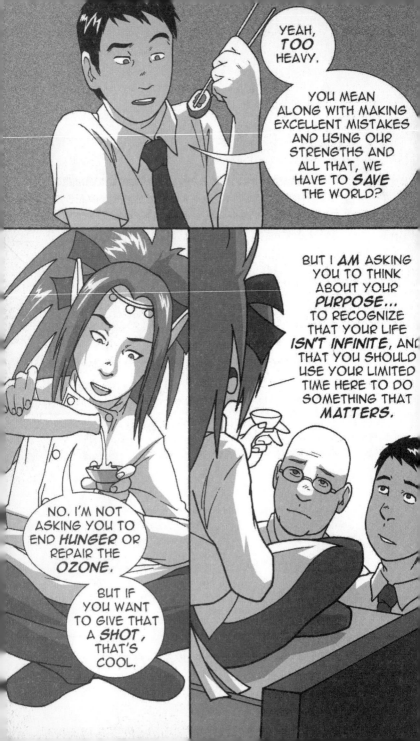

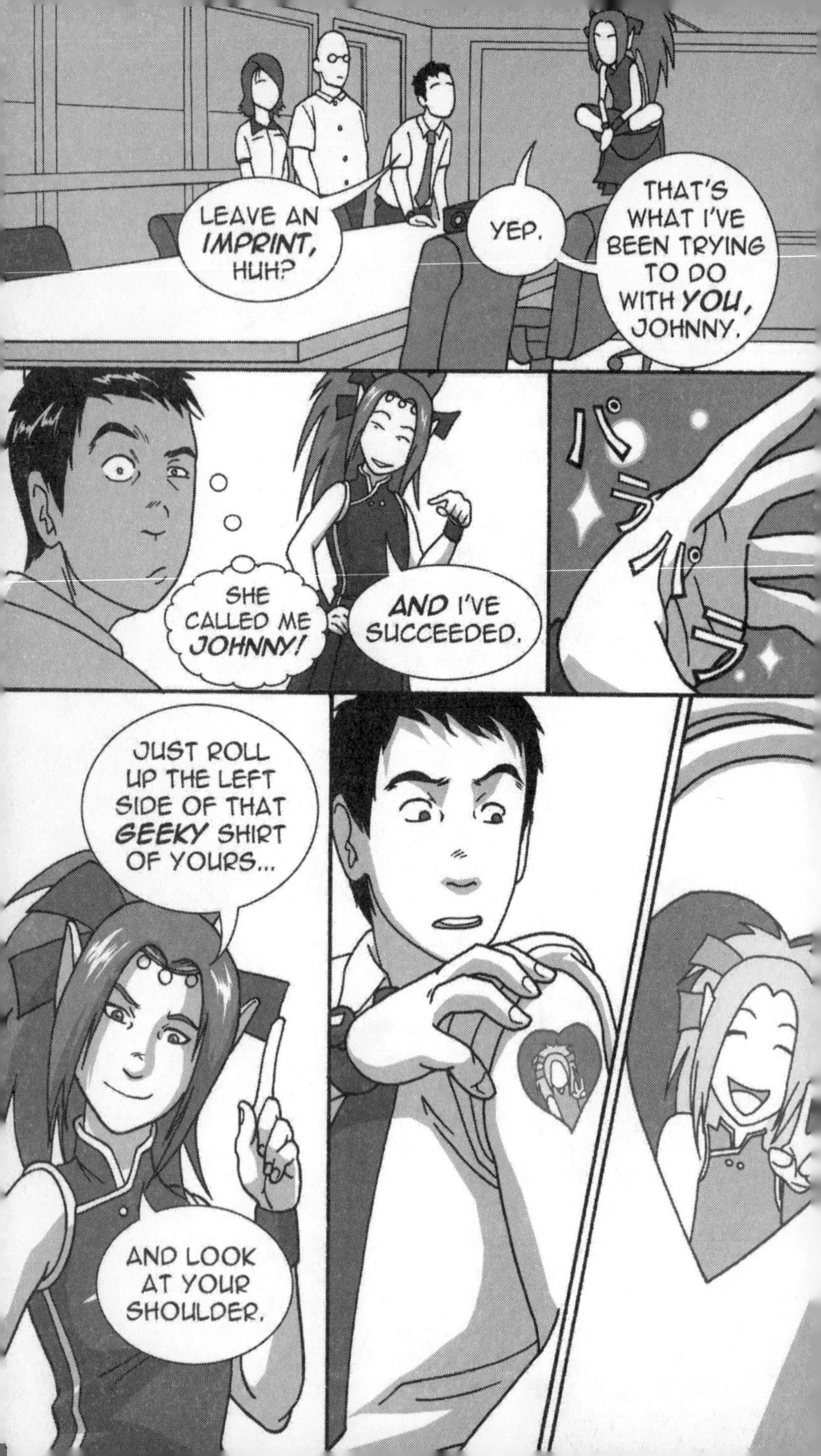
LEAVE AN *IMPRINT*, HUH?
YEP.
THAT'S WHAT I'VE BEEN TRYING TO DO WITH *YOU*, JOHNNY.
SHE CALLED ME *JOHNNY!*
AND I'VE SUCCEEDED.
JUST ROLL UP THE LEFT SIDE OF THAT *GEEKY* SHIRT OF YOURS...
AND LOOK AT YOUR SHOULDER.

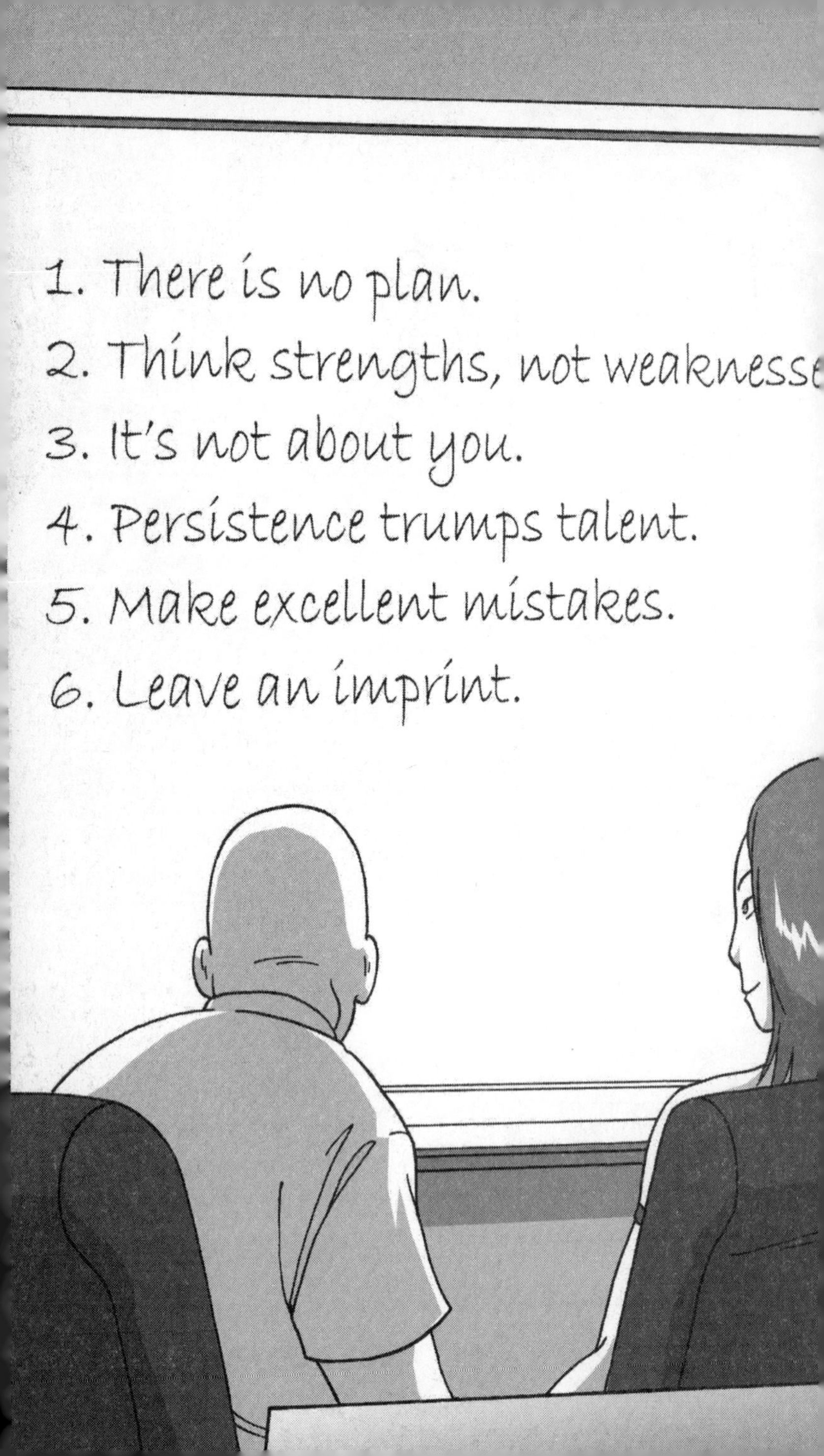
1. There is no plan.
2. Think strengths, not weaknesse
3. It's not about you.
4. Persistence trumps talent.
5. Make excellent mistakes.
6. Leave an imprint.

WWW.JOHNNYBLINKO.COM

FOR MORE, VISIT THE WEBSITE!

The author and artist wish to thank:

Pam Barricklow
Betsy Cavendish
Tiffany Estreicher
Lisa Katayama
Cliff Kellogg
Patty King
Geoff Kloske
Nathalie Kokke
Jessica Lerner
Jake Morrissey
Rob Pflaum
Eliza Pink
Sophia Pink
Rafe Sagalyn
Barb Schulz
Kosaku Shima
John & Sherry Ten Pas
Don Urness
Bridget Wagner
and
The Japan Society

FIRST PUBLISHED IN 2008 IN THE UNITED STATES BY RIVERHEAD BOOKS,
AN IMPRINT OF THE PENGUIN GROUP (USA) INC., 375 HUDSON STREET,
NEW YORK, NEW YORK 10014, USA

FIRST PUBLISHED IN PAPERBACK IN GREAT BRITAIN IN 2008 BY
HEADLINE PUBLISHING GROUP

1

CATALOGUING IN PUBLICATION DATA IS AVAILABLE FROM THE BRITISH LIBRARY

ISBN 978 0 7553 1873 5

PRINTED AND BOUND IN GREAT BRITAIN BY
MACKAYS OF CHATHAM LTD, CHATHAM, KENT

HEADLINE'S POLICY IS TO USE PAPERS THAT ARE NATURAL, RENEWABLE AND
RECYCLABLE PRODUCTS AND MADE FROM WOOD GROWN IN SUSTAINABLE FORESTS
THE LOGGING AND MANUFACTURING PROCESSES ARE EXPECTED TO CONFORM TO T
ENVIRONMENTAL REGULATIONS OF THE COUNTRY OF ORIGIN.

HEADLINE PUBLISHING GROUP
AN HACHETTE LIVRE UK COMPANY
338 EUSTON ROAD
LONDON NW1 3BH

WWW.HEADLINE.CO.UK
WWW.HACHETTELIVRE.CO.UK